P9-DEQ-701

THE RIDICULOUS RACE

THE RIDICULOUS RACE

26,000 miles.

2 guys. 1 globe.

No airplanes.

STEVE HELY

VALI CHANDRASEKARAN

A Holt Paperback

Henry Holt and Company

New York

Holt Paperbacks
Henry Holt and Company, LLC
Publishers since 1866
175 Fifth Avenue
New York, New York 10010
www.henryholt.com

Distributed in Canada by H. B. Fenn and Company Ltd.

Library of Congress Cataloging-in-Publication Data

Hely, Steve.
The ridiculous race : 26,000 miles, 2 guys, 1 globe, no airplanes / Steve Hely and Vali Chandrasekaran.—1st ed.
p. cm.
Includes bibliographical references and index.
ISBN-13: 978-0-8050-8740-6
ISBN-10: 0-8050-8740-0
1. Hely, Steve—Travel. 2. Chandrasekaran, Vali—Travel. 3. Voyages and travels—Anecdotes. I. Chandrasekaran, Vali. II. Title.
G465.H456 2008
910.4'1—dc22 2008003263

Henry Holt books are available for special promotions and premiums.
For details contact: Director, Special Markets.

First Edition 2008

Designed by Meryl Sussman Levavi
Illustrations by Tim Tomkinson
Printed in the United States of America

10 9 8 7 6 5 4 3 2 1

For our long-suffering parents,

who spent many sleepless nights

wondering why their sons

couldn't just vacation in Florida

like normal people.

Authors' Note

Everything in this book really happened to the authors between March and July 2007. We've changed names and identifying details where it seemed polite. Conversations are reconstructed from scratchy notes and memory.

INTERNATIONAL DATE LINE
ARCTIC
OCEAN
UNCHARTED
TERRITORIES
UNIMAK ISLAND
LONDON
RIVERSIDE IOWA
LOS ANGELES
PACIFIC
ATLANTIC
OCEAN
OCEAN
MEXICO CITY
GALAPAGOS ISLANDS
N
RIO DE JANEIRO
W
E
S

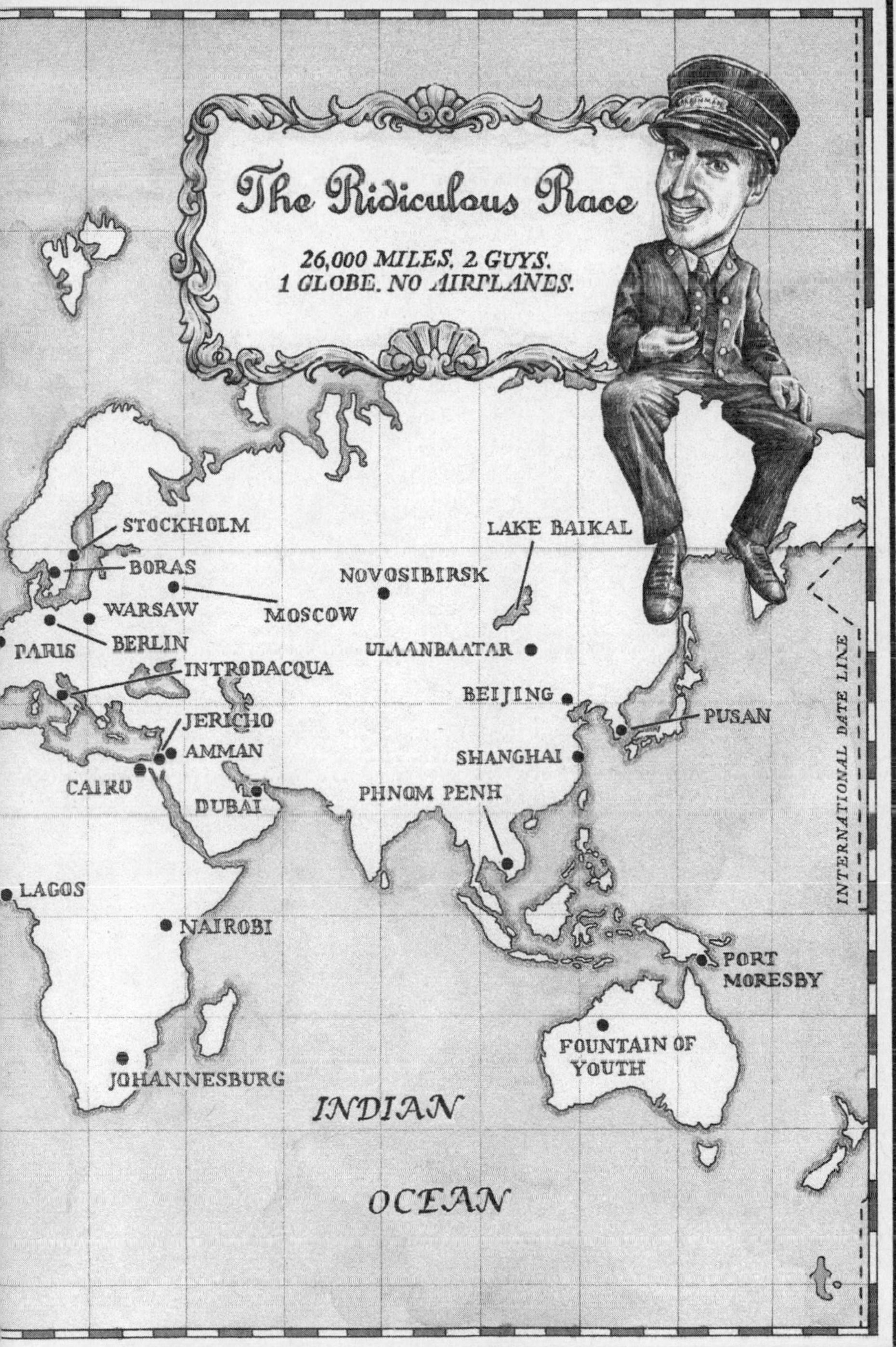
The Ridiculous Race
26,000 MILES. 2 GUYS.
1 GLOBE. NO AIRPLANES.
STOCKHOLM
BORAS
WARSAW
MOSCOW
PARIS
BERLIN
NOVOSIBIRSK
LAKE BAIKAL
ULAANBAATAR
INTRODACQUA
BEIJING
PUSAN
JERICHO
AMMAN
SHANGHAI
CAIRO
DUBAI
PHNOM PENH
INTERNATIONAL DATE LINE
LAGOS
NAIROBI
PORT MORESBY
FOUNTAIN OF YOUTH
JOHANNESBURG
INDIAN
OCEAN

THE RIDICULOUS RACE

STEVE: What to Expect

Off the coast of Kamchatka, Siberia, bundled up and standing on the deck of a German container ship, I gripped the railing with oil-stained gloves to avoid being pitched into a heaving ocean the color of a wet gravestone. Snow was falling *up*, a meteorological phenomenon which I did not then and do not now understand, but which I saw with my own human eyes. "Well," I thought, "I hope Vali is this miserable."

VALI: A Taste of What's to Come

I sat exhausted and disheveled, clutching my luggage in the backseat of a Checker taxicab driving north on La Brea Avenue, and wondered if Steve was already back in Los Angeles. Had he beaten me or was I the winner of the Ridiculous Race?

I looked out the window at the huge beige oil pumps and reflected on all I had experienced since I last saw them.

I smiled. I was proud of what I had done.

Did I, having circumnavigated the globe, consider myself to be some sort of better, modern-day Marco Polo? I wouldn't say that. People who know a lot about both me and Marco Polo probably wouldn't say that either. But some people, who know only a little bit about me and almost nothing about Marco Polo, might say that.

Those are the people I'm trying to impress.

STEVE: How It Started

This story begins on Sixth Street in Los Angeles, which can hold its own in any index of "world's craziest places." Sixth

Street is home to the La Brea Tar Pits, pools of tar and water where woolly mammoths used to get stuck and eaten by saber-toothed tigers, which would then also get stuck. Across from the still-burbling tar pits is the office of *Variety*, the showbiz newspaper devoted to reporting on which idiots just became millionaires. Just around the corner is the Peterson Auto Museum, where Notorious BIG got shot. Sixth Street runs past the barbecues of Koreatown, by Antonio Banderas's house in Hancock Park, and into LA's apocalyptically vacant downtown.

It was also home to the Sixth Street Dining Club and Magnificence Consortium, a society I'd founded. The members—myself, Vali Chandrasekaran, and our delightful young associate Leila—met weekly for the purposes of wearing preposterous suits, inventing cocktails, attempting to cook forgotten foods of the 1920s, drinking wine from the 99 Cent Store, sampling expired medicines, and proposing toasts to one another. Our meetings were held on Monday nights. This was a mistake. Members were often hungover disasters well into Thursday. But Monday was tradition, so Monday it remained.

Vali and I were Sixth Street neighbors, but we'd been friends at least since the time in college when I bailed him out of jail at five in the morning after he broke into the wrong building during an abortive prank. Five years later, he had cleaned up his act just enough to get a job writing jokes for actors playing well-intentioned rednecks to say on TV. My job was writing jokes for a cartoon alien, and, while this was incredibly fun, I sometimes wondered if I should try something more adventurous.

"See, some day all this will be over. We'll have wives and children and dogs, and we'll have to live responsibly."

I said this as Vali and I were sitting in the hot tub of his apartment building in the waning hours of a Monday night. I was drinking a bottle of ninety-nine-cent wine which contained some kind of kernels, and Vali was putting bubbles on his face and pretending they were a beard. Which doesn't sound all that funny, but he was really committing to the bit.

It's possible that I'm misremembering all this. Vali may have been pretending the bubbles were a hat.

"I assume my wife will be fine with me getting drunk and getting in a hot tub," Vali retorted.

"As of right now, my biography would be very boring to read," I said.

"Yeah, I've been meaning to give my future biographers more material."

"We should have an adventure." To get the last of the kernels out of the bottle of wine, I tilted my head back and pointed it at the stars.

"I'm in," said Vali. It's worth mentioning here that Vali was wearing boxer briefs.

"Should we become hoboes?"

"Mmm, too dangerous. I think these days hoboes are always getting stabbed."

"Maybe we should circumnavigate the globe."

"Maybe we should *race* around the globe."

"That would be something. That would be an adventure. But we would have to not use airplanes. Otherwise it would be too easy."

"No airplanes? Is that even possible?"

We didn't worry about that.

Once we thought it up, there was no way we weren't going to do it.

VALI: How It Started: Corrections & Amendments

The preceding is not even close to the truth of how Steve and I came up with the idea for this book. I have no idea why he fabricated the story. The truth is as follows:

One night I had a dream about lifting weights with Bob Dylan. During the workout, my trainer, Abraham Lincoln, told me I should race my friend around the world without airplanes.

The next night, I had dinner with Steve. When I told him about my dream, his eyes widened with amazement and he spit out his soda. I knew something big had happened because Steve really hates to waste soda.

"I had the exact same dream last night," he said.

Then we both knew what needed to be done.

STEVE: Circumnavigation: Why It's Awesome

In the next few days it became all I could think about.

It's not the craziest adventure ever. These days any men's magazine has an article by someone who backstroked the length of the Amazon, skateboarded the Kalahari, or Segway'd the Andes.

But 26,000 miles by sea and land is nothing to scoff at. Bear in mind that the first guy to try this, Magellan, ended up *dead*.

There's an old-fashioned grandeur to the idea. It's the kind of journey the great nineteenth-century adventurers dreamed up at the gentlemen's club and began on a whim. It summoned up cafés in grand, decaying train stations, and the bowels of steamships, timetables, and engine whistles and half-true tales told over card games with strangers.

The route is full of names that still ring with the exotic, even in a globalized age. The Forbidden City. Ulaanbaatar. Siberia. St. Petersburg. Warsaw. Cologne. Ohio.

Ironically, it may be harder to pull off than it was in Jules Verne's day. No one travels the oceans anymore. Long railway journeys are left to eccentrics. This trip would require stitching together transportation from the artifacts of the past and the new engines of the modern age. Vali and I were prepared to ride whatever beasts presented themselves, or to test the inventions of lunatic engineers.

Perhaps the best part would be that the "no airplanes" rule would keep us literally and figuratively close to the ground. We would *see* the world. We'd have to.

But to be honest, what I couldn't stop thinking about was me, in the near future, walking up to beautiful women, and saying this:

"Hello, my name is Steve Hely. In 2007 I circumnavigated the world by boat and train. I was competing in a race against a worthy and devilish foe. The prize was a bottle of forty-year-old Scotch. I won."

STEVE: The Rules

We agreed on certain details.

☛ **We would start in Los Angeles and go in opposite directions.** Because I'd done slightly more thinking about this than Vali, I quickly called dibs on heading west. My advantage would dawn on him over the course of the trip, when he lost an hour every time zone while my sleep was extended every two days.

☛ **No airplanes, helicopters, or hot air balloons.** Hovercrafts were a gray area.

☛ **Both competitors would cross every line of longitude on Earth.** You could do this any way you liked. If you went to the North Pole, ran around, and came back first, you'd win. But good luck getting to the North Pole without using airplanes.

☛ **The winner would be the first person back in Los Angeles.** Two glasses of Scotch would be poured and left in the care of Vali's roommate. The first man to round the Earth, arrive back from the opposite direction, and drink his Scotch would be the winner.

The schedule for network television has a two- to three-month gap, usually between the middle of April and the middle of June, when shows shut down production to prepare for the coming year. As a result, Vali and I both had two months off. That's when we'd go.

All we needed now was someone to pay for all this.

The authors would here like to express their sincere thanks to the corporate masters of the Henry Holt publishing company, who decided to fund our whim in exchange for this book. Readers can decide who got the better end of the deal.

STEVE: The Prize

The first thing we bought with our advance money was a bottle of Kinclaith 1969. This was the most expensive Scotch available in Los Angeles. It cost so much that upon paying for it I thought I might throw up. But this was a Ridiculous Race—it needed a ridiculous prize, a prize you could think about winning while you sat in some remote village choking down a warm glass of rainwater and ape blood.

STEVE: Planning

Back when the Ridiculous Race was just a funny idea, we debated about all kinds of crazy plans.

But then a gullible publisher decided to take us seriously.

The battle of wits began.

We agreed all planning had to be totally secret. Neither racer could let the other know what he was up to, or we'd risk falling into a trap set by our opponent. We'd need to outgame each other to win.

We agreed to start on April 14. This gave us about three weeks to plan our trips around the world.

That is not enough time.

We needed to get visas, work out timetables, map railroads, get vaccinations, buy equipment, and write taunting e-mails to each other. It turns out that planning a trip around the world, especially one without airplanes, is a lot of work

During all this Vali and I were at least nominally working at our "real" jobs for nine hours a day.

I tried to get a travel agent to help me. This was a mistake. He was used to setting up old ladies with package tours to Disney World. Meanwhile I kept calling with questions like "*Can* I rent a hydrofoil in the Ukraine and drop it off in England? I just need to know if that's possible." We agreed to part company. I'd plan alone.

I sent e-mails to billionaires Paul Allen, Larry Ellison, and the sheikh of Dubai, because they own the three biggest yachts in the world. I asked if any of them wanted to give me a ride across the Atlantic. An employee of the sheikh wrote back. He politely but firmly informed me that the sheikh was a busy man who had better things to do than help me win a stupid race. The Irish, British, and American navies expressed similar but more harshly worded disinterest when I asked if I could hitch a ride across the oceans.

Complicating all this was the Unspoken Awesomeness Contest. I knew Vali and I were in a game of chicken, a round of Adventure Poker. I intended to win the race, but I was also going to come back with the better stories.

Both Vali and I were about to crack under the stress of all this when Departure Day rolled around. We'd have to figure most of it out on the road. It was time to begin.

VALI: The Departure Debacle

Handcuffing someone is much harder than it looks.

I was awakened by a loud knocking on my apartment door. Loud noises are not my preferred wake-up mechanism. I prefer to be slowly massaged awake by a couple of bikini-clad ladies who know how to give a good compliment. Unfortunately, I also prefer not having to pay money to a bunch of ladies every time I wake up. This combination of preferences means I'm unhappy in the mornings no matter what. And the morning of Saturday, April 14, was no different.

I turned and groggily looked at my alarm clock. It was 9:00 a.m.—the time Steve and I agreed to begin the race. I should have insisted on a later start.

We had been out late the previous night at Trader Vic's where Steve and I spent a significant portion of our book advance throwing a party for ourselves. The consumed cocktails were now sloshing around my brain, affecting my balance. I rested my throbbing head against my bedroom wall for a moment, then made my way toward the knocking.

Before I swung the door all the way open, Steve leaped into

my apartment wearing a suit and tie, a scarf and sunglasses, and carrying a backpack that appeared to be filled with Tecate beers.

There was no way this was really happening. Five hours ago, Steve couldn't complete a sensical sentence. (Though he had been aggressively completing many nonsensical ones.)

Without even looking at me, he poured himself a tumbler of Johnny Walker and began drinking it. I was still in my boxer briefs and couldn't quite focus my eyes yet.

Jesus, I thought. I had seriously underestimated Steve. I've never read *The Art of War,* but there's probably something in there on never letting your opponent see you in your underwear. If not, I bet that subject is covered in Sun Tzu's sequel, *The Attire of War*.

If Steve's intent was to psych me out at the beginning of the race, it was working.

I had to pull myself into my shape. I told Steve I needed to "freshen up" and slipped back into my bedroom to take a Provigil—an antinarcolepsy drug that would help my body ignore both the effects of the hangover and the long day it was about to face. Then I quickly threw on a suit and rejoined Steve, who was now flipping through a copy of Alec Waugh's *In Praise of Wine,* which he had brought with him.

Why am I friends with this jackass? I wondered.

We sat down at my dining room table and opened up the Kinclaith 1969. I poured my glass first and took a long deep breath. It smelled Scotchy, like a drunk hobo in the morning. Then I slid the bottle over so Steve could pour his own glass. As he did this, I walked up behind my foe, slipped a pair of handcuffs out of my pocket, and cuffed one of his wrists.

Earlier in the week, I had purchased the handcuffs from the reputable Utah company Cuffs4Cops. When I ordered them over the phone, the saleswoman asked me if I wanted my police unit engraved onto the handcuffs. I thought for a moment, then asked if she could just engrave the phrase "keeping our children chaste" onto them. This aroused no questions. I'm not sure how much of Cuffs4Cops's business is actually 4Cops, but I would venture that the figure is closer to 0 percent than 100 percent.

My plan was elegantly simple: Just as Steve finished pouring his glass of Scotch, I would slap the handcuffs on him. Then, before he could process what had happened, I was going to affix two bumper stickers to Steve's body—one sticker for the front and one for the back. Both bumper stickers, which I had specially made for the occasion, simply read PEDOPHILE. I figured that the stickers combined with the "keeping our children chaste" message on the handcuffs would make it a bit more difficult for Steve to get the handcuffs removed and thus give me a nice little head start in the race. After I successfully restrained and stickered Steve, I expected him to laugh, congratulate me on a well-executed prank, shake my hand and bid me good luck. This is not what happened.

It turns out that people sometimes dislike getting handcuffed. Furthermore, it turns out that people can draw upon emergency reserves of strength while resisting arrest. Especially arrest by non-cops. So at the point where Steve was, according to my plans, supposed to be congratulating me, he was actually wrestling me on the floor of my apartment, fighting hard to prevent me from cuffing his other wrist. Largely, but not entirely, due to our hangovers, the wrestling match was incredibly pathetic—most of our energy was spent trying not to throw up.

After about two minutes of this nonsense, I finally pinned Steve to the ground and cuffed his other wrist, binding his hands in front of his stomach. I found this to be much easier than that behind-the-back garbage real cops insist on. I don't know why they bother. Showboating, probably. Then I fastened the PEDOPHILE stickers to Steve's torso.

Victorious, I started toward the door so I could begin the serious work of circumnavigation. Steve also started toward the door. Then he tackled me to the ground. And then he started choking me with the handcuff chain.

So this is why cops cuff behind the back, I thought.

While trying to maintain the unbroken status of my throat, I began to wonder how police officers ever successfully handcuff criminals. According to my experience with handcuffing, 100 percent of perpetrators should either escape with a free pair of handcuffs or choke a police officer to death. Then I realized cops had some advantages that I didn't have. *I wish I had a gun so I could shoot my friend Steve,* I thought.

Steve's face was now grotesque with anger. His mouth was fixed in a gargoyle's snarl. His eyes went what seemed like minutes between blinks. When he did blink, he did it with only one eye at a time—alternating left, right, left, right. . . . I assumed this was to ensure I didn't pull any other stunts while he wasn't looking.

"Vali, you have to uncuff me," Steve hissed at me through gritted teeth. "I can't explain now, but you're going to ruin the race and the book if you don't."

What was he talking about? Nothing, I would later find out. Steve was lying; he had nothing important to do that afternoon. Steve wasn't anxious to make a midmorning appointment. He was simply, and perhaps understandably, furious with me. Which explains why he started pummeling my head into my apartment floor between bouts of choking me with the handcuff's chain.

"Johnson, pull the car out front!" I screamed to my roommate. Thump. "This . . ." Thump. Choke. ". . . this is not going as planned."

Johnson, for some reason, decided to ignore my pleas and continue videotaping Steve's attempt at murdering me. On a parabola-shaped scale from one to ten where one is "poorly executed," five is "well executed," and ten returns to "poorly executed," this plan was a one (or a ten).

What was I to do? On the one hand I like oxygen getting to my brain, so I wanted to give Steve the handcuff key. On the other hand I found Steve's predicament incredibly funny, so I didn't want to give him the key. I decided to sacrifice my body for the joke. Besides, I hoped that if I could hold out long enough, Steve's eyeballs might dry out from insufficient blinking and fall out of his head. That would surely give me an advantage in the race.

After enduring another few minutes of abuse, my survival instinct kicked in. I pushed Steve off me, scrambled to my front door, and tossed the handcuff key outside.

"There, now I can't help you even if I wanted to."

Steve responded by silently storming over to the bushes where the key had landed. Worried that he would resume slamming my head/choking me if he couldn't find the key, I decided to leave immediately. I quickly loaded my belongings into Johnson's car and set off to the nearest Hertz auto rental location.

Just before I drove away, Steve freed himself from the handcuffs and ripped off the sticker I had fastened to his chest. However, in his fury, he forgot about the second sticker. As I left to begin my journey, I looked out the window of my ride to see Steve angrily walking home with a PEDOPHILE sticker on the back of his suit jacket. It was one of the proudest moments of my life.

STEVE: An Apology to the Reader, on Vali's Behalf, for the Stupidness of the Departure

When Vali, with a big, stupid grin on his face, took out his handcuffs, all I could think was *This was a mistake. I picked the wrong guy. This dude does not get it.*

He was so self-satisfied, so pleased with his own immaturity, his frat-dude vision of how the beginning of the race would play out.

Handcuffs?! Putting a sticker on my back?! It was all so juvenile. This was supposed to be the solemn commencement of a magnificent gentlemen's wager, in which Vali and I departed as both energetic opponents and high-minded sportsmen.

I'd tell my grandchildren about this race. And now Vali was ruining the start. How could I tell my grandchildren that the greatest event of my life had begun with an awkward wrestling match?

Even after his lame joke had collapsed into clumsy spectacle, it was obvious that I'd have to either choke him to death—an appealing option—or let him handcuff me. The latter would be less trouble in the long run

So I let him handcuff me. Within thirty seconds I'd found the key he'd "launched" about two yards into a bush.

Carrying myself with stunning dignity, I walked home. I did not realize there was a PEDOPHILE sticker on my back. I will leave out that part when I tell the story to my grandchildren. And I apologize to you, Reader, for allowing Vali to get this book off to such a boorish start.

But my revenge for the morning's debacle had already begun. The exhausted and now-bloodied Vali drove off into six weeks of pure exhaustion as I crawled back into bed.

VALI: Beginning with a Southward Diversion

People filter out any stimulus they experience frequently. Evolution has wired our brains to allow this. It is the only reason serious insanity epidemics are avoided in civilizations with dozens of whirring motors in every living space; the only reason homicide rates are not astronomically high in apartments above subway lines; the only reason we can stand wearing pants.

In Los Angeles, this filtration mechanism is particularly advanced: Angelinos have a highly developed ability to ignore stupidity. While their fellow Americans ignore the faint beeping of a neighbor's forgotten alarm clock, Angelinos ignore pornographers parking lemon yellow H2 Hummers in handicap spots in front of organic grocery stores.

"Which of your intermediate-sized cars can best handle jumps?" I asked the Hertz Car-Rental Artist.

"The Chevy Impala," he replied without hesitation. "We have one in red."

It was not yet noon, and I was wearing a crumpled-up suit, smelled like Scotch, and had requested a Mexican insurance policy that would cover bail up to ten thousand dollars. The jaded Rental Artist never even looked up at me.

I expect this kind of behavior from a teenager with three colinear green dots tattooed vertically below his lower lip and a safety pin through his nostril. But this Hertz employee—Nick, according to his rotary engraved name tag—was extremely normal, the kind of guy who always knows about daylight savings time at least twenty-four hours before it happens.

In the rental car lot, I found the Chevy Impala in a row of a hundred nearly identical American-made cars. According to the General Motors Company the car was Precision Red, a scientific color designed to help transport me from point A to point B as efficiently as possible. Despite his too-cool attitude Nick had hooked me up. Another color, like Run Out of Gas Yellow, would have been no good at all.

The Impala was the perfect vessel for the 2,100-mile drive to Cuernavaca, just south of Mexico City, where I had an appointment to buy a jetpack in three days.

VALI: An Advertisement for Craigslist

As measured by kidnapping efficiency, the United States is an embarrassingly poor performer on the world's stage. The "great nation" has fewer than ten kidnappings for ransom reported every year.*

Fortunately for U.S.-based abduction enthusiasts, a few things can be done to improve one's likelihood of getting kidnapped. The best way to get kidnapped is to be a beautiful nymphomaniac with rich and loving parents. Don't have time to cultivate a sex addiction and/or a loving relationship with your parents? No worries. You can always go to Mexico, the second most Kidnap Krazy nation on Earth.

Getting kidnapped would really set me back in the race, so I took some precautions. First, I mapped out a route that avoided the most dangerous and empty sections of Mexico. Second, I hired Juliana.

Juliana and I met for the first time a few days before the beginning of the race when she responded to a very vague Craigslist ad that I placed requesting a "Spanish translator who won't murder me." As I accelerated down the 10 East freeway toward Mexico, I was shocked to actually have her next to me, testing how far back the passenger seat reclined and judging my tastes as she scrolled through the music on my iPod. Why would any woman get into a car with an unknown man? Wasn't she concerned for her safety?

Then I got self-conscious. Was I really so obviously nonthreatening? That didn't fit in with the cool, devil-may-care persona I had invented for the Ridiculous Race.

And finally, I became afraid. Was Juliana going to abandon me at a Mexican rest stop, leaving me to stumble my way to Cuernavaca using only the North Star for direction and eating discarded sombreros for sustenance?

When we stopped for lunch Juliana told me something that explained her fearlessness. She was born and raised in

*According to Hiscox PLC, which prides itself on being the world's largest provider of "specialist kidnap, detention, and extortion insurance."

Colombia—the most Kidnap Krazy country on Earth, with a kidnapping incidence of over ten times its nearest competitor. I thought I felt a chill run down my spine, but it turned out to just be an ant.

Regardless, my fear intensified. The incredibly high Colombian kidnapping rate meant there was a good chance that Juliana had kidnapped someone at least once before. For all I knew she was the kidnapping queen of Bogotá, on the lam in Los Angeles.

I tried to remember if I had told Juliana that my parents loved me, thus implying that they would pay a hefty ransom if I were kidnapped. I didn't recall saying anything to that effect, but she might have figured it out on her own. Truth is: I'm extremely lovable; I'm like the Elmo of humans.

Until I could trust her (probably never) I needed to treat Juliana like a deadly assassin. This changed the way I processed even the simplest of our interactions. When the waitress brought over our lunches, instead of seeing an opportunity to eat, I saw an opportunity to get poisoned.

"What do you say we swap lunches?" I suggested to Juliana.

"What?" She was playing dumb. Very clever.

"Fine. We don't need to swap. How about you just take a bite of my food to test it?" Juliana's confused look tilted from me, down to my plate, then back up to me.

"I'm a vegetarian," she noted as she took another bite of her poison-free salad.

"My parents don't love me enough to pay out a ransom," I slyly noted.

I searched Juliana's face for even a microexpression of disappointment, but all I saw was confusion. She was a difficult read and I was starving, so I decided to flirt with death and dig into my ham steak. It ended up not being poisoned.

After I loosened up, I actually got to know Juliana.

For starters, she was beautiful. I'm not great at describing people, so bear with me. She was somewhere between zero and twenty feet tall and had mocha-colored skin. She had either two eyes or two mouths. Her hair was long, brown, and luxurious—like a brown Lamborghini. And her personality was even better than her looks. She was funny, smart, and sexy—like a slightly nicer brown Lamborghini. Once, while in Mexico, a waiter made eye contact with me, pointed to Juliana, and then gave me a thumbs-up. "Craigslist," I mouthed back.

For as long as Juliana could remember, she wanted to be an actress. So, after finishing college in Bogotá, Colombia, she sold a car that she had won in a raffle and bought a one-way ticket to Los Angeles.

After her tourist visa ran out, she found a fellow Colombian willing to sponsor her for a work visa. The sponsor owned a small company and agreed to fill out the necessary paperwork and put Juliana on his payroll. In reality Juliana was never paid by the small company. In fact cash flowed in the other direction; each month Juliana covered the payroll taxes that her sponsor paid the government. She earned the money through acting gigs, teaching salsa dancing lessons, and participating in the occasional adventure with a charming Indian American stranger.

Juliana exclusively referred to her sponsor as "the Asshole." And since the Asshole made exactly zero dollars on the whole sponsorship arrangement, I naturally assumed he did it hoping to earn a few smooches. Juliana confirmed this assumption.

Everything Juliana was doing, by the way, was illegal. But it didn't seem like it should have been. She was simply working hard in pursuit of a goal. She wanted to be an actress, so she left everyone she knew in Colombia and moved to Hollywood. What money she did not spend on rent and covering payroll taxes she spent on acting classes. When she wanted to take more expensive acting classes, she started teaching more salsa dancing classes. She had big dreams, gumption, stick-to-it-ive-ness, and a go-getter attitude. She was an American born in Colombia.

And by the end of our first meal together she had charmed the crap out of me; I would have been thrilled to get kidnapped by her.

VALI: Peering Over the Edge of the United States into Mexico

Somewhere, deep in Arizona, road signs began listing distances in kilometers instead of miles. The truck to car ratio skyrocketed. I got the feeling I was the only man for miles who had never been in a fight.

I pulled into a roadside motel in Nogales, less than a mile from the border. The clerk sat behind a bulletproof glass window. I paid for the room by sliding money along a bank-teller-style recessed metal curve that went under the glass. Then the clerk pressed a button, unlocking a door with a loud metallic click so Juliana and I could access the room. The sum effect of this setup made me feel less rather than more safe.

At the end of the first day of the Ridiculous Race, I was frustrated. I had hoped to make it to Guymas on the Mexican coast. But it was already midnight and Guymas was still four hours away, assuming we sailed across the U.S.-Mexico border without any problems. There was no way I could've driven that much longer. My dose of antinarcolepsy drugs was losing its potency and I didn't want to dig into the stash twice on my first day of travel. I had only twenty pills and at least fifty more days to go.

God, I wanted this whole tedious stunt to be over.

STEVE: My First Three Days

Imagine you're just about to start the biggest, craziest race imaginable, a crucial event for which you've prepped for nearly a month, a head-to-head competition against a vicious rival. The pistol goes off—and in your first step, you trip and fall facedown in the muck as your opponent sprints off.

That's a decent metaphor for what happened to me at the start of the Ridiculous Race.

April 14. The day had loomed in my brain like Christmas

to a Nintendo-less child. As it drew near, the first stages of my trip were all in place. But just to double-check, on April 12 I called down to Long Beach to make sure my ship would be leaving as scheduled.

"Yes, I'm calling to check on *Hanjin Athens*? I'm supposed to be a passenger on that ship."

"*Hanjin Athens*? Looks like there's a delay," said the voice on the phone, belonging to a man I'd dubbed Hanjin Matt. "She won't be leaving until the eighteenth."

"WHAT?!"

"It happens," replied the unabashedly indifferent Hanjin Matt.

Just like that, because of some union problem in Oakland, or a weather system in Korea, I'd lost crucial days in a round-the-world race. I would literally have to wait for my ship to come in.

Of course I couldn't reveal this to Vali. My one edge was psychological: I knew Vali looked at me and saw a globe-savvy, bold-hearted, reckless foe who would endure any misery, use any opportunity, and accept any risk to defeat him. I was half-expecting him to give up before the race had even started.

So I played it cool and revealed nothing. The night before our scheduled departure, I challenged Vali to a drinking contest, knowing full well that I'd be able to spend the next day sleeping off the Singapore Slings while he'd have to start crossing a continent.

But after Vali's messy failed handcuffing, and the official launch of the race, I was left with three extremely restless days.

An industrious man would've used this time to, say, learn Russian or study maps.

I did not do this. Instead I developed and tested an optimistic theory that a person can "store up" hygiene in advance of unpleasant conditions. So I took five showers a day.

Knowing that I'd soon be in bizarre lands where I'd be expected to eat chicken foreheads and such, I bulked up at my favorite LA establishments. I ate at Astroburger and Fatburger, the La Brea Bakery and my favorite food landmark of all, the Most Unfortunate Honeybaked Ham Franchise in the World, tragically located in the heart of an Orthodox Jewish neighborhood.

I practiced meditating. On this trip I'd be spending a lot of time with no one to keep me company except my own mind, so we'd best be on good terms. I packed, unpacked, and repacked, wondering whether I'd really need more than three pairs of socks, or more than thirty-six antidiarrhea tablets. One item I was looking forward to trying was my Never-Wash underwear.*

I paced around my apartment like a caged badger. Vali had been gone for three days. He must've made it to the Atlantic by now. I wondered how I could persuade the Coast Guard to send back all eastbound shipping.

And every day I called Hanjin Matt, whose patience never flagged. Finally, on April 17, he told me to report to Pier T the following morning and be ready to ship out.

VALI: Crossing the Border

I awoke in Nogales to find Juliana in workout clothes, rolling up a blue yoga mat. She had clearly gotten a good night's rest. I, on the other hand, had spent most of the night unable to sleep, waiting to hear a spray of gunshots ricocheting off the motel clerk's bulletproof glass followed by the revving of truck engines and the smell of charring carpet and faux wood paneling as our motel burned to the ground.

"Hurry up and get dressed," Juliana chided. "There's a pretty good continental breakfast downstairs."

After some hard-boiled eggs and coffee we drove to the border. Security was shockingly lax. An official waved us through before I could even slow the Impala down.

Ten kilometers later, we saw a sign requesting foreigners to stop and purchase a tourist visa. A sign. That was it. No border guards. No checkpoint. Overland border control into

* I don't know where Steve is getting this—I was with him when he bought this item. It was "Quick-Dry" not "Never-Wash" underwear.—Vali

Mexico appeared to be on the honor system. The sign might as well have read, PLEASE SNEAK INTO MEXICO: WE'RE PRETTY BORED.

Since I was driving a car with U.S. plates, I figured it'd be wise to fill out the necessary paperwork, pay the necessary fees, and pee in the necessary bathrooms. So I pulled over and confidently marched straight up to the tourist visa desk.

"Passport?" requested the immigration agent.

I didn't have my passport.

VALI: Susie, the First of Many People I Encountered Who Thought I Had a Learning Disability

To be honest, when Steve and I dreamed up the Ridiculous Race, I didn't think we'd be able to trick any fancy New York City publishers into financing not one, but two, around-the-world boondoggles. I was wrong.

So with only one month before Departure Day, I found myself forced to plan the trip. My first step was to get other people to do as much of the work for me as possible. To obtain visas, I enlisted the help of Susie.

Moments after we first met, Susie looked up from the list of countries I needed visas for with an expression that told me my request was impossible. Then, while maintaining the expression, she said the same thing with words. *Calm down. I get the point,* I thought.

"Please get me these visas," I begged Susie. "I'm racing my friend Steve around the world and if when we're done he has better stories about more interesting places than I do, I'll never be able to hit on girls at the same party as him again."

"But some of these visas take a long time to get."

"I'm prepared to spend as much of my publisher's money as necessary."

"I'll do my best."

VALI: Crossing the Border (Continued)

Unfortunately, Susie's best wasn't enough to speed up the Belarussian embassy in New York. They had my passport.

Fortunately, I had done my research and knew that until the summer of 2008, a U.S. citizen can enter Mexico by land with a government-issued photo ID and a birth certificate. I slid these two items across the counter.

"This is a *copy* of your birth certificate," the passport official correctly noted. "We need the original. Or your passport."

I turned to Juliana and whispered, "Get him to change his mind."

"Why don't you have your documents? Why do Americans think they can go anywhere they want without following the rules?"

"Please," I begged, "just persuade him to let it slide."

"How?"

"I have a condom you could use," I joked.

Juliana shot me a look that you often see heroines in romantic comedies give the hero early on in the film. On the surface the look conveys a lot of anger, but we all know that it is really the moment that the heroine starts falling in love with the hero. I've watched enough romantic comedies to know that women are always falling in love with me.

Juliana spoke to the passport official in Spanish for a few minutes while I tried to look as helpless and pathetic as possible. I slouched my shoulders, ate dust from the countertop, etc. Finally the official caved and gave me a tourist visa. Later Juliana told me that the hardest part was convincing him that I was American. He didn't buy that someone named Vali Chandrasekaran was born in the United States, so he thought my photocopied birth certificate was a forgery. Just before issuing my visa, he turned to Juliana and threatened, "He is traveling at his own risk. If he gets caught doing anything wrong, we'll deport him back to India."

Forty-eight hours into my journey I had already discovered a new route to the Far East. I was on pace to discover El

Dorado by nightfall and the Fountain of Youth by the end of the week. I wished Columbus were still alive so I could gloat about how much better I was at exploring than him. He seems like a guy who'd get real steamed about that sort of thing.

VALI: Driving in Mexico Is Like Driving in the United States Except You Always Think You Are About to Die

I drove down Highway 15, the well-maintained interstate that runs down half of the west coast of Mexico before dog-legging left, toward the capital city. The drive along the coast was mostly through a barren swath of desert and mountains. Very few other cars shared the road with me. It looked and felt like the drive through the desert from Los Angeles to Las Vegas on a weekday morning. Except every two minutes, I passed a small white cross memorial. According to my back-of-the envelope calculations, 100 percent of drivers on Highway 15 are killed. On the other hand, I never saw any car accidents. Perhaps the white crosses were a scheme by the Mexican Department of Transportation to remind people to drive safely. Another common sight during the drive was a huge fire burning the tall wild grass in the median or along the side of the road. The ones I saw were each at least a hundred feet long and a few dozen feet deep. What were these? Portals to hell? Advertisements for matches? Nobody seemed to know.

A few times per day Juliana and I passed through towns, each of which looked like movie-set versions of Mexico. I had seen places like them so many times on television and theater screens that the real thing looked fake to me. The streets were crowded with extras and the brightly colored buildings looked artificially aged by a sandblaster.

Once the sun went down, the Mexican highway acquired additional dangers. The roads were rarely lit so I drove along at a hundred kilometers per hour toward the blackness just beyond my headlights. At one point, I accidentally merged onto a two-lane, bidirectional, non-toll portion of Highway 15, frequented by eighteen-wheeler trucks. The road was so narrow that every rig passing from the opposite direction pulled—shook—the Precision Red Impala into the other lane, each time bringing Juliana and I within inches of a nasty car wreck before suddenly releasing us.

But the scariest danger was highway robbery by banditos who, according to the guidebooks, occasionally held up cars at night. My strategy for dealing with armed bandits—allowing myself to get badly beaten up, robbed, and left for dead—was alarmingly suboptimal, but I asked around and it appeared to be one of the better strategies out there.

Fortunately, I had Juliana helping me. She translated the road signs, followed our progress on the maps, and occasionally drove. Best of all, the two of us got along famously. We had been acquainted for less than forty-eight hours but acted like we had been in a serious relationship for years: Juliana constantly checked to see if I was tired or hungry as I drove; we revealed personal information to each other; she made me talk to her mother on the phone; et cetera. We were aware of the absurdity of our close relationship, developed in such a short time frame. We addressed it by behaving as if we were in a parody of a long-term relationship. We called each other "husband" and "wife"; whenever she returned from the bathroom, I would accuse her of having an affair with her tennis coach; she would pretend that I was not the most awesome and hilarious dude she had ever met in her life.

Without Juliana, I would have probably intentionally driven into one of the mysterious highway fires. She was the only thing keeping me sane. I wondered how Steve was staving off boredom on his journey across the Pacific. By this point he was probably talking to his nose hairs.

VALI: Into Mazatlan

Late into my second day of driving, Mexico mounted a serious assault on my sanity.

I saw a sign informing me that I was thirty-two kilometers from Mazatlan. A few minutes later, another sign claimed I was thirty-five kilometers from Mazatlan. There were only two explanations for this phenomenon: (1) I was driving away from Mazatlan and Mexican drivers prefer to know what cities they are driving away from rather than what cities they are driving toward or (2) I was driving the Chevy Impala so fast that I was tearing holes in the space-time continuum. Neither explanation was particularly comforting, but I hoped for the second since it probably meant I was breaking the land speed record.

I turned up the air conditioner, blasting the cold air directly onto my face.

Thankfully, it turned out that I was driving in the correct direction. Around 3:00 a.m. we made it into town. Around 3:01 a.m., I found myself driving the wrong way down a one-way street. And thirty seconds after that, I found myself staring blankly at two Mexican cops. Less than twenty-four hours in Mexico so far and I was about to book a one-way ticket to Bombay on my "lost" passport.

I had come to an intersection with no signs and accidentally turned onto a one-way street. After driving fifty feet, I realized my error and turned around. There was nobody else on the road. None of these specifics mattered to the fat Mexican Justices of the Peace. They saw my Tennessee license plates and smelled dollars.

Juliana pleaded with the cops.

"They say you could have caused a serious accident," Juliana translated. "We need to go down to the station and fill out a lot of paperwork with them."

"Offer them some money," I whispered to Juliana.

"No. I hate corruption in Latin America. We're not giving them any money until they ask for it."

I was so tired I had to concentrate to make my heart beat

and Juliana, who had been napping for the last hour, wanted to engage in civil disobedience. I was livid. Her heart may have been in the right place, but it wasn't getting me to sleep any faster. I was too tired to care about principles. In that moment I would have punched a baby seal in the face in exchange for another hour of sleep.

I decided to take matters into my own hands. I rested my head against the steering wheel and tried to nap. Then Juliana hit me.

"They just asked me for some money for coffee," she informed me through a satisfied smile.

Finally! I hadn't withdrawn any pesos yet, so I handed one of the cops the only bill I had—a $20 note. He shot me a smile so wide that the ends of his lips actually met on the back of his head. I had paid him a 300 percent premium on the standard bribe of $5. Thrilled with his windfall, the cop became our new best friend. He welcomed us to Mazatlan, then recommended a few nearby motels with reasonable rates.

During my entire drive through Mexico, I was pulled over three times, was stopped at two sobriety checkpoints (I hadn't had a drink either time), and once had soldiers thoroughly search the Chevy Impala. Thanks to Juliana's stubbornness and pleading eyes, I received zero tickets and never paid another bribe.

VALI: My Parents Prefer Safety over Awesomeness

It wasn't until the third day of driving through Mexico that I finally started to relax. I got used to the idiosyncrasies of the road: the occasional military checkpoints with young soldiers on the lookout for drug runners; the sections of the highway where flashing lights accentuated the divider line and shoulder, giving me the sensation of driving a giant Jupiter-sized car along the milky way; the unhidden prostitutes who waited just beyond every set of toll booths in the cold nighttime desert against silhouettes of trident cacti.

I was finally confident that I would make it to Mexico City alive and on time.

To celebrate the surge of confidence, Juliana and I took a short driving break in Guadalajara, Mexico's second largest city, for a drink.

The waitress at the bar brought over two beers, which were served as Micheladas—a beer-based Mexican cocktail. As with any cocktail, preparations vary. Our Micheladas were prepared by adding Worcestershire sauce, salt, lime juice, and salsa to the Coronas. They were reminiscent of Bloody Marys. And they made me very happy. It's exciting to discover a new alcoholic breakfast beverage.

After the drink, I walked outside to call my parents and let them know my heart was still beating. They were pretty concerned for my safety during this race. I tried to assuage their fears by pretending to be taking a lot of precautions. But they saw through that. My parents knew me too well.

To keep in touch with loved ones (my family) and romantic idiots (Steve), I convinced the Irridium Satellite Phone Company to loan Steve and me two phones for the duration of the race. In exchange, we agreed to mention Irridium satellite phones in *The Ridiculous Race*. I wish I could say that the phones were fantastic and easy to use and a marvel of technology. But I feel obligated to tell the truth.

I fucking hated the phones.

They worked only if one had direct access to the sky. So calls from inside cars or near trees were not possible. And, as it turned out, I was spending a lot of my time inside cars or near trees. When the phones did work, the connection was awful. I've gotten better sound quality out of two paper cups connected by some string. Because of these shortcomings, I spent several minutes every day on Mexican street corners loudly screaming my American-accented English into a massive and boxy 1980s-looking cell phone. Somehow, I was never robbed. Probably because I was such an obvious target, thieves assumed it was a trap.

"Vali, where are you?" asked my mom.

I looked at the small group of Mexican men across the

street. They were staring at me while talking among themselves.

"In a five-star hotel in Mexico."

"Be careful!"

Nothing could be safe enough for my parents. If they had their way, the Ridiculous Race would be about me sitting in my bedroom while an armed guard kept watch outside the door.

VALI: Next Time I Race Around the World, I'm Going West

At the end of my third night of driving, I stopped in Morelia. I planned on sleeping for five hours before continuing on to Cuernavaca, making my noon jetpack-purchasing appointment.

"Why does the clock say one a.m.?" I asked. "I thought it was midnight."

Juliana didn't respond because we both knew the answer. We had crossed into another time zone, our third in three days. Practically this meant we would get one less hour of sleep. This caused some emotional distress.

Every country observes time differently. Some maintain only one time zone. Some run their time zones along major geographical boundaries such as mountain ranges or rivers. Some countries practice daylight savings time. Some do not. As a result, there are over thirty time zones in the world. For simplicity's sake, let's assume that the Earth is divided into twenty-four wedge-shaped time zones, one for each hour of the day, each containing fifteen-degree lunes of the globe. That means, assuming I circumnavigate the globe in my goal of fifty days, I will cross into a new time zone *every other day*. Every other day I'm going to lose an hour of sleep if I want to catch scheduled ships, buses, trains, meet foreign heads of state, et cetera. As if that wasn't bad enough, it meant every other day Steve was going to *gain* an extra hour.

My only solace was imagining Steve shivering in the hold of a container ship amid thousands of pounds of plastic bound for a factory in China where it would be molded into SpongeBob SquarePants lunch boxes.

More than ever, I really wanted the jetpack to work.

STEVE: Two Weeks Before the Mast

"So it will take you fourteen days."

"Yes."

"You will be on this ship for *fourteen* days?"

"Yes."

The questions were coming from my buddy Doogs, who'd driven me to Long Beach Harbor. We were at the counter of the Bake 'n' Broil for my last land-based meal: the country-fried steak special with two eggs, hash browns, toast, a blueberry muffin, and lots of coffee.

"Did you bring any books?"

"Oh yes." I held up a grocery bag loaded with epic tomes, spines as yet uncracked.

"Will there be any other passengers?"

"I don't know."

"What kind of cargo will the ship be carrying?"

"I don't know."

"What's the food like on this thing?"

"I don't know."

"Are there storms and things?"

"I guess."

"Are you going to get seasick?"

"No, I got this medicine you put behind your ears."

Doogs considered this. "The sailors are going to make fun of you for that."

"Probably."

"So, there are still pirates. I read that. They use machine guns and stuff."

"Yes." There were 266 acts of piracy on the world's oceans during the previous year. I'd memorized this.

"Are you going to be attacked by pirates?"

"I don't know."

"Are you going to die?"

"It's possible."

"Would you like some pie, hon?"

That last question was asked not by Doogs but by our buxom waitress. She looked like she'd be happy to give me the hug I very much wanted.

"Yes please. Apple crumble."

"Do you want ice cream on that?"

"Yes please, very much so."

I've wanted to take an ocean voyage since age six, when I tried to float from the beach in Marshfield, Massachusetts, to Portugal* on an inflatable raft, venturing out as far as I could before my mom started shrieking and sent my dad out to drag me back. I built foot-long model ships, then wondered how to cram them into bottles. In high school I interned at the New England Aquarium, where I stuffed vitamins into frozen squid, fed cuttlefish by hand, maintained tubs of lobster larvae, pulled algae off of coral with my fingers, and tested sea otter water until my clothes stank of brine. This did not help with girls but I was very popular with cuttlefish. My iPod is loaded with scratchy recordings of old sea chanteys, songs with titles like "Haul On the Bowline," "Come All You Gallant Fishermen," and "The Handsome Cabin Boy." (Spoiler alert: The handsome cabin boy is no boy at all; this causes a number of problems.)

But as for actually going to sea, I'm too lazy.

It's a shame, because from *Captains Courageous* to *Cabin Boy*, there's a great tradition of sea voyages making a man. At some point in my sea madness I'd come across *Two Years Before the Mast*, published in 1840 by Richard Henry Dana. While attending Harvard, Dana discovered his eyesight was failing, so he decided to cure it the sensible way: by signing up for a three-year sailing voyage to California. The resulting book is terrific, although if you read it I suggest you skip the dozens of pages given over to hide-tanning methods. But the point is

* For now-obscure reasons I thought that's where Chef Boyardee lived.

clear. If you're a pasty nerd with bad eyesight, a good long sea voyage will set you right.

I'd fallen into a lazy cycle of landlubberdom. I ordered apple crumble pie with ice cream and hoped the waitress would hug me. A hard sea voyage would do me good.

As the crow flies, or the unusually straight-swimming dolphin swims, the trip from California to Asia is some 6,522 miles. But the real problem with crossing the Pacific isn't the distance. It's that nobody wants to do it. Those are 6,522 vacant, humanless miles that no casual vacationer wants to see.

But I'd agreed to a wager of honor. No airplanes.

So I started thinking about cargo ships. If I could hitch a ride on one of those, I'd be delivered across the Pacific as efficiently as a forty-foot container of frozen steaks. I hoped that, like those steaks, I would cross the ocean without turning rancid or leaking blood.

But you can't just stroll down to the port and ask for rides. Port security guards are among the least-amused people in the world. Even if some captain had agreed to take me, freighters run on changing routes and schedules, going where the cargo needs to go. I'd be likely to end up in Laem Chabang (the nineteenth most commonly visited port in the world) or Keelung (number eleven)—both fine cities, I'm sure, just not great launching pads to beat Vali.

With the help of the daring traveler's greatest friend, the Internet, I learned of a German company called NSB (short for Niederelbe Schiffahrtsgesellschaft Buxtehude, which at no point in my trip did I hear anyone pronounce). NSB is Germanically efficient. They realized that automation on their container ships meant smaller crews, and that meant empty cabins. For the equivalent of about $144 a day, to pay for my food and cover the insurance risk, they'd let me ride along on one of their "ocean-going giants," enormous ships contracted out to various shipping companies. *Hanjin Athens* ran a set four-point route from Long Beach to Oakland to Korea to Shanghai. All I had to do to come along was receive a barrage of immunizations for various sailor-borne diseases.

NSB, to its credit, doesn't oversell the attractiveness of these trips. "Watch containers being loaded and unloaded in highly mechanized terminals" is one of the main selling points on its Web site.

So I found myself at Pier T of Long Beach Harbor on the afternoon of April 18 watching containers being loaded and unloaded in a highly mechanized terminal.

You know that special magic that occurs where the land meets the sea? In Long Beach, they've figured out how to eliminate that. Don't be fooled by its romantic and melodious name: Pier T is an enormous asphalt lot, dense with alleys of stacked containers.

Hanjin Athens wasn't romantic, either. It is a massive oceangoing behemoth, 304 yards long and so wide it can't fit through the Panama Canal. It looked as though joyless accountants and squinting engineers went over every inch stripping off character. No one will paint an oil painting of it, or wax poetically about how her lines meld with the wind and waves. It—no need to stand on that "she" nonsense with container ships—is a hollowed-out shell of steel. About a third of the way from the stern there's a narrow superstructure, five stories high. This is the only habitable part of the ship; all the rest is essentially a flatbed truck, with containers stacked on top of the ones below. You could build a very accurate model of the *Hanjin Athens* out of LEGOs.

Even the quirks—the After 8 bar, for instance, tucked into a cranny on the outside of F Deck—look prefabricated. A single tiki torch was propped against the wall, as though consultants in Germany had determined that was the exact minimum of "human" touch that would keep a sailor from going insane.

BE VIGILANT IN PIRATE AREAS warned the poster that hung outside the galley. Below these words was a drawing of two sneering, unshaven, knife-wielding goons crawling onto the deck under a night sky, while their lanky associate slinked over the rail with an automatic pistol. These weren't parrot-and-eyepatch pirates—they were slice-off-one-finger-a-day-unless-you-pay-ransom pirates.

"You don't need to worry about that," said Alex. "We

wouldn't be going near Somalia, or the Indonesian straits, the bad pirate waters."

Maybe not. But I was locked into spending the next two weeks in an unfamiliar world with its own rules and dangers. Its own posters.

Alex was the first officer, and he did not appear to be a match for these poster pirates. He didn't really look like a sailor at all, at least not as I'd pictured one. He was kind of doughy. In a lifeboat situation he'd be the guy I'd vote for eating.

That first afternoon he displayed his affable style as he showed me around: from A Deck, where banks of computer screens showed how the engine was doing; to D Deck, where I'd eat in the officers' mess; to E Deck, where I could sign out cans of Pringles and read old shipping magazines on the couches in the officers' lounge; up to F Deck, where I'd be living; and on to the bridge, at the moment offering a panoramic view of tugboat traffic.

All six of the officers, including Alex, were German. In theory they all spoke English, although none of them seemed to have gone past Chapter 8 or 9 in the textbook. English was the language the Germans used to speak to the eleven crewmen, who were all Filipinos.

I was the only passenger they'd had in months. That was just as well. I didn't want to spend time with anybody who was unbalanced enough to do what I was doing.

The scariest aspect of my tour was that Alex kept referring to the captain as "the master," which gave the whole thing a spooky Teutonic tone: "the master will decide when we depart," "the master will take your passport," "the master is quite fond of basketball."

So I was surprised to meet the master himself and discover that he was a mild-mannered and balding middle-aged man who looked like Mr. Belding, the principal from *Saved By the Bell*, but with a bushy German mustache.

My cabin was about equivalent to a room at the Holiday Inn, although it had the disadvantage of rolling from side to side, a problem I have not noticed at most Holiday Inns. I had my own shower and mini-bathroom, which would be the scene of some slippery antics. The window offered a glorious view of the backs of crates HJCU 1904 02 6 and 7819635.

Aside from trying on my snug, plush orange survival suit, and getting a seat assigned in the lifeboat, *Hanjin Athens* seemed about as exciting as a giant floating Kinkos.

STEVE: Is Fourteen Days on the Pacific a Grand, Romantic Adventure or Crushingly Boring?

The short answer is "crushingly boring."

By the time we left port, it was clear that the greatest danger facing me wasn't pirates or storms. Or sharks. Or giant squid. Or flesh-eating jellyfish. Or being raped and stabbed by sailors. Or stingrays.

It was keeping my idle mind from destroying itself.

Entire days I spent staring at the ocean. I read so much that my eyes broke and I couldn't see words.

But I was determined to prove that fourteen days on *Hanjin Athens* is truly boring only to the Vali-level intellect, a childlike mind ruined by the cacophony of the electronic age, demanding to be constantly amused with flashing pictures and loud sounds. To anyone willing to dig a little deeper, a freighter voyage is full of surprising pleasures.

STEVE: The Surprising Pleasures of *Hanjin Athens*

Friendship. On our first night at sea, I found one of the Filipino crewmen on watch—his name was Glen—and we shook hands. After that there was a silent, awkward pause. Part of this might've been that Glen's English wasn't so good, and I'd picked up very little Tagalog on the streets of Needham, Massachusetts.

We also didn't have much to talk about. I was at sea because I was participating in a ludicrous wager; Glen was at sea because the $6,000 a year he makes wiping down decks supports his entire family in the Philippines. I was giddy and nervous; Glen looked bored and tired. I'd read about the sea in obscure books; Glen had lived on it in nine-month stretches since he was fifteen.

So I mentioned the one thing that might bridge the gap between us, the only Filipino entry in my personal encyclopedia of Stuff I Know About.

"Glen, do you know Manny Pacquiao?"

The Story of Manny Pacquiao

When Manny Pacquiao was a twelve-year-old kid in the slums of General Santos City, he ran away from home after his drunken father killed and ate his beloved dog. This left Pacquiao with some unresolved anger issues, so he became the greatest superfeatherweight boxer alive.

In his native country, Manny Pacquiao endorses, among other things, brands of socks, gin, health food, vinegar, a vitamin supplement for fighting roosters, and a kind of karaoke microphone. He released a hit single, "Para Sa Yo," and appears in the video, soulfully crooning while stroking a punching bag. In Filipino movies, Pacquiao has played a supernatural version of himself who can shoot fire from his mouth. Pacquiao's wife once called one of his girlfriends and threatened to sew her eyes shut.

The Filipino people love him as the National Fist. When his fights are broadcast, the violent streets of Manila are silent and crime free. Sixteen years after the alleged dog eating, Pacquiao is the most famous Filipino in the world.

I had never heard of him until a year ago, when my friend Nick Khan, sports superagent, told me stories about how the very sight of his client made Filipinos burst into tears of rapture. Nick kindly got me a press pass to see Pacquiao fight Erik Morales, the Terror of Tijuana, in Las Vegas. There were eighteen thousand fans in the Thomas and Mack Arena, screaming invective in English, Spanish, and Tagalog.

Watching this fight might've been the most intense

thing I've ever done. In the third round, Pacquiao knocked Morales out.

Before the match, Pacquiao had been sick and feverish and begged to have it called off. It was too late, the manager told him. His best bet was to win fast. So that's what he'd done. Manny Pacquiao is that awesome.

Glen looked at me as his eyes widened with joy.

"YOU know Manny Pacquiao?"

"Yes!" I said. "I saw him fight Morales!" I demonstrated to Glen the way Pacquiao had nudged Morales's head into position before smashing him directly in the face.

From that moment on, I never lacked for friends on *Hanjin Athens*. My fame spread across the ship. Filipino crewmen I'd never met came up to me, screamed "Pacquiao!" and insisted we high-five. They told me that Pacquiao was running for Congress in the Philippines, so sometimes the greeting was "*Congressional Candidate* Manny Pacquiao!" in the same "ain't the world nuts?" tone you might say "*Governor* Arnold Schwarzenegger."

That night, and every night thereafter, I had an invitation to the crew rec room. This was a cranny down on B Deck that looked like a finished basement. Out the windows the Pacific rolled by, but inside we'd sit, drink San Miguel beers, and watch old Pacquiao fights on DVD.

That was how I spent my evenings for two weeks.

Shore Leave: San Francisco. On the first morning of our trip, *Hanjin Athens* turned into San Francisco Bay, which afforded me a great chance to see what the Golden Gate Bridge looks like from underneath, a view known only to mariners and suicides.

Come into San Francisco by water, and the miraculous accident of its geography is clear. From a bobbing ship its hill-protected harbor seems as welcoming as your grandmother's bosom. You get why hundreds of sailing ships chose this as the place for disgorging prospectors and their accompanying prostitutes.

Our ship docked at Oakland, and as we took on cargo a few lucky officers had a day to go ashore. I hitched a ride with them into town.

"Terrific!" I thought. "We'll tear the place apart!" These being sailors, I assumed I was in for a day of brothel-hopping and whiskey-pounding, and that I'd go to sleep that night with a tattoo and some wounds from a knife fight.

This was incorrect. The third officer was going to the dentist. The chief engineer wanted to do some shopping. Worst of all, the captain and the fourth mate, a young lady named Liesel,* were going to rent bikes and cycle across to Sausalito.

It was enough to make a nineteenth-century sailor choke on his grog. Deciding I had to uphold the honor of the ship, I headed to the Buena Vista. It's claimed that Irish coffee was invented at this bar, but my own guess is that the first Irish guy to ever have coffee also came up with the idea of putting whiskey in it.

Knife fight or not, sitting at a bar, drinking whiskey for breakfast, and waiting to ship out for China gave me a swagger. Out the window of the Buena Vista you can see docked an old merchant ship, *Balclutha*. I scoffed at it. Poor old rat trap probably couldn't hold ten containers. With a deep-throated laugh I threw down my drink and strutted out with a sailor's insouciant pride. Pretty much that whole day I spent strutting around with a sailor's insouciant pride.

When a ship the size of *Hanjin Athens* enters or leaves a port, a local harbor expert—a pilot—comes aboard and guides the vessel through the tricky process of docking or undocking and steering through traffic. Leaving San Francisco our pilot was just what I'd hoped for, a red-cheeked old man with a fisherman's cap and a boat-calling voice, a chantey voice, who bellowed out orders across the bridge as he guided us past Alcatraz.

"Have a last look at your country," the captain said, as the Golden Gate Bridge faded away in the dying sunlight. Yeah, that's right. I watched the Golden Gate Bridge fade away in dying sunlight.

* Name changed; you'll see why.

OCEAN STARING: Most days I spent at least an hour just looking at the ocean. I came up with Crayola-style names for its shifting colors. Some days it was slick black—Wet Chalkboard. Some days it looked gray—Canned Bacon Grease. Some days it appeared almost oily—Salmon Skin. But many days it was big, full, Squeezed Blueberry blue.

FINE DINING: The first meal I had aboard was something called "labkous," made of chopped beef topped with a fried egg. "It looks like dog food!" Alex commented, almost admiringly, "but it's quite good."

When I tasted it I suspected it quite possibly *was* dog food and that tricking me into eating it was an ancient maritime initiation. If these guys were funny enough to trick me into eating dog food, kudos to them.

The food did not improve. It was German cuisine as interpreted by a Filipino cook, which is the punch line to a joke about the world's worst possible food.

The meals were thick and serious—veiny sausages, drenched meatballs, salty, cow-chunked soups. About two-thirds of the dishes involved a fried egg on top. The second engineer told me that on his last trip, his boss had keeled over from a heart attack, mid-cigarette. Given the diet I was surprised when our own trip was coronary-free.

"Yes, this is manly," I would think as I slathered Düsseldorf-style mustard on a bratwurst and tucked into a pile of boiled potatoes. "I am a manly man, who has had a man's day at sea, and I require this man-food." This after a day of strolling around on the deck looking at seagulls and lounging half-dressed in my bed flipping through an old issue of *Vanity Fair*.

The surfeit of lard began to wear on me, so I tried eating Filipino food with the crew. They were eating steaming piles of stir-fry vegetables over rice, and they seemed delighted that I'd gone over to their side. Proud of my democratic, man-of-the-people tastes, I asked them the best way to season my food. Somebody handed me a glass bottle of something that I dolloped out generously. As soon as I tasted this stuff I concluded it must be turtle mucous.

One day we had a barbecue. A suckling pig had been brought aboard, and it was stuffed with onions and carrots and then roasted for an entire day over a grill made of half an oil barrel. The crewmen generously offered me the finest part, the crispy ear, but I declined. This baffled and saddened them.

The Germans played a mix CD comprised almost entirely of house remixes of old Bond movie theme songs. San Miguels aplenty were on hand, and soon the tone grew almost maudlin. The conversation turned to poetic recountings in half-English, half-Tagalog of the virtues of various wives, girlfriends, and mothers left behind. One of the crewmen, Oliver, told me about how he never met his father, how his mother supported eight children selling fish in the market in Manila, and how he cried the first time he went to sea. I thought of my own mom, and we both would've broken down in lonesome tears had someone not lifted everyone's spirits by proposing a toast to Pacquiao.

WORSHIP: One Sunday I was invited to attend "Sailor's Church." It turns out this devout ceremony consists of the officers gathering to drink a beer and watch the captain's vacation videos. These videos were heavy on dissolve cuts between sunsets and were all overlaid with gentle Spanish guitar music. It was my misfortune, for storytelling purposes, that my captain was more Mr. Rogers than Ahab, but the canon of sea literature does not contain many captains who are masters of iMovie, so at least I'm broadening the field.

MENTAL CHALLENGE: My second night aboard, I agreed to a chess match against Oliver, arrogantly assuming I'd prove a match for him. He promptly beat me eleven games in a row. He took to beating me without bishops. Then without knights or bishops. Our nightly games became a kind of chess Harlem Globetrotters show. Oliver would call which pawn he was going to checkmate me with, then do so. He'd studied the games of Spassky and Fischer and Kasparov, and memorized thousands of openings. It struck me as a tragic waste that this guy's job was doing things like spraying freshwater tanks with chlorine.

SEA STORIES: I'd talk to the officers, too. Most of them had grown up in East Germany. One of the engineers, Gunther, was six foot five, and I asked him the biggest difference about life before the Berlin Wall fell. He told me that, in those days, he could never find clothes that fit. This is hardly the greatest tragedy of the Communist era, but he said it in such a sad, frustrated way that I almost wanted to cry picturing Gunther walking about, ankles exposed, as he yearned for longer pants.

One day the captain suggested I join him for a beer out on the deck as the sun went down. I immediately launched into a flurry of questions—about his home, his kids, his mustache.

Suddenly I remembered the film *Crimson Tide*, where Captain Gene Hackman invites the young Denzel Washington to take in a sunset from their cruising submarine. Denzel keeps his mouth shut, and when the two go back inside, Captain Hackman compliments his officer on his discretion. "An egghead," he says, "would've talked the view away."

I realized I was being an egghead and promptly shut up. The captain and I sat in contented silence for half an hour. Once again the films of Denzel Washington had guided me through a crucial life test.

Just when I was getting disappointed that both the officers and the crew seemed exclusively to be level-headed, well-disciplined professionals, I met the cook. I had ducked into the kitchen to see if I could unravel the turtle mucous mystery when he gripped me by the arm.

"You been to the Bermuda Triangle?" he asked me.

He looked at me out the sides of his eyes, as though he suspected I might be in league with the Bermuda Triangle.

"I heard it's terrible!" I assured him.

"Don't go there. Many ships lost," he said in his somber Filipino accent. Then he leaned in and whispered, "Maybe it's magnets."

He then began to list his girlfriends. He was accounted

for, ladywise, in Shanghai, Hong Kong, Manila, Vladivostok, Tokyo, Houston, Long Beach, and Tianjin. He suggested I should accumulate such an arsenal. "They cook for me. They always cry, cry. I tell them stop cry, cook."

I made a nightly ritual of talking to him. This was hard, because he spoke largely in a language of his own invention.

But I never stopped listening, because sometimes an incredible detail would emerge. He told me about a ship he served on that got caught in a crossfire during the Iran-Iraq War in the '80s. He told me the water itself was on fire from burning oil, but as ships exploded some men stripped down to their underwear and jumped overboard. What still sticks with me is the way he pantomimed sailors pulling their rings off their fingers and handing them to friends before plunging.

Then he told me where to find prostitutes in Korea.

The best stories anyone had, however, were pirate stories. Oliver told me of an attack on a ship he was on off the coast of West Africa, when a gang of miscreants were discovered on the stern, hacking off tow ropes. They were chased off, but the desperation of men who'd attack a ship to steal rope was not lost on him. The captain told me a story of a gang of pirates who snuck aboard and managed to grab the first mate, hold a knife to his throat, and force the handover of a safe full of cash.

FLIRTING WITH THE ONLY WOMAN ABOARD: This was a challenge, because Liesel's shift on the bridge was between 2:00 and 6.00 a.m. But seducing a woman on a cargo ship would ensure victory in the Awesomeness Contest, so my body managed to sleep-flirt for a few minutes every night, waking itself up, proceeding to the bridge, making a terrible joke about the International Date Line, then going back to bed. I'd fall asleep wondering if two miles directly below my bed a ten-foot spider crab was picking apart the wounded body of a monstrous sun star.

LEARNING ABOUT NAVIGATION: I'd brought with me a plastic sextant, and one noon I stood out on the deck and took a sunsight. In times past this was the only way to determine longitude. The knowledge of this ancient art has been lost to younger sailors, a fact bemoaned by the captain. He kindly took the time to work through the navigation tables with me and calculate our position based on my measurement. He seemed confused when he realized we must be somewhere in Montana. He did not adjust course.

EXERCISE: Should I cross paths with Vali during this race, I'd need to be in peak physical condition. So every day I lifted weights in the ship's tiny gym. My arms grew from the puniness of tender young saplings to the strength of slightly thicker saplings.

As this was a race, and the end might come down to a sprint, every day I put in a few miles on the exercise bike. Riding an exercise bike on a violently pitching ship works out not just your thighs, but your brain's dizziness receptors.

The gym also had a pool, which was empty, but Alex kept offering to fill it up for me. This was his favorite joke, as the seawater was about forty-eight degrees. I kept declining, and he kept offering, and the joke went the full circle, through annoyingly not funny and back around to funny. It was usually funniest right after I'd gotten off the exercise bike.

I also competed in a basketball tournament. Apparently teams on the ship were always divided along racial lines, so I ended up on the German side.

It should be noted here that despite a lanky stature and two developmental years during which I refused to drink any fluids save those served in a Boston Celtics 1986 commemorative glass, I am terrible at basketball. Yet on the half-court on the stern of *Hanjin Athens*, I dominated.

It was a classic matchup of skilled but small players—the Filipinos—versus the tall but gawky Teutonics. The Filipinos would duck and weave and execute picks and set up passes, only to have their perfect shots swatted from the air by my flailing, pasty arms. No Filipino eye was safe from the stray elbows of the whites, and the two games ended first in a clumsy tie and then a German victory.

At the end of this, Fourth Mate Liesel pointed out in her halting English that "almost your every shot you made went in!" Damn right—and was romance blooming?

SIGHTSEEING: The ocean should have historical markers. The Filipinos might've been more inspired if they'd remembered our game was taking place in the Tsushima Strait, where two of the greatest underdog victories in naval history occurred. In these waters, in 1281, the fleet of Kublai Khan was destroyed by a typhoon, the famous "kamikaze" or "divine wind," and puny Japan was spared from invasion. Six hundred twenty-four years later, Russia and Japan were at war. The Russian Baltic Fleet sailed all the way around the world, only to be destroyed here by the Japanese in a single day.

Twenty-one of the tsar's ships were on the ocean bottom somewhere under the waters around us. But unfortunately, on the surface, historical ocean looks a lot like regular ocean, so I quickly lost interest.

TEXTING VALI: Every few days I'd brave gale winds to stand out on the deck, point my satellite phone upward, and text Vali:

Already in China. Have fallen in love, been elected mayor of small village.

He'd reply:

I know you're on the ocean. I hope you're bored out of your mind.

SHORE LEAVE—KOREA: The first foreign country I visited in this race was South Korea, when we stopped in Busan to take on and take off some cargo. Busan is South Korea's second biggest metropolis, an ink-splotchy mess of mountains and crooked-finger harbors on the southeast corner of the peninsula.

The captain invited me to go ashore with him and Liesel. He kept encouraging us to talk—had he noticed the romantic sparks after the basketball game? As if chaperoning a date, he led us into the mountains to the lovely Beom-Eo Sa Buddhist temple.

Once again my stereotypes about sailors were smashed, because the captain seemed to be quite an expert on Shilla period Buddhism. He drank deeply from a spring fountain, and then bounded forth as he led Liesel and I on a vigorous march up through the forested mountains. Both Liesel and I thought this was a lunatic idea but were obliged to trudge along.

On we went back to town, and through Busan's enormous fish market, where elderly women tend buckets of sea cucumbers and keep Coke bottles cold in bins that house spider crabs. We did not, however, visit Texas Street, where the cook had advised me I might find pliant women of all nationalities. As the captain explained to Liesel, "It's just for gentlemen."

That night the captain hosted the officers and me for a Korean feast in a restaurant overlooking the harbor. Hite beers were enthusiastically ordered and consumed, and perhaps by design I was sitting right next to Liesel, but our romance was not to be, because she started talking.

I'm willing to give her the benefit of the doubt and say that her remarks about the demographics of Baltimore, Maryland, were garbled in translation rather than racist. But any hopes for freighter travel romance were substantially dimmed.

LEARNING ABOUT GLOBAL COMMERCE: One day, somewhere way off British Columbia, Alex and I were walking around the bow of the ship. He was explaining to me the ridiculously cushy job of Suez Canal light guy (you come onboard, switch on a light, and take a nap for twelve hours) when we passed under a container that had a sickly sweet smell, like the jacket of a disheveled old man on a bus.

"That must be cowhides," Alex said. "That's the smell of their preservative."

The stink of these cowhides blending with the briny air, the forty-foot aluminum container they were in, the economic logic of their going to China, the fact that the port they came from was a boring parking lot—all this can be traced to a man you've never heard of named Malcom McLean, who started out driving tobacco trucks in North Carolina during the Depression and rose to run his own shipping company.

Back in the 1950s, the process of loading a ship with cargo was not unlike packing a Volvo with vacation gear. It was done almost entirely by hand, with burly longshoremen stuffing crates of oranges and sacks of coffee and sheet metal and lumber wherever it would fit.

This struck Malcom McLean as stupid. He decided he should just lift the forty-foot trailers off the backs of his trucks and stack them onto ships.

"Using boxes of the same size" doesn't sound like that brilliant of an idea. But it made shipping so much cheaper and easier that it blew open the world economy. Economists know what a big deal this is, so they came up with a smart-sounding name for the use of same-size boxes: "the container revolution."

Malcom McLean's idea is why Wal-Mart can keep prices so low, why cargo nets are now only for gym class, and why the movie *On the Waterfront* is a charming anachronism. It's why San Francisco and Manhattan convert their docks to condos while Laem Chabang and Newark handle the world's cargo.

In about fifty years the entire world has changed, from a chaos of loading jumbled-up messes off piers by hand to a system of stacking giant aluminum boxes in an organized, uniform pattern that could calm the nerves of the obsessive-compulsive.

Except for the fact that, because you can't see inside them, any one of those containers might be a nuclear bomb.

Best not to worry about it. The crew of *Hanjin Athens* didn't. First Officer Alex was in charge of the containers—"cans," as he and everyone else who works with them call them. Alex knew what was in any cans listed as hazardous—helium, batteries, paint. But it would just be too much paperwork to bother with the rest of them. So he had no idea, unless he could smell it.

He did let me in on a fact that nearly made my brain explode. Because the United States imports so much stuff from China, and exports so little, empty cans stack up in Long

Beach while the Chinese run out of them. So 65 percent of the cans we were carrying were empty. They were going back to Shanghai to get filled up with more stuff for Americans. *Hanjin Athens* was a physical demonstration of our trade deficit.

I didn't power myself across the Pacific. But the Adidas shoes I was wearing were made in Vietnam. So was the Eagle Creek backpack I was carrying. My iPod was assembled in China, which is also where my raincoat was made. China is where my trusty Never-Wash underwear came from, too. So I helped, in a tiny way, to power the economic engine that was driving *Hanjin Athens* across the Pacific. That's almost as good as rowing.

PROFOUND THOUGHTS ON THE NATURE OF LIFE: One day at four in the morning we sailed through a narrow channel off Unimak Island, in the Aleutians.

These days it's kind of pointless to try and describe what something looks like. You could go on the Internet and discover jaw-dropping photographs of the giant volcano on Unimak, one of the ten most active in the world, and see for yourself how glaciers cut up valleys and slope up mountains capped by otherworldly spires of ice. You'll save reading time and I'll be spared the trouble of coming up with phrases like "otherworldly spires of ice." That's good, because I have difficulty describing these mountains without alluding to cake or frosting.

What you can't get from pictures is a sense of what it feels like to stand out on the deck just before dawn, fingers freezing in your gloves as you try and squint through binoculars, ears near-falling off from cold, eyes watering from the wind, nose dribbling snot, but unwilling to go inside because every now and then the fog breaks and you can make out bulging castle formations of ice that would dwarf the Manhattan skyline.

Sometimes, as I stood out there, the constant ripples of the water would be broken by an inkspot of smoothness, followed by a dense pack of mysterious seabirds. Out of these spots would arch the calloused back of a whale, its spout firing with a very satisfying PFOOOSH noise.

As if all this were not surreal enough, stretched out behind us was a slow-motion highway of container ships with the names of lines painted on their hulls—China Shipping, Maersk, Evergreen.

Out there in the water whales were eating krill and birds were diving for fish, their every part an evolutionary adaptation in the endless flow of killing each other and reproducing themselves, energy back into energy, nothing wasted. From the algae through the flying fish and the whales and tube-worms it was one giant blob of shifting life, a perpetual motion machine that stretched out and filled the whole ocean. These ships were part of it, too, metal beasts with shapes that reflected their own evolution to carry cowhides from one land to another. I was part of it, too, standing out here, waiting for a breakfast of stringy bacon and fried eggs. So was Alex, inside the bridge, half-asleep and mixing himself some Nesquik as he lazily watched the monitors that made sure we didn't crash into a volcano.

All this is just to say either that (1) while standing on the deck in the Aleutians I had an epiphany about the connectedness of all things that alone made the two weeks of sailing worth it, or (2) if you stare at the ocean for too long you will go crazy.

I should also add that I'd purchased a bottle of Johnnie Walker from the ship store. That might've affected my epiphany.

But as I stood out there off the Aleutians, I remember thinking, "I hope Vali gets to see something like this."

This was a rare moment of generous thinking where Vali is concerned.

VALI: Jetpack!

Juliana and I arrived at Cuernavaca in the late afternoon. It is a beautiful stucco and pastel exurb of Mexico City, a universe away from the concrete, kidnappings, and poverty that afflicted the capital.

It was an ideal setting for the fortuitous meeting that would ensure my victory in the Ridiculous Race. After purchasing the jetpack, I would be able to speedily fly across the oceans without breaking the agreed-upon "no airplanes" rule. As a bonus, rocketing across the azure Atlantic and angry Pacific would be superfun and awesome as opposed to monumentally tedious and uninteresting like taking a ship across the oceans.

Juan Lozano greeted us in a greasy T-shirt and jeans. He apologized for his attire, explaining that he was working. Then I apologized for my attire, even though I was dressed great. Sometimes I can be too much of a follower.

In 1963 NASA demonstrated its prototype jetpack, or "rocketbelt" as those in the biz prefer to call it, at the American Space Expo at a polo field in Mexico City. Also in 1963, a seven-year-old Juan Lozano became obsessed with jetpacks. Coincidence? No. Anticoincidence? Yes. Is there a word for that? Probably.

Instantly smitten, Juan begged his mother to take him

back to see the jetpack the next day and the day after that and each following day until the Expo left town. As absurd as it may have seemed, she did. It's not that strange to hear of a young boy obsessed with rockets or dinosaurs or ninjas. But it is a bit strange to hear of a forty five-year-old man obsessed with them. At some point between seven and forty-five, most boys discover girls, beer, and football. The others, a few weirdos, retain their focus. And those weirdos would call Juan an obsessed weirdo. A weirdo among weirdos.

Juan Lozano is awesome.

Juan's estate was massive, with space divided equally between living quarters for his family and that dedicated to research. Juan's workshop, a converted two-story garage, was stuffed with rockets. Small rockets, large rockets, rocket bikes, rockets for helicopter blades, and . . . yes! The jetpacks!

There were four of them: two prototypes, one pink rocket belt that Juan's daughter uses, and finally Juan's own rocket belt. It was beautiful. A hard white fiberglass chassis attached to a shiny metal hydrogen peroxide fuel tank festooned with tubes, whachyacallems, and doodads. When in flying mode, tubes from the fuel tank transport liquid industrial-grade hydrogen peroxide (that Juan makes himself) toward a catalyst. The catalyst enables a chemical reaction that converts the hydrogen peroxide into hydrogen gas and water. One cubic centimeter of the hydrogen peroxide yields five hundred cubic centimeters of hydrogen gas. That reaction produces a ferocious force. That force propels the jetpack wearer into the air. Then the jetpack wearer looks really cool.

Juan is the first individual not affiliated with a government institution to build a working jetpack. And he did it without any formal training as an engineer. He did work as a commercial pilot for a short period of time, but quit because the job didn't leave him enough time to build rockets. Like many of history's great weirdos, Juan is self-taught.

Juan's company, Tecnologia Aeroespacial Mexicana, lists the rocket belt price at "only $250,000" (about 2.5 million pesos) on its Web site. This might sound expensive, but the price includes a machine to make industrial-grade hydrogen peroxide (retail value $15,000), training on how to fly the rocket belt, and food and lodging during training.

Needless to say, I didn't want to be the idiot who paid sticker price for a new jetpack, so I readied myself for a fierce negotiation: I tried not to act too interested in the jetpack; I casually lied that I had purchased a jetpack before; I generally let Juan know that I was an informed buyer. It seemed to work and Juan seemed to like me, so I was confident that I could haggle him down at least to $240,000. If negotiations went particularly well, I might even be able to take the food left over from my training period. That could save me up to $100 while on the road.

Juan's negotiating tactic was to claim price didn't matter because jetpacks are an absurdly attractive investment. He explained that a jetpack owner could and should charge $25,000 for "shows." Then, assuming $0 in overhead costs, a jetpack owner could begin making money on his investment after only ten shows. That's not even counting the profits one would make from selling fuel-grade hydrogen peroxide to the general public.

I was convinced. But I didn't want to buy the car (jetpack) before I kicked the tires (jets). So I asked Juan if I could test one of the Rocket Belts. As he strapped the pinnacle of modern engineering to my back, he told me three things:

1. The jetpack can hold only thirty seconds worth of fuel. Adding more fuel makes the jetpack too heavy to consistently take off. So until another safe fuel with a better weight-to-stored-energy ratio can be found, thirty seconds is the maximum amount of time a jetpack will fly. It turns out that's why NASA abandoned its jetpack program. I asked Juan if it would take longer than thirty seconds to fly across the Atlantic Ocean. He said yes.
2. It takes three months for Juan to build a new jetpack, customized to the weight and center of gravity of the purchaser. Then the purchaser needs to train for sev-

eral weeks with tethered flights before acquiring the skills to fly solo.

3. The jetpack is crazily dangerous. When Juan was landing at the end of his last flight he made a slight error and ended up breaking four ribs and a wrist. Juan also has a plate with eight screws in his clavicle and grafts on his legs from other rocket-related mishaps. Oh, and he almost killed his wife by shooting her in the face with a rocket. The jetpack was, in short, a flying coffin.
   3a. The failed landing that ended the jetpack's last flight inflicted damage that Juan had yet to repair. In other words, there were no jetpacks currently in working condition.

In hindsight I had nobody to blame but myself. I should have asked some follow-up questions after I e-mailed Juan Lozano in April asking if I could buy a rocket belt and he responded "yes."

A lesser man, with my same motives, might have found himself in an impossible situation. I was in a race around the globe that forbade the use of airplanes. The very thought of wasting three weeks of my life crossing the Atlantic and Pacific oceans on a boat made me want to crush my head in a vise. And my attempt at circumventing the rules by flying over the oceans in a jetpack had ended in failure. Fortunately, I was prepared for the possibility that the jetpack wouldn't work. . . .

VALI: The Best Grocery Store in Mexico City

Juliana and I left Cuernavaca and made our way north, back toward the U.S. border, by car. Driving a car after having a jetpack strapped to your back is a lot like eating cardboard after tasting unicorn tenderloin. It was a serious letdown. On the other hand, I enjoyed the flexibility of being able to travel in increments longer than thirty seconds.

Juliana wanted to pick up a few Latin American snacks that she hadn't tasted since leaving Colombia, so we asked three different locals to recommend a good Mexican grocery store. Each directed us to the nearest Wal-Mart.

The place was packed. As I wandered the aisles, I tried to parse my feelings on Mexicans buying their groceries from Wal-Mart. It was easy to feel saddened by it. There was an obvious villain: the enormous American company. There were also obvious victims: tourists hoping to shop in grocery stores with dirt floors and chickens running through the cereal aisle. I came to Mexico City hoping to find people with desires completely alien to my own but found instead that they all want the same things I want: convenience, low prices, deliciously seasoned Doritos snack products, and dozens of Kelly Clarkson CDs.

I wandered through an aisle of microwavable Kraft brand pasta and cheese combinations and reflected on my trip thus far. I had three goals for my time in Mexico:

1. Buy a jetpack
2. Learn to move objects with my mind
3. See Mexico

I had failed at goal number one, succeeded at goal number two, and—I suddenly realized—failed at goal number three.

I had driven millions of inches through Mexico and I had seen almost nothing. Speeding through a country like this allowed me to make only the most uninformed judgments: people in Guadalajara are more curious than people in Mazatlan, evidenced by a waitress in Guadalajara who asked me where I was from; people in Guymas are nicer than people in Morelia, evidenced by how one gas station attendant returned a smile a half second faster than the other; Mexicans eat tacos. I was moving too quickly to learn anything meaningful about the places I passed through.

And much of what I had seen did not fit in with what I knew, or thought I knew, about Mexico. I had been through the country's two largest cities (Guadalajara and Mexico City), two of the state capitals (Morelia and San Luis Potosí), and a very wealthy suburb (Cuernavaca). Between those cities and the well-maintained highways, life appeared to be pretty good for Mexicans. However, I knew that hundreds of thousands of Mexicans attempt the dangerous border crossing to enter the United States illegally every year. Some attempt several times, risking jail time if caught. For what? The best they can hope for in the U.S. is a low-paying job as unskilled workers or laborers. They flee Mexico for what most of us would consider a terrible life. How bad must their lives in Mexico be to make them want that? Where were these miserable poor Mexicans?

I didn't know. All I had learned about Mexico was that it was possible for the rich to never see the poor.

My motivation in the Ridiculous Race was supposed to be simple: I was racing Steve around the world. But really, there was more to it than that.

Let's be honest. I was making this trip for the sole purpose of writing a humorous book.

It's not uncommon for writers to interview someone or attend an event for an assignment. But in our case, Steve and I *were* the assignment. We were writing a book about the experiences we had while racing around the world. And knowing we had to write a book about our experiences affected what we decided to experience.

For example: A few days after leaving Mexico, I found myself in Birmingham, Alabama, staying at the same hotel as a Harley-Davidson convention. I also found myself incredibly exhausted. Had I been racing around the world for the sole purpose of racing around the world, I would have gone to bed early, woken up early the following morning, and continued traveling as quickly as possible. But I had a book to write and thus experiences to collect. So I felt it my journalistic responsibility to go down to the hotel bar and talk to some bikers.

Within minutes I was overwhelmed with boredom. A Harley-Davidson convention, it turns out, has little in common with the fearsome Hell's Angels rallies of the 1960s.

There was no one named Buzzard or Tiny or Smackey Jack and no Old Ladies or Mamas or Strange Chicks. No waitress had her teeth yanked out with a pair of pliers as punishment for delinquent slice-of-pie deliveries. There was just a flock of old people with a taste for beer, fried foods, and leather vests with patches. They looked like *Far Side* characters with beards.

In other words, the night turned out to be pretty uninteresting. However, I didn't regret my decision to talk to the bikers because it *could* have been interesting. That's why when, the next night, I found myself in a similar extremely exhausted situation in Nashville, I didn't think, *Tonight will probably be a bust just like last night, so I'll get some rest.* Instead I thought, *I have to go out because something awesome might happen if I do. Plus I know nothing awesome will happen if I don't.*

The pressure of having to accumulate experiences was exacerbated by the fear that Steve might be having cooler and more interesting experiences than me. Every time I did something banal—eat, rest, pump some gas—my mind's engine would kick into overdrive, trying to guess what Steve was doing at that very moment. Had he talked his way onto a military submarine, getting an ancient one-legged admiral to transport him from California to the Far East in exchange for having a character named after him on *American Dad*? Was he doing cocaine with the pope?

The possibilities drove me insane. I was fine with losing the race around the world. But there was no way I was going to lose the Awesomeness Contest.

VALI: Good-bye, Juliana

Juliana and I shared our final meal together at a highway BBQ joint in south Texas. A sign outside the restaurant advertised showers for six dollars or three dollars "w/dine in," suggesting that the joint opened during the great sign-ink shortage of '98.

What the restaurant lacked in full words it made up for in greasy deliciousness. Even the toast had enough fat on it to soak through the wax paper it was wrapped in. It tasted like a stick of butter with breadcrumbs sprinkled on top.

"Since we dined in, could I get a shower for three dollars?" I asked the waitress.

"Yes, sir."

"How about two showers for five dollars?"

She responded with the silence of deep thought. After thirty seconds of hemming and hawing, the waitress decided to elevate my request to the on-duty restaurant manager, a stocky woman who had figured out a way to incorporate denim into every article of clothing including her earrings. Her decision came swiftly and without hesitation: "No. There is no bulk pricing on showers."

After our good-bye meal, I drove Juliana straight to the Austin airport. Curbside, under the thundering of departing airplanes, I gave her the parting gift of a coupon for 50 percent off a green card marriage to me. (Market value: up to $5,000.)

A few months after the conclusion of the Ridiculous Race, Juliana's relationship with "the Asshole" soured and he discontinued her visa sponsorship. With only one month to spare before becoming an illegal alien, Juliana frantically tried to get married to a citizen. She met with over twenty men in four weeks. None of the meetings resulted in a marriage, primarily because every man wanted more money than Juliana had. We spoke frequently during this period. Neither of us ever brought up the coupon, a joke that had transformed from barely funny to crass extremely quickly.

In early 2008, Juliana moved back to Colombia. She has promised to name all of her sons after me.

VALI: Let's Address a Thing

All right, it's going to be hard to ignore this any longer. I cheated.

English is armed with several slang terms for cheaters: chiseler, flimflammer, Judas, sharper, Brutus, jerkhead, etc. A lot of those words hurt my feelings. I guess it's true that sometimes words can cut deeper than knives. Not all knives, though. I've never seen a word cut through a shoe or a metal pipe or anything like that. So I guess words can cut deeper than dull knives. But I suppose that says more about the dullness of the knives than the sharpness of the words. You know what? If you need to cut someone, just play it safe and use a knife.

Back to why I cheated. The world is a different place today than it was one hundred years ago. Off the top of my head, I can't think of any examples as to how, but I'm pretty sure that's correct. And nobody hates how much the world has changed more than Steve Hely. His own words on why circumnavigating the globe without airplanes is awesome are as follows:

> 26,000 miles by sea and land is something worth bragging about. There's an old-fashioned grandeur to it. It's the kind of journey the great nineteenth-century adventurers dreamed up at the gentlemen's club and began on a whim. It summons up cafés in grand, decaying train stations, and the bowels of steamships, timetables and engine whistles and half-true tales told over card games with strangers.

Steve was not being campy when he wrote that. He really believes it. Reader, by now you've gotten to know Steve a little bit. If you don't mind, I'd like to deepen your understanding. Consider the following:

- ☛ When Steve was in college, before he had ever had a real job, he wrote a book titled *The Senior's Guide to Retirement.**
- ☛ In 2006 he sent somebody a telegram.

* The book is now out of print, but if you write a personal letter to Steve care of the Henry Holt Publishing Company, I'm sure he'll send you a copy and add you to his Christmas card list.

- His first words were probably, "Things aren't as good as they used to be."
- He only dates women in their nineties.

The dude loves olde tyme things.

I, on the other hand, lack Steve's enthusiasm for the days of yore. For several reasons, the past means almost nothing to me. First, I personally do not have much of a past. (For more on this read almost anything written by an Indian not born in India.)

Second, I don't believe the past that Steve is nostalgic for ever truly existed. He longs for an imaginary era that combines the best aspects of today with the wonderful aspects of yesterday. Let's be honest. There were no Vali Chandrasekarans allowed in any nineteenth-century gentlemen's clubs.

But I understand the spirit of what Steve longs for. I want adventure, too. I also want to understand the modern world better. There is so much information about so much change happening so quickly. The world is at war with radical Islam. Asian nations are lifting themselves out of third-world status faster than any country in the history of the world. Europe is struggling to stay relevant. What does all this mean? I didn't know. I thought personal observation might help me figure it all out, at least a little bit. However, I couldn't go see South America, the Middle East, and the Far East in two or three months if I was limited to the transportation of the past. I needed to take airplanes.

Also, I really wanted to fuck with Steve.

VALI: But First, More Driving

The first flight destination was Rio de Janeiro, Brazil. I could have flown there easily from Monterrey, Mexico, or Austin, Texas, but I didn't want readers to think I was cheating out of laziness. So I booked my first flight out of Atlanta, requiring me to race across the continent to reach it in time. Also, the flight out of Atlanta was much cheaper.

So newly Juliana-less and with dreams of Rio bouncing around my head, I drove across the American South. It quickly became clear how much Juliana spoiled me during my first week of driving. With her I was never bored. Without her the Impala felt empty and lame. Her perfume was replaced with the smell of banana peels. Her voice was replaced by actual banana peels. Making matters worse, I had run out of the bananas Juliana had left behind for me.

I tried to occupy myself by taking in the landscape. The rocky sands of Texas eventually gave way to the wet marshes of Louisiana. The pillar-supported highway passed over the reed-filled and lush tree-lined bayous.

However, the excitement of seeing new landscapes was short-lived. Soon I began playing mental games to keep myself entertained and alert. For over an hour, I tried to form a sentence using all twenty-six letters of the alphabet. I only thought of one: "Qwerty, whose nickname is Yuiop, was born in the mythical town of Dgjzv." After accomplishing that I moved on to manufacturing longer and longer palindromes. The longest one I thought of was "zz." It's the sound of a guy taking a short nap.

VALI: How Not to Experience Bourbon Street

On the Friday night in April, the hotel lobby was crowded with middle-aged people well on their way to drunk. I was surprised by the size of the pink wobbling herd. I asked a hotel employee if anything special was taking place that night in New Orleans—a Hawaiian Shirts Worn with Braided Leather Belts convention or something. "No, Mr. Chandrasekaran," he responded. "Just another Friday night in N'Owleans."

"Mr. Chandrasekaran is my father's name," I told him. "Please call me Sir."

Apparently tourism to the city's French Quarter resumed with force once the major hotel chains reopened after Hurricane Katrina. The herd of old pink drunks, with their sweaty dollars and footlong beers, were helping rebuild the city. What patriots!

Eager to do my part to revitalize New Orleans, I quickly made my way to Bourbon Street. Well-worn and ornately designed multistory hotels flanked the streets. From over their white metal second- and third-story balconies, drunk frat boys have, in the past—and will, in the future—tossed bead necklaces down to any girl able to muster up an appropriate response to "Show us your tits!" (Appropriate responses include ignoring the specifics of the request and tastefully flashing some vagina.) Bars pumped loud dance music and advertised cheap drinks. Streetside stands sold hurricanes, sugary shots, and $1.00 cans of beer to partiers who didn't want to waste time going inside. Four guys lounged near a brand-new cherry red Ford Mustang with gigantic gleaming rims and listened to hip-hop blaring through the open doors. Any passing female who showed the slightest sign of interest, including crossing the street to avoid the guys, were invited to sit in the Mustang and have a drink.

The scene was actually quite tame compared to the Mardis Gras insanity I've seen advertised on television. But the street was still packed with drunks and soon-to-be-drunks. I tried to integrate myself with one of the herds, but my heart just wasn't in it. My conversations never got much past "hi" and "Los Angeles" and "Yes, I'm alone."

After about an hour and a half of trying not to look creepy, I returned to my hotel room. For the first time since leaving Los Angeles, I missed Steve. I knew that if he were with me, we would be having a fantastic time drinking, screaming, rebuilding New Orleans together, and threatening to set each other on fire.

I pulled out my brick-sized satellite phone and called Steve.

"Hello?"

"Vali?"

"Yeah. How are you man?"

"I'm freezing my butt off."

"What are you doing? I know you must still be on a boat. So don't try and lie."

"I'm the only passenger on a freighter with an all-German crew. There is one woman. I plan on seducing her."

I tried to imagine what a female German sailor would look like. I decided that she was really fat.

"What are you doing to keep yourself occupied?" I asked.

"I'm halfway through *Infinite Jest*."

Oh my god. The poor bastard was working his way through a one-thousand-page novel. I couldn't wait to hear him tell other people stories about the Pacific crossing. I couldn't wait to hear what bullshit he'd conjure up to hide the fact that he spent most of his time reading in an effort to stave off suicide-inducing levels of boredom.

"Where are you?"

"New Orleans." I thought about lying, but I figured he would never believe I was only to New Orleans one week into the race. Besides, I was elated that Steve was, according to any objective measure, having a terrible time.

"What are you doing?" Steve asked.

"Doing coke with the pope."

VALI: How Much for That Snake Oil?

I woke up with only one goal in mind for my day: to put a hex on Steve. Thankfully the French Quarter of New Orleans was home to a few voodoo establishments that looked like they could accommodate my needs. I wanted a hex that would ensure that Steve's around-the-world journey would continue being the most miserable experience of his life. I didn't want him to die or anything drastic like that. I simply wanted him to be mildly tortured by secret police or lose ten pounds in two hours due to diarrhea or get exposed to some nuclear waste, rendering him impotent for the rest of his life—funny stuff like that.

Having never purchased any voodoo, hoodoo, or occult services before, I was worried about getting scammed. I didn't want to pay good money for a voodoo priestess and end up with a snake oil salesman or some other quack. Unfortunately, there isn't a lot of reliable information on voodoo practitioners. The establishments are not rated by AAA, Zagats, or Michelin guides. So I had to rely on a well-established time saver: stereotypes.

I used my preconceived notions to create a dossier for my ideal voodoo priestess. Obviously, and most importantly, she needed to be black. Additionally I thought she should (1) be abnormally tall—a physical manifestation of her superiority over Normals—and (2) have very bad, but still intact, teeth—proof that her relationship with the occult protected her from pedestrian concerns like gingivitis and other gum diseases.

After designing my perfect priestess, I walked into the first place I saw advertising voodoo consultations.

"I'll take one consultation with your tallest priestess."

"We don't have anyone available for consultation right now. But you can visit JT down the street. He's a very gifted tarot reader."

"Is he, you know . . . legit?"

"He's not black, if that's what you're asking."

JT's tarot reading room was a card table set up next to a chain-link fence along the edge of his back patio. Potted green ferns and small trees crowded the corners, lending the space the ambience of a Kmart garden shop.

JT wore a faded T-shirt, khaki shorts, and no shoes. He appeared more homeless than mystical. He had warm eyes that may have been enhanced by certain smokeable relaxants and a confident smile that sat slightly too close to the bottom of his face.

At first JT said nothing. My anger built in the silence. This hexing-Steve adventure was supposed to be a fun lark. JT had a very simple, but specific, role to play in that lark. Instead he was acting like a regular dude, making no effort to draw me into a world of angry spirits and dark forces. In his hands voodoo dolls, tiny humanoid bundles of twine, looked kitchy and silly. I knew he didn't believe they accomplished anything.

JT was providing me with the experiential equivalent of a tour through Colonial Williamsburg led by a guide wearing a space suit.

Finally JT unfolded a batik print cloth revealing an aged tarot deck whose corners had been worn fuzzy from use. As he laid out my tarot reading, JT launched into memorized patter. He began by explaining his multiyear journey to becoming an ordained voodoo priest. I don't know where he underwent his training but judging from his girth the place probably had a lot of Peanut M&Ms. The patter got more absurd as it continued. At one point JT claimed to have spent a night in Africa alone in a hut with a tiger.

Before JT could tell me the meaning of my first card, I had changed the goal of my visit. I no longer cared about hexing Steve. Instead, I just didn't want to give JT the satisfaction of thinking I bought into his bullshit.

"I sense that you have not yet been tested in your life," JT said.

"Yup."

Seeing that the portentous conversation starters weren't going to work, JT switched to a subtler tactic. He slowly started speaking softer. Without thinking, I leaned in to hear better. Then he got even softer. I leaned in a bit more. He began speaking at subwhisper volume. When I realized that JT was purposely getting me to lean forward, to place myself in the physical arrangement of a seeker straining to hear the wise oracle, I shot back in my chair and didn't move for the rest of my visit. For twenty minutes I sat back, unable to hear anything JT said, occasionally nodding when I sensed he needed a response in order to move on. I have no idea what the tarot divined about my future on that day.

After the half-hour whisper session, JT showed me a photo of the largest python I ever saw.

"Isn't she beautiful?" he asked. "I keep her upstairs."

I rolled my eyes. There was no way he had anything upstairs other than a lot of pot and a SEGA genesis. I decided to call him out.

"Can I see her?"

"Um . . . she just ate." *Of course she did.* Then he continued: "But wait here. You should meet Jolie-Vert."

With that he scampered up the stairs.

A minute later he returned with a young albino python draped around his neck. Jolie-Vert was a five-foot-long piece of smooth muscle. Her skin looked like a shiny tight-fitting knit sock that faded from the light yellow of her top to the pale white of her belly. Her terrifying head hung alert, just under JT's chin.

"I'm going to give you the first test of your life. Hold out your hand."

"No."

All I knew about pythons was that they killed by constriction. And I had an aversion to being squeezed to death by something that looked like a giant yellow penis. Maybe one day a psychologist will help me get to the bottom of that.

"During the tarot reading, we agreed that you needed to be more open to surprise opportunities."

"I wasn't listening to anything you said."

"Jolie-Vert is sweet. Hold out your hand."

I really didn't want to, but I would never forgive myself if I turned down this experience.

As I extended my trembling hand I felt the thumping of my heart against my rib cage. Jolie-Vert snaked her head toward me. Oh shit oh shit oh shit. Then she rested her head on my palm and began flicking it with her tongue.

I dropped my hand and jumped back.

"It's okay. She won't hurt you."

JT was right. Jolie-Vert was stunningly calm. But even if her killer instinct wouldn't cause her to attack me, I was afraid she would sense my fear—something that wouldn't be tough since I was shaking with the frequency of a struck tuning fork—then become fearful herself, which would lead to the spirited constriction and subsequent death of yours truly. Like many of my theories, this theory had no basis in knowledge of the subject (in this case, the subject being living organisms).

"Try again," JT instructed. "Let Jolie-Vert rest her head on your palm until you calm down."

I did. Two minutes later she was draped around my neck. Jolie-Vert slithered her diamond-shaped head up my chest until her face was level with my own and pressed her smooth snout against my cheek, flicking my nose with her lightning-fast forked tongue. For the first and hopefully last time in my life, I had charmed the socks off a snake.

JT smiled. The crazy quack had helped me pass my first test.

As Jolie-Vert snaked her tail up my shirtsleeve, I wondered what book Steve was reading at that exact moment.

VALI: Leaving the United States

After a very late night in Nashville, which ended with me sleeping for a few hours just inside the door of my hotel room, I somehow piloted the rental car to Atlanta, where I finally dropped it off.

Before returning the keys I ran my eyes across the now dusty Precision Red Impala and reflected on all we had experienced together. In nine days of driving I had put 4,525 miles on the car. To get an idea of how far that is, imagine driving one mile 4,525 times.

I had driven across an entire continent for no real purpose, other than to observe it. I saw a bunch of stuff. Most of it was road. Some of that road was asphalt, some of it was concrete, none of it was edible. I had seen some interesting things, but nothing too exotic. It was time to change that.

As I rode the yellow Hertz shuttle to the main terminal, I decided to leave, in the Ridiculous Race, a picture of Mexico and the American South so complete that if the regions were to suddenly disappear from Earth they could be reconstructed out of my words. I think I succeeded quite nicely.

At 9:00 p.m., I boarded Delta flight 61 from Atlanta, Georgia, to Rio de Janeiro, Brazil.

STEVE: Shanghai'd

Around sunset, fifty miles out of Shanghai, *Hanjin Athens* anchored. In longitude terms, I was now 33.15 percent of the way around the Earth. But the next .1 percent or so would be incredibly hard.

I could tell we were close to land by the swarm of fishing boats that darted around, picking up buoys. You wouldn't want to buy seafood you knew had been in one of these boats. Sanitation did not appear to be a priority. The boats appeared to be made out of rust and plastic bags. Even the gentle coastal waters were enough to toss them about like corks in a whirlpool. If one of them were to be cut under by the bow of *Hanjin Athens*, the boat would be sucked beneath and spewed out our stern as scrap metal and her crew chummed and immediately devoured by fish, which would then be devoured by birds. They were a slight wrong turn away from becoming seagull poop.

The Chinese sailors appeared unafraid. Boats jockeyed and vied against each other. They bobbed right below our decks, and the captains were maneuvering in a kind of three-dimensional video game while the crews tried to keep their hands from being severed as they hauled in nets being raised and lowered as though in the power of a lunatic elevator operator.

If I'd been a better guy, I would've thought to toss them the remnants of my Johnnie Walker. Watching them, I did not want to miss seeing China.

At the moment that was the danger.

The problem was Shanghai harbor is a mess. It is the maritime equivalent of the worst-ever freeway off-ramp in the world. Heading into Shanghai in a container ship is like heading into Manhattan at rush hour in an RV.

First of all, Shanghai is one of the busiest ports in the world. Second, winds blow sand from the northern deserts, giving the air an eerie yellow tint that doesn't make steering any easier. Then there are the sandbars. A deep-draw vessel like *Hanjin Athens* can only make a run at it during high tide. At low tide traffic backs up, so once the tide changes dozens of ships are waiting for the Chinese pilots to steer them in. Add to that that Chinese vessels can go for it without pilots, and you can imagine the crush as everybody guns it into the funnel at tidal rush hour. There is no glorious freedom of the sea in Shanghai harbor. Up on the bridge the radio was a steady screech of captains howling at one another.

It was the evening of May 1. Somewhere in Shanghai was Amy, the Amester, a lovely Pennsylvanian expat and friend of mine whom I'd hired to translate for me as I crossed China.

That night she received a series of frantic text messages from me.

I had a ticket for the Trans-Mongolian Railway, leaving Beijing at 7:40 a.m. May 5, four days from now. Getting that ticket had been the biggest logistical headache of my frantic planning phase. It had required timing out visas and working out foreign schedules, but from Beijing that train could take me a quarter of the way across the surface of the Earth, depositing me in Moscow—halfway around the world, well on my way to tasting the sweet burn of Victory Scotch.

But Beijing was some eight hundred miles away. If I missed my train, it would cause a cascade of bureaucratic nightmares, and cost me hundreds of dollars, and I might not make it out of Russia before my visa expired. If I didn't get on land, I would see nothing, probably lose the race, and possibly end up in a Moscow jail cell.

The delay leaving Long Beach had cost me two days in China already. The Forbidden City, the Great Wall, pandas, Szechuan, Hunan, all the other words I knew only from menus—it was slipping away.

The race was important to me, but my victory wouldn't mean nearly as much if I didn't get a chance along the way to plunge into China.

I was fishing-boat distance from the Middle Kingdom, the land of Yao Ming and Mao Tse-tung, the country of the future that economists are constantly warning us about. It would take a thousand lifetimes to see China. As is I was cutting it close with three days.

The captain was less than comforting. We'd anchor out here, he said, and maybe get a Chinese pilot aboard to take us in with the morning tide. But I shouldn't get my hopes up.

"You never know in Shanghai," he said. "Sometimes it takes days or a week to get in. Once, in the seventies, we waited out here for two months."

"Two months?!"

"Yes." The captain smiled. "They had to bring out fresh water on a motorboat! We took our shirts off and played basketball."

I peered over the deck again and wondered if I could zipline to one of the fishing boats and have it take me in. They did not look welcoming.

But I resolved to give it a try the instant the captain's shirt came off.

It was to my immense relief then when I woke up around four-thirty the next morning and felt the whole superstructure shaking like an aluminum can. We were moving. I threw on some pants and raced up to the bridge.

Oliver was at the wheel, with the captain presiding behind him. Both were accepting orders from a young Chinese pilot who looked like he was trying his hardest to fill out the broad shoulders of his uniform. An older Chinese pilot, face gaunt and indifferent, was ravaging a hamburger that the cook must've fried up for him.

Now I'd seen two Chinese people. One billion, two hundred ninety-nine million, ninety-nine hundred thousand, nine hundred ninety-eight to go.

Out the window was a ship menagerie. Alex helped me identify various forms: South American half-cargo/half-passenger vessels, pilot boats, tugs, local ferries. The tankers you could tell by their giant NO SMOKING signs. There were roll-on, roll-off ships ("RoRos"), dredgers, fragile fishing boats, and testudinate* car carriers. Through the dust I could barely make out the factories and cranes alongshore.

* This word means "turtlelike" and I've waited a long time to have a chance to use it.

I was lucky to have any view at all. The captain told me he'd first visited this harbor on East German ships in the '70s. Back then, he said, Shanghai harbor was a secret. The Chinese had been so suspicious of the Soviets, Soviet allies, and foreigners generally that the local boarding pilots would kick everyone out of the bridge, lock up the binoculars, force the crew into their cabins, and steer the ship in themselves to keep strangers from learning the intricacies of their harbor. No charts existed. Often, the captain said, coming into the harbor, he'd feel his ship smash into local junks in the night. But the Chinese pilots would always press on.

"You'd hear the ships crushing at night," he said. He shrugged. "What could we do?"

Before I'd left the United States, I'd sent a blind e-mail to an assortment of Chinese history professors at American universities. I'd explained to them that I was going to race around the world, and while doing so I'd pass through China. I mentioned that, as I didn't have much time to immerse myself in that nation's history, I'd be very grateful if they'd summarize Chinese history for me in under fifty words.

I'll acknowledge it's a little obnoxious to ask someone to summarize the field to which they'd devoted their lives in fifty words because I'm too busy to learn. I thought the more fun-loving among them might be game to give it a try.

I'd overestimated the "fun-loving" nature of academic historians, because only one of them wrote me back. But if only one professor of Chinese history is going to respond to your juvenile challenge, you want it to be Jonathan Spence of Yale University, the silver-bearded dean of the field. I'd read, or flipped through, two of his books, including his biography of Mao. The quotes on the inside covers say things like "no other historian could even conceive of beginning to write a book this good." Among English-language historians of China, he's, like, the guy.

Professor Spence's e-mail to me was two words long. But

they were two very handy words when trying to figure out China. I will save them for one paragraph to build suspense.

Thirty-five years ago I wouldn't have been allowed to look at this harbor, let alone visit. Now, out on the river, I could see the flags of ten countries in my view. From out here, as best as I could tell, the Shanghai skyline consisted of nothing but construction cranes. I looked at the first Chinese pilot, whose main focus was his hamburger. I looked at the second Chinese pilot, whose main focus was his colleague's hamburger distracting him as he tried to thread this vessel of American cowhides and batteries through the jumble of international commerce.

Professor Spence had summarized the history of China thusly: "Constant change."

STEVE: 旅行 (Road Trip!)

My accomplice Amy is a strikingly beautiful woman of grand stature. She looms over most Chinese, who have been known to gape at her and ask in trembling voices how much milk she drinks a day, it being well known in China that Western physiques are the result of prodigious milk ingestion. But unlike most strikingly beautiful women, Amy also looks as though she could punch your nose into your brain if she got ticked off. Chinese men would see her, become mystified by her half-Asian features, and begin to speculate among themselves whether she could understand Mandarin. She would then wheel around and inform them in pitch-perfect Shanghai slang that she didn't appreciate being muttered about. The men would tremble. The Amester doesn't truck with nonsense. She'd be a perfect guide.

Most of my time in China I'd be on the move. As every American knows, when you need to combine forward momentum with adventure/experience, there is but one answer: a road trip.

I'd apply that genius American idea to the countryside of

China. I'd known Americans who'd been to China, studied there, and lived there. I didn't know anyone who'd driven across it. Most Western visitors jet around from city to city. What I wanted to see was the middle.

Even Amy was startled by the idea. She didn't know anyone who'd tried driving in China, either. She ran the notion by her Chinese friends.

"They all seemed confused," she told me. "They kept asking, 'Why doesn't he just fly?' I told them it's a long story."

Here is what I pictured: myself at the wheel of a rented Dodge Stratus, Amy fumbling with a map in the passenger's seat, ice-cold Cokes in the cup holders, a half-eaten package of yak jerky resting on the dashboard, windows rolled down as we burned past gawking peasants on the Chou Enlai Expressway or whatever.

My knowledge of China was not very sophisticated.

These days the Chinese authorities may let you look out the window of a container ship, but they're not thrilled about the idea of foreigners driving around, following the wind and the smell of freshly steamed dumplings. It turns out, in fact, that it's illegal for foreigners to drive anywhere outside the city limits of Hong Kong, Macao, Guangzho, Beijing, and Shanghai.

Of course, that settled it.

If the Chinese government didn't want me to drive from Shanghai to Beijing, they should've had an official meet me at the dock with keys to a Dodge Stratus and a mix CD. "I put some great old Johnny Cash stuff on here for you, tracks I got off a Sun Records anthology, think you'll really dig it," the official should've said. "Anyway, enjoy your drive!"

This would've convinced me that driving in China was boring. I would've headed to the train station immediately. But once I learned that the government didn't want me exploring the in-between country, I became obsessed.

Amy thought of the solution: We'd hire drivers, Chinese citizens with a car. She somehow managed to find two Shanghai dudes with an old Buick who didn't ask questions after she'd promised I'd pay generously in cash. Actually, I doubt they asked questions beforehand either. They just kinda rolled with it.

The three of them, Shanghai dudes and Amy, were waiting for me when I climbed down the gangway of *Hanjin Athens*.

Our drivers conveniently had easy-to-remember Chinese names.* Li was the cool guy of the duo, with greasy long hair, a habit of leaving his shirts unbuttoned, and an enthusiasm for singing soulfully along with the cheesy Chinese ballads that dominate the radio. Chen, his associate, seemed a bit more suspicious of the whole enterprise. But Amy kept him in line. They were both afraid of Amy.

There was no "getting to know you" period. This trip would be the equivalent of driving from Boston to West Virginia, across uncertain roads. There wasn't a lot of spare time. Within minutes of leaving the ship we were moving.

I could describe what I saw of Shanghai, but by the time you read this it would already be irrelevant. There's a statistic which people like to repeat—I heard Pat Buchanan say it on *The McLaughlin Group*—that Shanghai employs 25 percent of the world's construction cranes. I've since looked into the origin of this supposed fact, and as best I can tell the mayor of Shanghai made it up one day. But Shanghai is very much under construction. Amy told me stories of how the government would assign thousands of people to new homes as they bulldozed according to grander schemes.

The Chinese government is really into slogans, which are printed on huge banners crossing the roads. Amy translated two of them for me: STRONGLY DEVELOP SHANGHAI ECONOMIC PRACTICE OF TRADEMARKING! and PROTECT CREATIVITY, STRENGTHEN INTELLECTUAL PROPERTY! Both of which I plan on doing.

As I looked out on Shanghai, I stuck to my own personal slogan for China: *Constant Change!*

*Note: I have changed their names, to keep them from getting in trouble and because I forgot their actual, hard-to-remember Chinese names.

STEVE: The In-Between Country

Allow me to describe for you China's In-Between Country, as seen from the back of a Buick.

On the radio, ballads so maudlin and weepy they would make a drunken Irishman blush are playing, and Li croons along unabashedly. Chen is driving, and it's terrifying. In China apparently it is perfectly acceptable to stop in the middle of the highway, do a U-turn, and drive for a spell against traffic. If you want to pass someone, you may wish to pull up next to him and engage in a running argument for a few miles—that's okay, too. Or you can just stop for a minute while you adjust your groin, as Chen does frequently.

No one has thought to bring a map, except me. And mine is of course in English. So it's a running multilingual argument when we need to figure out whether we want to go toward Huaiyin or Huai'an.

Chinese gas stations are exactly like American gas stations, except that your gas is pumped by teenage girls wearing matching blue jumpsuits and burdensome amounts of makeup. You'd think when you pumped gas for strangers and wore a grease-stained blue jumpsuit you wouldn't bother too much with the lipstick and so forth, but these girls were done up for a Dallas prom.

Chinese rest stops are exactly like American rest stops, except that there's apt to be a giant playground-climby thing shaped like a dragon or a World War II fighter plane, and a huge store that is only a third full, that third being filled exclusively by (1) plastic dolls with intense, creepy expressions and (2) huge bags of rice candy.

Along the road through tangles of green half-jungle I saw sets of houses, enclosed in a collapsing wall at the end of a winding trail, like an Ewok village. A bucktoothed, elderly, leather-skinned woman hunched under a bulging sack of wood waddled along between two rough-dug irrigation ditches, and it occurred to me that this was the first time I'd ever seen a person actually *waddling*.

There were scenes—a cart where the role of the horse had been replaced by a motorcycle engine, for example—that made me feel as though I were in some bizarre alt-history novel, or a bad episode of the old TV show *Sliders*,* where cars exist in the Middle Ages.

"Rapidly developing" is a handy go-to phrase to describe China if you're an investment banker trying to fill air at a meeting, or a commentator on CNBC. Before I'd been there, I could've told you that China was a rapidly developing nation. I would've said it with conviction, I would've sounded informed, and I would've been right. Maria Bartiromo would've wanted to kiss me.

But in the In-Between Country I saw what "rapidly developing" really means. It means "China is very poor, but it is becoming unpoor *super* fast." If I were on CNBC tomorrow, and I had to talk about how China is rapidly developing, I would talk about Lianyungang.

There's an old harbor in Lianyungang, but we drove through maybe twenty miles inland. From out there, it appears that Lianyungang is an idea of a skyscrapered metropolis that is being imposed on dust. The streets are mostly theory, voids between semifinished buildings, and they're crowded with trucks and farm equipment and filthy cars. It looks as though some lunatic just decreed that a city ought to be here, and everyone began racing to pull it off. Given China's recent history, that may be exactly what happened.

Amid all this, it was easy to get lost. Li and Chen were content to drive around aimlessly, but Amy was calling the shots, so we pulled off for directions. Li and Chen spoke with a Shanghai accent, which Amy and I agreed sounds like the growly chatter of a cartoon bear. The blue jumpsuit girl in Lianyungang, face made up enough for the Miss South Carolina pageant, spoke in a dialect very different. If you'd like to approximate it, open your mouth halfway and try saying "Wo yong de hua zhuang pin zenme zheme duo?"† without moving your lower jaw.

Even I, who didn't speak any Chinese, could tell this was

* Joking of course (there were no bad episodes of *Sliders*).
† "Why am I wearing so much makeup?"

weird. As we drove away, Chen and Li were doing impressions of this poor girl. Then Amy tried one. Well, naturally I couldn't resist joining in on the fun, so I did an impression, too. Which of course made Chen and Li darn near die from laughing, not because I was funny but because I was just saying nonsense syllables that sounded like Chinese to me. For the next hour the four of us took turns doing riotous impressions of the gas station girl.

Beyond Lianyungang, as we drove through coal-mining country, I discussed with Amy how China seemed to collectively sweep in wild new directions every so often.

"Yeah," she said. "China is like the Borg. But, like, a friendly Borg."

Now this could've launched us into a very interesting discussion of whether China is, indeed, like the massive robot collective depicted in the *Star Trek: The Next Generation* television show and subsequent films. For instance, is any one person or group of people ever really "in charge" of China, directing its events and momentum? Can China be "controlled"? Or do the tensions and needs and drives of one billion people swell together and move in infinitely complex, unpredictable patterns?

We did not discuss these matters. The mention of the Borg launched Amy and me into a game of "Remember the *Star Trek* episode when . . ." which occupied us all the way to Qingdao.

China is full of "minor" cities that are secretly enormous. By "secretly" I mean "nobody bothered to tell me." By some estimates, Qingdao has over seven million people, yet it had first appeared on my radar when I was staring at my world map shower curtain and decided, "Huh, 'Qingdao.' Never heard of it. Maybe I could stop there on the way."

At a hotel I ducked to the restroom as Amy took care of checking us all in. When I returned, she told me that Chen and Li had decided not to stay there.

"Wait, isn't part of the deal that I pay for their hotel rooms?"

"Yeah," Amy said, "but they'd rather just have cash." She leaned in and whispered. "*They got prostitutes.*"

"What? I've been gone for, like, three minutes!"

Amy shrugged and pointed in the direction of two ladies in gas-station-level makeup.

Who was I to judge? I gave Chen and Li their cash and off they went.

The next morning I had a permanent grin as I asked Amy to translate for me.

"Ask Chen and Li if the evening afforded them any opportunity to avail themselves of Qingdao's rich cultural offerings." I was pretty pleased with myself.

Amy rolled her eyes and obliged but her translation perhaps didn't capture my salacious, locker-room tone. They both replied that they'd gone right to bed.

STEVE: Feast in Qingdao

Ordinarily, I make it a rule not to eat:

- Sea monsters of unknown phyla
- things with eyes that stare back at me accusingly
- limbless, tube-shaped creatures
- anything cooked within five feet of an overflowing toilet.

But on my second morning in China I ate all these things, because of the brewery tour.

Qingdao—formerly Tsingtao—is home to the Tsingtao Brewery, founded by Germans in 1915. This was the first morning in two weeks that I'd woken up on land, and it seemed like I'd earned a reward. So first thing in the morning we trotted down Beer Street.

Brewery tours are the same the world over, and they all end with free beer. In this regard the Tsingtao brewery goes above and beyond. So it was that I sat across from Amy, pounding the table in enthusiasm.

"This, see, *this* is what this whole race thing should really be about!"

"Right on," replied the Amester.

"See?! You know, what's, like, the rush? Let's just enjoy our beers!" The rush was that I was competing in a race around the world, but that notion was shoved backward in my brain behind a swell of Tsingtao-fueled goodwill toward humanity. "Why aren't Chen and Li drinking with us?!" I demanded to know.

"They have to drive."

"Right, right. Remember when they got prostitutes? Those guys!"

"The seafood here in Qingdao is supposed to be awesome," said the Amester, who knows an opportunity when she hears one.

"Yes! Exactly!" I said, pointing emphatically at nothing in particular. "That's what we should be doing! We should have, like, a feast!"

"We could go down to the beach and find a place. We'd still get to Beijing by tonight. You'd have all day tomorrow to see it."

"Yes! Tomorrow is when I should do stuff, and today is when I should have a *feast*! Chen and Li! Let's throw those guys a feast! That's what's the freakin' *important* thing about the race right *now*!"

So it was that Chen and Li drove us down to the shore, to a torn-up strip of road at the top of a seawall. The buildings had my all-time favorite aesthetic, Decrepit Seaside Resort, with the peeling paint and worn facades battered by decades of saltwater wind.

In front of houses that doubled as restaurants, old aunties sent children out to pull at my pant legs and plead for my business, while Amy, Chen, and Li got down to a careful survey of which house had the liveliest temporary bin-aquaria. Amy haggled over the prices of unidentifiable mollusks and sea insects, letting the owners crack a few open to demonstrate their batch's vitality.

For something like twelve dollars, the four of us ate sautéed garlic cucumbers, spicy diced potatoes, and oysters as big as late-'80s cell phones. We picked apart a whole pan-fried fish that stared back at us with a "Guys! C'mon! Quit eating me!" expression. I ate pieces from as far away from the face as possible.

Amy tried to explain something to me about the Chinese philosophy of mixing "cold" dishes with "hot" ones, wherein some things that are actually hot count as cold, and vice versa. I interpreted this to mean I should stab randomly with my chopsticks and hope for the best.

After we'd burped and had tea, and I'd slid past the cooks frying away in the kitchen to relieve myself in the fly-infested hole-bathroom, and we'd all piled back into the car, I immediately fell asleep.

As a result, I can't report much about what China looks like between Qingdao and Beijing. From time to time I'd wake up, look out the window, and see a farmer on a tractor-cart, or some strangely grand but half-abandoned factory, and I'd think, "Right, China, Constant Change, et cetera" and I'd slump my head against the seat again and nod off.

By the time I was fully cognizant again, it was nearing midnight and Chen and Li were engaged in the delicate procedure of getting us into Beijing.

STEVE: Hutongs, and Why You Shouldn't Eat Fried Silkworms

Due to personal eccentricities, I own a pamphlet called *A Pocket Guide to China*. This handy book was published by the United States War Department in 1942 and was issued to servicemen deployed in China. It's full of helpful facts—for example, GIs are advised that the Chinese like jokes as much as we do: "Their stock jokes are the same as ours—about professors, and doctors, and Irishmen, the Chinese equivalent for the Irish being people from Hunan Province."

The piece of advice this book hits most strongly is not to lose your temper. It stresses that the Chinese have an ancient tradition of courtesy, of not criticizing one another directly.

This makes perfect sense when you see the *hutongs* of Beijing.

Hutongs are traditional alleyways, mazes of narrow streets with small abutting houses opening onto communal courtyards. These hutongs are often occupied by generations of the same families, who must have an incredible tolerance for one another's annoying qualities. I'm considering pitching a reality show called *American Hutong*, in which several average families from a culture without a tradition of courtesy squeeze into a Beijing hutong for a week. Within hours the contestants would be shooting one another's dogs and slashing one another's tires and throwing aluminum bats and lawn chairs through one another's windows. Someone would be blasting Nickelback while someone else screamed "SHUT THE HELL UP!" and shirtless toddlers wrestled in a pile of discarded Fritos bags and Mountain Dew cans. Yet somehow Beijing's hutong dwellers manage to keep their cool. You could tell the domestic space was sorted out, owned and regulated down to the inch, where at invisible borders one family's laundry or trash ended and another's began. Perhaps the residents had drawn up elaborate treaties on the subject. These neighborhoods are among the oldest in Beijing, so they must've worked out something. By contrast, on day three of *American Hutong* the whole place would be burned to the ground.

Not all of Beijing is laid out in the ancient style. Even at night we could see evidence of the various frantic gussy-the-place-up projects that were under way in anticipation of the 2008 Olympics. But our hotel, the Beijing Hebei Guest House, was in the heart of one of the hutongs. Locating it was far beyond the mapless navigation Chen and Li practiced—they had to bribe a local cabdriver to guide us in.

If you are looking for a traditional Chinese hotel experience, allow me to recommend highly the Beijing Hebei Guest

House. It has all the classic elements: the traditional architecture, the picturesque courtyard presided over by stone lions, the paper-thin walls, the rock-rigid mattresses, the spider-infested showers, and the desk staff of young women who all appear petrified that you might start talking. When I walked in, these ladies put on a comedy-dance routine as they each tried to jockey out of the way of any questions I might have. When Amy started speaking Mandarin, they all let out great gasping laughs of relief, as though they'd almost fallen for a terrible prank.

From the Hebei Guest House you can walk to a long row of street food vendors. I don't know its Chinese name, but Amy kept referring to this place as "Snack Street," which can't be improved upon, description-wise. At least one hundred people wanted to sell me skewers of chicken, lamb, fish, shrimp, grilled snake, scorpion, and mysterious lumpy black things.

"Oh, that's silkworm," Amy informed me.

The Qingdao feast had infused me with food courage. "I'll totally eat that," I said, making sure I said it loud enough for some nearby European women to hear.

Now, the outside part of grilled silkworm tastes fine. It's crunchy and salty, not unlike bacon. If it were all outside part, you'd get it down, no worries.

Here's the problem: The inside part of a grilled silkworm is leathery and so chewy that you can't swallow it faster than your brain can compute "you are eating grilled silkworm, and this is the gooey innards part." What follows is a very unpleasant forty-second struggle between mouth, mind, and will.

This experience sort of jerked my senses alert. The post-feast reverie was gone—time to focus on seeing China.

It was the night of May 3. The next day would be my only chance to see Beijing, one of the world's great capitals, a city containing fifteen million people, with an area of sixteen thousand kilometers, and buildings that date back half a millennium.

I told Amy to wear comfortable shoes.

STEVE: How to See Beijing in One Day

I'm confident I sorted out the dense labyrinthian universe of Chinese history and culture in a day of frenzied sightseeing. Should any traveler wish to do the same, just follow my simple steps.

Wake Up, Walk Around: Any truly great city like Beijing maintains a steady supply of spectacle to keep the pedestrian entertained. Two hours of walking around Beijing are a better and more compelling visual treat than *The Bourne Supremacy* in digital HD. And I loved *The Bourne Supremacy.*

In our morning walk from the hotel to dumplings, I saw two dogs where it was clear from their expressions that they'd had a history of fights but were now attempting to each "be cool." We walked past a morning wedding. I pegged the bride's age at seventeen. The poor girl was having a tough time of it because at least three people were trying to stage-manage the event. Obeying various screamed commands the groom kept picking her up and putting her down, and carrying her back and forth through a hutong archway. In the confusion some kids weren't sure when to fire off their handheld confetti cannons and couldn't resist the temptation to blast them in one another's faces. Amy and I stood by as a proper parade was organized, and the now-exhausted groom managed to get his bride to the waiting red convertible without dropping her. To my great delight Amy translated some overheard remarks to the effect of "Shi Qi has a foreigner at her wedding?"

Eat Dumplings: Despite her genetic advantage I defeated Amester nine to eight in dumpling eating.

See the Forbidden City: The Forbidden City has 980 buildings. I allotted two hours, for a very generous seven seconds per building.

The Forbidden City is so called because for five hundred

years your average Chinese person was not allowed inside without the emperor's permission. This must've been extremely irritating if you were trying to walk from Fuyou Jie to Wangufing Dajie—the Forbidden City is big enough to force you a mile out of your way. Probably the whole walk you muttered to yourself, "Man, we should overthrow the emperor. Definitely within the next thousand years."

If you did see the inside, and someone explained, "Oh, you see that huge building over there? The one that's the biggest thing you've ever seen? That's just so the emperor has a place to rest between ceremonies," then you'd still be pretty steamed when you got back to your hut, where you lived with your wife, two kids, mother-in-law, and some chickens if you were lucky.

The *Lonely Planet: Beijing* guidebook has a canny sense of what visitors such as myself are interested in when they come to the Forbidden City and devotes a whole page and a half to the subject of eunuchs, which answers questions you might have such as "Why would anyone become a eunuch?" ("in the hopes of advancing their station") and "How did you become a eunuch?" (you sat in a special chair and they sliced your testicles off) and "Sounds great, I would like to sign up—but is there any risk to me, the eunuch applicant?" (yes, more than half the applicants died of the testicle slicing).

Trying to "see" the Forbidden City is a futile project. Within about fifteen minutes your brain has been swamped by grandeur and cannot possibly process any more epic gates or delicate woodwork. A truly wise person would visit the Forbidden City in fifteen-minute intervals every day for a lifetime.

But such a person wouldn't do well in a round-the-world race. On I went!

Walk Through Tiananmen Square: Everywhere we could see the bizarre but jolly images of Beibei, Jingjing, Huanhuan, Yingying, and Nini—the Five Friendlies, four-fingered, smudge-eyed cartoon mascots of the Beijing Olympics. These characters were created by the Communist government, in the hopes that foreign observers would see them and think, "Aw, those little chubbies could NEVER torture dissidents or conquer Tibet! We must've been wrong about China!"

On the street, Amy and I were the objects of endless friendly attention. Moms passing us would nudge their school-age children toward us for English practice:

"HELLO! WHERE ARE YOU FROM?"

"We're from the United States."

"HELLO I AM CHINA GIRL!"

"I guessed as much. Nice to meet you! I'm Steve and this is Amy."

"NICE TO MEET . . . AH, YOU!"

These interactions were impossibly charming, and I suspect the government may pay a bounty to kids to talk to white people in an effort to win us over. It's working! But I would here suggest to Chinese teachers of English that they work on conversation closers, as the children seemed never to know what to do except smile for a decent interval and then walk away. I don't mean to knock their English too hard here. At least they're trying—I doubt when the Chinese visit Times Square they are besieged by American kids forced by their moms to practice their Mandarin.

Of course, just as these kids are winning you over in Tiananmen Square, you can look up. Looming over everything is the famous portrait of Chairman Mao, looking down from the Gate of Heavenly Peace. In 1989, during the prodemocracy protests, a guy named Yu Dongyue threw some paint at Mao's portrait. For this crime he spent seventeen years in prison. Two of those years were spent in solitary confinement, and when he was finally released he was hardly recognizable to his family and barely capable of speech. There were rumors that his jailors kept him outside, tied for days to a metal pole.

I'm not sure what to do about a story like that except tell it to as many people as possible.

Go See Mao: The man whose image you can't deface is preserved and displayed in a mausoleum (or "Mao-soleum," in a clever pun which I'm doubtless the first to think up) across the square. I would've liked to have seen him, so I could later compare his waxy corpse to Lenin's and decide who's holding up better, but the place was closed for the day.

In lieu of a description of Mao's body, here is a paragraph of facts about him.

Mao Tse-Tung

Mao was absurdly casual about nuclear annihilation, once pointing out that even if the Earth were destroyed, it wouldn't be a very big deal for the universe. Or that a nuclear war wouldn't really matter for China, since even if half the Chinese died there'd still be four hundred million people left. In his early writings he made it very clear that he believed in no morality except his own will. He loved having sex, with underlings supplying fresh women. Sleeping with Mao was bad work if you got it. When Mao would contract venereal diseases, his solution would be to have more sex, his argument being "I wash myself inside the bodies of my women." Mao would wash his mouth out with green tea instead of brushing his teeth. To get to sleep he would take near-fatal doses of sleeping pills, then lie in bed as assistants massaged his feet. He exuded a weird charisma: When Nixon and Kissinger met him, he was eighty, but they agreed Mao would've commanded any room he walked into. And these guys had been in rooms with John F. Kennedy and Elvis. Still, it's indisputable that Mao was an asshole, personally. Khrushchev, who, let's remember, knew *Stalin,* thought Mao was a jerk who treated people "like furniture." Mao had reason not to get too attached to anybody. By the time he was thirty, his wife and two of his brothers had been executed. Sorting out all this in retrospect, the current Chinese regime takes the tack that Mao was "complex," and leaves it at that. But Mao was either partly or entirely responsible for the deaths of seventy million people and the miseries of millions more.

Anyway. This isn't *The Gloomy Depressing Geo-Historical Crimes Race.* On we go.

Eat Duck: The next important thing to do if you only have a day in Beijing is to eat Peking duck. The best place to do this, at least according to Amy, is at Quanjude Roast Duck.

Peking duck is made in a perfectly logical way—a cavity is created between the dead duck's body and its skin using an air pump. Then the skin is boiled, rubbed with molasses, dried for half a day, and then baked.* Whatever—the point is it's fatty and delicious.

At Quanjude Roast Duck, there are other things to get, too. The menu has pictures, so you know what "deep-fried duck liver with whole scorpions" looks like before you eat it (it looks like a circle of scorpions, tails curled up, preparing to assault three brown rectangles).

In 2001 my parents visited China. They were so afraid of the food that they devoted a full third of a suitcase to granola bars and peanut butter. At the time that seemed sensible, but now that I'd had one of the best meals of my life in Qingdao, and eaten a silkworm without major harm, I decided my parents were charming provincial rubes. "What a wonder two adorable naifs such as them produced such a grand culinary cosmopolitan as me!" I thought with a smug smile.

I was thinking here of my dad, who built me a crooked but fantastic tree house, complete with rope swing, and my mom, who took me on at least thirty trips to see the mummies at the Museum of Fine Arts back when I was super into mummies. (I'm just trying to get you good and riled up, Reader, so that you will gleefully anticipate my inevitable comeuppance.)

"Yes, my parents are foolish American rubes, and I am a glorious sophisticate!" I thought as I ate piles of fatty duck.

*I kept thinking about how weird Chinese food is, but at some point I remembered that, where I'm from, the most famous delicacy is a garbage-eating crustacean, boiled alive until it changes color, served with butter, and eaten with the hands.

The boiled duck webs in mustard sauce I was a bit less smug about. I'd ordered them in arrogance, but when presented with a plate of floppy disembodied duck feet, it just seemed tragic. Still, I ate one. Just out of snobbish scorn for my parents. (Wait for it.)

Visit the Beijing Underground City: It's not easy to find the Beijing Underground City, in part because the whole project was a secret. How anyone planned to build something like seventeen miles of tunnels crisscrossing one of the densest cities in the world is beyond understanding. This was all Mao's idea. The tunnels were designed so that Beijing—or at least the three hundred thousand best-connected Beijingers—could go underground in the event of a nuclear war with the Soviets. In the 1970s Mao had pissed off the Russians and thought this scenario not only curiously amusing but likely.

If you can find the Underground City entrance—which is hard, because the residents of the surrounding hutong enjoy giving totally made-up directions—then one of several chipper teenage girls dressed in full camouflage will lead you on a tour. Neither Amy nor I could find out whether this girl was actually in the army. If so, then we should not worry about the Chinese conquering the world. She was pimply, adorable, and enthusiastic—had I known her in high school we would've been debate team nerds together and I would've asked her to the prom. She spoke to us in English and kept apologizing for her "British accent."

A British accent was not the problem with her English. For instance, she had to repeat the words "British accent" five times before I understood what she was saying. She was from Harbin, which is either a "very cold," "very cool," "vary code," or "vatty coo" city. I listed these options from most to least likely. From what I've learned of Harbin I've ruled out a fifth possibility, that she was comparing it to the Vatican City.

Had the Sino-Russian Nuclear War ever happened—and our guide kept stressing it was the Russians they were worried about, not us—it would've been bad times even down there.

The tunnels were shoddily built, like most Chinese projects of the 1970s, and would've immediately collapsed if bombs hit. Ideally there'd be enough time for everyone down there to realize what'd happened and punch Mao in the face.

About midway through the tour, the tunnels filtered in to an enormous, high-ceilinged underground assembly area. This, our guide told us, was designed to be the hospital. Now it was redesigned, laid out with long tables of silk. Four other girls, also in uniform, stood standing by.

"Do you guys want to buy some silk?"

"No thanks," I replied, more baffled than anything. By way of explanation I said, "Silkworms are for eating."

STEVE: Barren Mountain Tears, or, Constant Change in My Stomach

Now, the point of this trip was to get around the world fast. Not to saunter about the globe attending curious theatricals. That would be a great but very different trip. Possibly a much better book—we may never know.

However, here in Beijing was the start of a railway network that connects all the way to London. All I had to do was ride it.

Besides, I was confident that by this point Vali was either (a) somewhere in Florida, realizing all too late that it wasn't as easy as he thought to bribe a retiree with a powerboat to speed him across the Atlantic, (b) somewhere in Europe, having crossed the Atlantic on a container ship and deciding that he should take a few weeks just to "unwind," (c) in Las Vegas, wondering what to do now that he'd gambled away his entire travel budget, or (d) back in his apartment, sleeping in his boxer shorts, having given up.

Meanwhile, I had one free night in Beijing. What I wanted to do was attend a Peking opera.

A Peking opera begins with clanging gongs that launch a barrage of traditional string instruments that sound to the untrained ear like a high-pitched, shrieky cacophonous mess. Presumably it sounds better to the trained ear, because a ticket to the cheap seats at the Chang'an Theater is, like, fifty bucks.

The stories tend be ancient, well known, and campy: A loyal concubine kills herself, or a princess loves a rebel. There's a famous short one that's just about a concubine getting drunk. In my Peking opera writing workshop I advise all my students to include a princess, a concubine, or both.

Part of the hook is that traditionally all these concubines and princesses were played by men. Opera companies often had a side business going in boy prostitutes who pretended to be ladies.

The point is that attending a Peking opera sounded weird and foreign. So Amy and I got tickets to that night's performance of *Barren Mountain Tears*.

Now, in a Peking opera, a problem is often hinted at just as the story gets started. So it was with me. We got to the theater a little early and sat having a cup of tea as Amy explained Chinese dating (apparently the move for a Chinese guy working a foreign lady is to ask her out for an hour of "language exchange"). I had trouble listening, because I felt, flopping around in my stomach, a discontented duck web.

Sweat formed on my face as I excused myself with as much dignity as possible, sprinted to the bathroom, and promptly un-ate my lunch.

After a solid three minutes in a frenzied head-shaking hurricane of violent vomiting, I reeled back on the bathroom tile and felt fine. It was over. Whatever Chinese parasite had invaded me was now very much expunged. On with the show!

Barren Mountain Tears got off to a great start when a tiger—played by a person—ate somebody.

Amy did her best to whisper translations into my ear, but it was hard even for her to follow. There's a saying about the Peking opera: "No sound but a song, no movement but a dance." To understand how the "songs" sound, imagine a kitten singing jazz standards accompanied by what sounds like two broken violins and a kazoo. Under it all, Amy would whisper, "Okay, this woman's lover is on a mountain? Maybe? But she's afraid the tiger ate him. And some officials are demanding taxes."

Not naturally compelling stuff, perhaps. Nonetheless I was enthralled, because the man playing the main woman was just astoundingly feminine. He had tiny little lady feet, and he moved with unspeakable subtlety and grace. It's not like I was ready to inquire about she-boy prostitutes, but this dude was a pretty foxy lady.

Then my stomach started rumbling again. Sweat formed on my face.

The situation was dire. We were pent in, our fifty-dollar seats on the inside, and the exit was two rows down. I felt churned-up duck starting to work its way upward in my throat as the unknowing Amy tried to explain the tax problem facing the family onstage. I needed to move, fast.

Sometimes, in extraordinary circumstances, people attempt and achieve seemingly impossible athletic feats. As the Astounding Man-Lady sang a lament onstage, I stood up on my seat, bent my knees, and managed to hurtle over the heads of two rows of Chinese spectators, dashing out the door before they even realized what happened.

A man at a urinal was the only witness to a Peking opera performance of my own—no sound but a wretch, no movement but a defiantly unfeminine upchuck—as I spewed what I thought was the last of my lunch into the Chang'an bathroom trash can.

Then, convinced I'd licked the problem, I walked with solemn dignity back to my seat.

The bug or whatever was out of my system.

Incorrect. As the second act dragged on, I felt feverish sweat beading on my forehead, the dreadful tingle in my fingertips, and the awful, ominous nausea in my stomach.

I refused to give in. "I will tough this out," I decided. "I will make it to the end of *Barren Mountain Tears* if it kills me." It nearly did. But I tried to focus my attention on the Man-Lady, wonder at his weird feminine power, and keep the last of my Quanjude duck retained.

At the end of *Barren Mountain Tears*, most of the audience

was moved to tears because the officials are dead (I think) and so is the lady (she faints, at least) and the tiger, or taxes, or some combination have really screwed everybody over. For me the ending was incredibly cathartic, but not because I'd followed the plot. Because I had to puke. Like, immediately.

"C'mon, c'mon, it wasn't *that* good!" I thought, as the audience applauded for agonizing seconds. Finally the folks followed my lead as I stood up. They started to file out. We filtered into the main aisle as I shifted on the balls of my feet, praying I'd make it to the bathroom. It looked like I would, just barely.

Then, a murmur. All eyes turned to the stage. The Astounding Man-Lady was being brought out. For an encore.

Shrieks of delight! A sudden turn of the entire crowd as they shoved one another in a dash to get back to their seats! The Man-Lady bowed, gently, and began a lilting shriek-song.

I reeled my head back, and with violent, uncontrollable contortions, I launched a spray of yellow, soupy duckfoot vomit into the air.

As my body like a human geyser shot forth its viscous tide, I looked at the stage and realized in a flash, "Wait, that's not a Man-Lady! That's just a straight-up lady!"

It was indeed. This was a fully modern Peking opera, where the female lead was played by a woman, a lovely, fully lady songbird named Zhang Hui Zhu.

Meanwhile, I had not seen where my regurgitated lunch had ended up after it'd been blasted from my throat. I didn't stick around to find out. I booked it out of the now-befouled Chang'an Theater as fast as possible. Amy found me fifteen minutes later trying to look as casual as it is possible for a six-foot-two curly-haired white guy to look in a Beijing theater.

I will spare you, Reader, a detailed description of the rest of my night. Suffice it to say that I suddenly realized how wise and sensible my parents are. The Peking opera version of this story ends with me bowing to them in filial piety.

At around midnight, convinced I was finally, this time *seriously*, fine, I ate some chicken grilled by a jolly mustachioed vendor on Snack Street. I probably would've kept this down.

Except that when I looked up, Amy was eating an entire skewered octopus.

So I repaid Beijing for the spectacle she'd given me. The round of gastronomic misfortune that followed was a piece of impromptu street theater that enthralled and delighted a number of Beijingers of all ages. It ended with me, exhausted, shirt sullied, hollow-eyed, sitting on a stool that had been provided for me mid-hurl by two generous Beijing dudes who ran a tiny convenience store. Amy later related to me the conversation that took place over my weakened body:

"Is your friend okay?"

"Yeah. He ate something bad."

"Foreigners' stomachs are weak."

"Yeah."

"Well, he'll be all right. He should rest tomorrow."

"He can't. He's going to Mongolia."

"Oh. Well, that's not so bad. He can sleep on the plane."

"No, he's taking the train."

"The train?! To Mongolia? How long does that take?"

"Two days."

"Why doesn't he just fly?"

"It's a long story."

VALI: The Plane

The 220,000-pound Boeing 767-200 tore through the evening sky. Two jet engines thrust the plane forward at 550 miles per hour. Pressure created by air flowing around the carefully engineered wings lifted passengers up into the clear expanse of sky that exists above the clouds.

About a hundred years ago the Wright brothers, two bicycle makers—one of whom hadn't even finished high school—built the first working airplane. Their first flight lasted twelve seconds. What the history books don't tell you is that the flight, which was only supposed to be eight seconds long, arrived late. Also, the airline lost Orville Wright's luggage (a case filled with monocles and those bicycles with huge front wheels).

On my first flight, I sat on the left edge of the center aisle. In front of me a seat-back television screen allowed me to check the time and weather in Rio, track flight progress by watching an airplane-shaped icon slowly slide down a world map, or view one of a dozen recently released Hollywood films.

I sipped a plastic tumbler filled with whiskey and hollow cylinders of cloudy ice and thought about Steve. Most likely, he was nearly alone on some mode of transportation that he wouldn't be allowed off of for several days. As I was flying he was undoubtedly bearded and shirtless, staring into a mirror while repeating: "This is fun. This is worthwhile. This is not the most boring experience of not only my life but anyone's life in the history of the world. This is fun. This is worthwhile. This is not . . ."

I actually felt guilty, not for cheating but for being less miserable than Steve. I decided to find an in-flight movie involving boats and, as penance, watch it no matter how bad or boring it was. Thankfully, there weren't any. So instead I watched a movie about two rival magicians who tried to destroy each other's lives.

VALI: Why Brazil?

It started with a movie.

In college I saw *City of God*, a beautiful gangster movie set in a favela, or shantytown, of the same name outside Rio. A lot of awesome stuff happens in the movie, including the murder of a drug lord by a gang of six-year-olds.

I could beat the crap out of a gang of six-year-olds, I remember thinking as the credits scrolled up the screen.

What most people don't realize about six-year-olds is that they're light enough to be easily swung around, yet heavy enough to function as a weapon. So if a gang of, say, nine or ten six-year-olds attacked me, I'd punch the first one in the mouth, real fastlike. Then I'd grab her by the ankles and swing her around forcefully, until I'd knocked all the other little runts unconscious. The specifics of the situation would determine what my next move would be. Most likely, I'd search the kids' pockets for candy.

With that plan to become the most powerful drug lord in all of Brazil, I made my way to Rio.

Also, the country's capital city, Brasília, was built in 1956 in the shape of an airplane. Brazil was the perfect place to begin cheating.

VALI: Losing My Touristyness

Rio's Sugerloaf Mountain is supposedly shaped like a loaf of sugar—a thing nobody alive has ever seen or heard of. I thought it was actually shaped like a regular mountain. Perhaps the Brazilians agreed but, since Mountain Mountain isn't a very catchy name, they decided to go with something else.

Not far from Sugarloaf, the 130-foot-tall milky white statue of Christ the Redeemer towers over the city. Christ stands open-armed staring straight ahead, looking like he's about to take a backward trust fall into the waiting embrace of the lush green Tijuca forest.

I had seen these images so many times on posters and magazine ads beckoning tourists to Brazil, I decided not to visit them. I wasn't going to spend my time in Rio using my digital camera to reproduce postcards. Instead I was going to take to the streets and find out what the place was really about.

My first stop was downtown.

There I saw that Rio had much in common with a major American city. For example: much like in New York, gravity existed in Rio, drawing objects toward the earth with a force inversely proportional to the square of the distance between the earth and the object. I also observed some differences. For example: everyone was Brazilian.

My plan for my first day in Rio was to begin integrating myself into Brazilian society. I eyed everyone I passed, hoping to pick up on some Brazilian idiosyncrasies that I could emulate in order to fit in better. Cool travelers, such as myself, hate the idea of looking like a tourist. Ideally we'd be indistinguishable from the locals. Failing that, we'd accept looking like a smelly backpacker. Looking like a tourist is in last place, shortly behind looking employable.

Fortunately, my name is Vali Chandrasekaran and I grew up in a rural northern Pennsylvania town of about seventeen thousand people. So I was something of an expert on assimilation.

VALI: The Vali Guide to Assimilating Yourself in a Foreign Land

The most important factors for assimilation are as follows:

Adopt the Local 'Look': This was actually pretty simple in Rio. Locals wear the Western standards of pants and shirts and racially range from European white to Haitian black. The place is seriously multicultural, largely due to an influx of Japanese, Portuguese, Spanish, German, and Italian immigrants who came over to work in the coffee fields after the abolition of slavery in 1888. When I stepped off the plane, I already looked like someone whose family could have lived in Brazil for over a century.

Never Look Lost: Locals, I observed, never stood at corners looking for street signs and consulting maps. Tourists, on the other hand, did a lot of that. So I ditched the maps and started walking around confidently, like I knew where I was going. This was tremendously successful. I immediately stopped looking lost. Instead, I started actually being lost. But that sort of thing happens to locals too.

Eat the Local Cuisine: Indians are famously finicky eaters, unwilling to stomach even the thought of eating something not made with curry and seasoned with saffron. Once, upon being told that I had a three-week vacation to Italy planned, an Indian family friend looked at me with fear in his eyes and, without irony, asked, "Three weeks in Italy? What will you do for food?"

Thankfully, I'm not like that. Some sort of genetic mutation must have saved me from gastronomic conservatism. If a reliable source told me that the local delicacy was cat hair sautéed in worm fat and served over a bed of mixed greens, I would have tried it.

Brazilian cuisine wasn't quite that exotic, but it did taste better than my hypothetical meal probably would have. Waiters in churrascaria restaurants walk from table to table with two-foot-long skewers of chicken hearts, pork, duck, and beef. Fresh from the glowing charcoal grills, the seasoned and marinated meats spit hot juices into the air, filling the room with a smell that would cause a bowl of dust to salivate.

My favorite dish was *feijoada* as served by the corner restaurant near where I was staying in Santa Theresa. The stew of black turtle beans, salted goat meat, and smoked pork sausage was served with rice, two circles of sliced fresh oranges, and collard greens chopped into ribbons. One day I ate it for both brunch and dinner.

Relax Like the Locals Relax: In Rio this means going to the beach and watching soccer.

Rio's deservedly legendary beaches run for six kilometers from Leblon to Ipanema to Copacabana. On a map, the beach looks like one wide shark's tooth. It might even be advertised as such if people weren't so squeamish about associating sharks and beaches. At ground level, the beaches looked manufactured for summer perfection. There was Chex Mix colored sand, water the color of your favorite movie star's eyes, well-oiled bodies that would have looked great fully dressed and looked even better partially dressed, and mountains looming dramatically in the background.

All beachgoers are equal on the boardwalk that ran along the edge of the beach. But on the sand the beach is separated into twelve sections, each about five hundred meters long and attracting a distinct clientele. They're like little neighborhoods for each of Rio's socioeconomic groups. For example, Post 9 is where Rio's whitest and most likely to have a personal trainer maintain their bronzes. Post 6 is where the favela kids hang out. Post 5 is for homosexuals and transvestites. Post 3.14159265 . . . is for irrational number enthusiasts.

After a day of relaxing on the beach, I went to a soccer game with a group called Be a Local that arranges events for non-Portuguese speakers. I was shocked they even agreed to take my money given how masterfully I had already transformed myself with all the wearing of T-shirts, ignoring of maps, and eating of *feijoada*. According to this company, locals spent a lot of time clustered around guides wearing white DON'T BE A GRINGO! BE A LOCAL T-shirts.

The game between the local team, Botafogo, and Coritiba was important for the Brazilian national soccer championships. If I understood the situation correctly (extremely unlikely), Botafogo would advance to the next stage of the tournament only if they tied or beat Coritiba. A loss would end their hopes for the title.

With so much at stake, the fans took to their feet before kickoff and never sat back down. Directly in front of me, a curly blond-haired baby sucked on a pacifier and tried to sleep on his father's shoulder. When Botafogo slipped the ball into the goal, just out of reach of the diving Coritiba goalie, the stadium erupted. The baby suddenly awoke with a nubby-toothed smile and pointed his chubby forefingers into the air, instinctively celebrating "Botafogo, Number One!" with the rest of the dancing crowd.

The match ended in a 3–3 tie, less than ideal, but sufficient for the fans. Happy drunk songs echoed through the hallways of the Rio stadium at the end of the night. Souvenir T-shirts, depicting a woman wearing a rival soccer team's jersey while going down on a grinning man in Botafogo's black-and-white-striped jersey, sold especially well that night.

The Result: On my third day in Rio, a couple of hayseeds from out of town asked me for directions in Portuguese.

Assuming they asked me "What direction are we walking in?" I smiled and pointed straight ahead. That's how I learned the Portuguese word for "Thank you."

VALI: Rocinha—the Largest Favela in Rio

I rode on the back of a motorcycle taxi, zigzagging up a hillside road to the top of Rocinha, Rio's largest favela. The driver wasn't reckless, but he was more at ease with sudden movements than I was. I don't think I've ever clutched anything as tightly as I clutched him. If I fell, I was determined to take my driver down with me.

In the less than five-minute ride up the hill we passed thousands of Rocinha residents going about their lives. Kids ran around shirtless, wearing faded shorts and primary-colored flip-flops. Men sat on plastic crates stacked to a comfortable height shooting the shit, sipping coffee, and eating food wrapped in newspaper. The air was crowded with the smell of engine exhaust and the sounds of dozens of revving motorcycle engines.

An estimated 20 percent of Rio's population live in one of the city's favelas. Rocinha is the largest of the shantytowns with a population of 200,000. To get an idea of how many people that is, consider a pile of 200,000 bodies. If arranged properly, it could be up to 133,333 feet tall! Improperly arranged, it could be as little as eight inches tall.

My guide, Mario F. Balthazar, led the way on another moto taxi. Until two years ago Mario had been a Rio lawyer who, like most Cariocas, had never set foot in a favela. The lifestyle didn't suit him, so now he arranges excursions for too-cool-for-school tourists like myself.

We dismounted our motorcycle taxis at the top of the hill. From there we could see all of Rocinha—tens of thousands of small mostly clay red or cement gray houses. We could even identify the "richer" and "poorer" parts of the slum. Those terms are, of course, very relative. Houses in the richer section were occasionally painted and had light blue water tanks on top. Those in the poorer section, located against the gray-brown cliffs on the perimeter of Rocinha, were shacks with thatched or corrugated tin roofs.

The beaches of Ipanema beckoned from just past the bottom edge of the slum. Sugarloaf Mountain stood to the west. People in Los Angeles pay millions of dollars for houses with views half as good as this. People in New York would roll around in a mixture of broken glass and salt for the same. In Rocinha nobody pays a cent. Everyone lives illegally.

"I come here every day, so the people know me," Mario explained as we walked. "So we are safe. You can take pictures of anything, except anybody holding a gun. Those are drug dealers and they fear photos of themselves appearing in newspapers or on the Internet where police could identify them."

Science hasn't yet created a machine that can measure the tiny amount of time that passed between our hearing the words *drug dealers* and seeing one. It was as if simply uttering those words caused him to appear—a cocaine genie.

The dealer couldn't have been a day older than twenty and his already dark complexion was burned even darker from sitting shirtless in the sun every day for months. His gun rested in an open holster attached to his belt. And a walkie-talkie lay in his lap.

Nobody gave the armed kid any notice. Next to him an old man sold flowers laid out on a towel. I guessed that meant everything was normal. If the locals started panicking, I was fully prepared to crumple to the ground and begin sobbing and soiling myself.

The dealer recognized Mario with a wide smile. They hugged then spoke in Portuguese. I assume the conversation went something like this:

DRUG DEALER: Who is this really tough looking Indian guy?

MARIO: Correction—tough and *handsome* Indian guy.

DRUG DEALER: They don't make 'em like him anymore, do they?

MARIO: No they don't.

DRUG DEALER AND MARIO (IN UNISON): I wish he was my dad.

When we resumed walking Mario explained that the gang that controls Rocinha, Amigos dos Amigos (Friends of Friends), stations people at several strategic points around the favela. They watch out for the police, who only entered the favela to arrest someone. Drug dealers, it turns out, don't like getting arrested. So any cop sighting is radioed to every nearby drug gang member. Then the shooting starts.

Linha Da Morte (The Line of Death) was spray painted along one particularly bullet-scarred corridor, referring to many fatal meetings between cops and dealers that took place along the passageway.

Despite all the drugs and violence, Rocinha was a surprisingly smoothly functioning community. There was an official post office, toy-filled day care facilities, stores that sold TVs and radios off dusty yellow and green shelves, and small bakeries serving ham croissants (perfectly fine, but not great). Life in the favela was, relatively speaking, not so bad. That's probably why the residents tolerate the drug gangs. If the cops were to come in and enforce laws—force people to pay taxes and buy their land from the government—the lives that so many have built up would collapse. So by keeping the cops out of the favelas, the drug dealers actually protect the poor in a strange way. The drug gangs are the reason why the favelas are dangerous places for the poor to live but also the most livable.

Toward the end of my tour, a small group of kids began following me. I assumed they knew I was a tourist and were hoping for a handout. But then the boldest of the group, unable to contain himself any longer, started waving at me and shouting, "Helio! Helio!" Mario looked at me, then laughed.

"They think you're this Brazilian comedian named Helio de la Penya," he explained. "You actually look like him."

I looked over toward the kids with a big smile and, with the best Brazilian accent I could muster, screamed back,

"*Obrigado*." As I left, I saw them excitedly run off, eager to tell their friends they had just met the hilarious and generous Helio de la Penya.

VALI: Out on the Town in Rio Part *Um*: The Scenarium

The prostitutes in Rio are infuriatingly attractive. It was Thursday night and I was walking through the upscale Lapa neighborhood on my way to a recommended club.

The girls were unavoidable. These program girls—the word *program* apparently being a Brazilian euphemism for "sex for money"—stood right out in the open, on the edges of the sidewalks, leaning against cars and barely covering their tremendous bodies with tight halter tops paired with short shorts or mini miniskirts. Most underwear is less revealing than these outfits. Groups of them chatted as well-heeled locals walked by on their way to dinner, bars, and concerts.

My destination was a samba club called the Rio Scenarium. Before leaving the house, I told my host, Favoretto, where I was going. He responded with a warning not to accept any drinks from strangers and made me promise to never leave my cocktail unattended. What was going on? He must have had me confused with his daughter. I thought about taking advantage of this confusion by asking him for pizza money.

Then Favoretto explained a Rio scam involving romance, cunning, and intrigue. I've always loved romance and cunning. Intrigue I could do without.

The scam, as Favoretto explained it, begins with a pretty Brazilian girl flirting with an aw-shucks tourist. While she charms the tourist, one of her associates drugs his unattended drink. A few minutes later, smooching commences. This, understandably, excites the tourist, causing him to think that although in his native country he is pretty run-of-the-mill, in Brazil he is some sort of exotic Adonis. As this rationalization courses through the tourist's brain, a telling expression flashes across his face. The expression, a cocky smile with deeply focused eyes, betrays a newfound confidence. It lets the pretty Brazilian girl know her hooks are in his heart. Then she abruptly stops the flirting, hair stroking, and kissing to lean in and, in charmingly broken English, suggest going back to her apartment. The tourist, now convinced that he has the biggest dick in all of Rio, immediately agrees. On their way out the girl might think something along the lines of "I hate my life" while the aw-shucks tourist thinks "Girls have such a great attitude, here in Brazil." Shortly after arriving at the pretty Brazilian girl's conveniently nearby "apartment," the drugs kick in, causing our tourist to lose consciousness. Then he gets robbed.

Under normal circumstances falling victim to the above scam would be an awful experience. But I was writing a book! And what a great story that would make: How I Was Drugged and Robbed by a Beautiful Brazilian Vixen, by Vali Chandrasekaran. I would follow it with the sequel: How a Beautiful Brazilian Vixen Couldn't Go Through with Robbing Me Because We Fell in Love Just as the Drugs Hit and Then When I Woke Up She Was Having Sex with Me, by Ilav Narakesardnahc. (I publish my more salacious stuff under a pseudonym.)

Obviously, I really didn't want anyone to drug and rob me. But I did want someone to try.

The Rio Scenarium was one story of scene tucked beneath two stories of arium. On the first level, a band played to a crowd of samba enthusiasts.* Floorless centers on the second and third levels of the Scenarium allowed patrons to lean against a balcony and check out the sambaing taking place on level one. The walls of the Scenarium were covered with antique farming implements. Now that sounds weird. But it looked cool so I didn't question it at the time.

Once in the Scenarium, I marched straight to the bar and ordered a rum and coke. It wasn't a typical order for me, but I

*Or salsa or tango enthusiasts. To be honest, I don't believe there are any differences between South American dances. I believe the different names exist purely so the fat cats in the dance-lesson industry can make more money.

wanted something dark-colored to allow for easy drugging. I placed the drink on the bar and acted like I wasn't paying attention to it though I really was. Then I made my aw-shucks out-of-town-ness explicitly clear.

"I don't understand this metric system of yours," I said loudly to the bartender.

His response was confused and brief, something along the lines of "What?" or "Excuse me, sir?"

Over the next hour and a half, I loitered in over a dozen sections of the Scenarium. The only time anyone talked to me was to ask if I was in line for the bathroom. Everyone else was sambaing with their partner or engrossed in fascinating conversations with their friends. Nobody seemed interested in robbing me.

Rio seemed to be much safer than Favoretto had led me to believe. Bummed, I left the Scenarium. I decided that if I couldn't do anything dangerous I was going to do the next best thing: something fun. So I walked down the street, past a different crop of prostitutes, and followed a group of young locals into a bar where a live band played Portuguese rock.

VALI: Out on the Town in Rio Part *Dois*: A Bar I Don't Remember the Name Of

The venue was filled with a crowd of twenty-somethings dressed in crisp linen blazers and dresses that made girls look like upside-down flowers when they spun around. Though many young Brazilians know English, they often found my American accent intimidating. In case you are wondering, affecting a French accent didn't help at all. My situation was particularly maddening at this bar since it was teeming with cute ladies. What I needed was a conversation starter that was light on words. Thankfully, my friend Leila had prepared me for exactly this situation.

VALI: A Primer on Leila

The night before Steve and I left Los Angeles, Leila handed each of us a sealed manila envelope with instructions not to look inside until we had left town. I, of course, immediately went to the bathroom and opened mine. The note within read as follows:

> I know you don't have a lot of space in your luggage, but I thought you should have a pack of cigarettes. I've been told that it's a fool's errand to try and pick up a girl in any country other than the U.S. without cigarettes. Also if you end up in some kind of Turkish prison, they might come in handy.

Attached to the note were a pack of cigarettes and six pages of dialogue snippets of Batman lecturing Robin from the *Batman* television series starring Adam West.* I'm serious.

VALI: Out on the Town in Rio Part *Dois*: A Bar I Don't Remember the Name Of Continued . . .

Back at the bar in Rio. I had no wingman to support my lady charming but, thanks to Leila's generosity and foresight, I did have the next best thing: cigarettes.

In the quieter back section of the bar I spotted a group of sultry young brunettes passing around a hinged shiny cigarette case, each pulling out and lighting a white paper-wrapped conversation starter.

* My favorite of which is:

ROBIN: "You can't get away from Batman that easy!"
BATMAN: "Easily."
ROBIN: "Easily."
BATMAN: "Good grammar is essential, Robin."
ROBIN: "Thank you."
BATMAN: "You're welcome."

I opened my pack of Lucky Strike unfiltered cigarettes and threw two of the smokes away, masterfully creating the illusion that I had smoked two cigarettes recently.* Then I walked straight up to a tall olive-skinned girl with a green dress, red-orange lipstick, and smoldering eyes. I placed a cigarette in my mouth and pantomimed lighting it. I must have looked like a movie star.

She smiled as she lit my cigarette for me.

"Do you speak English?" I asked, sucking in warm mind-stimulating smoke through the end of my new best friend, the unfiltered cigarette. It was my first drag ever. According to every after-school special I've ever seen, this moment was supposed to have come over a decade earlier in my life, in the stalls of my middle school lavatory. But it didn't. Perhaps because I spent my middle school years so excited about learning I hated taking bathroom breaks.

My first cigarette drag was . . . glorious. The warm smoke tasted earthy and smelled of confidence.

"Yes," nodded the Brazilian girl. "I speak English."

The advertisements were right! Cigarettes help you meet beautiful women! Who cares what the nerds in the lab coats say? This experience was worth getting cancer!

Before responding, I took a second drag. This time I inhaled into my lungs. Then I entered a violent coughing fit that only ended several seconds later, after I had thrown up a little bit into my own hand.

I have had a fair share of terribly embarrassing experiences in my life. And even before I finished vomiting, I knew this one was an instant classic. I was done.

I never saw the reaction of the girl in the green dress. Keeping my eyes trained on the floor, I slinked out of the bar.

VALI: Out on the Town in Rio Part *Três*

Embarrassment quickly gave way to anger as I walked back to Favoretto's house. In the coming weeks, I was going to be

*Gentlemen readers: feel free to use this trick yourself.

spending a lot of time alone in non-English-speaking sections of the world. I now realized how ill-prepared I was for that. I hadn't met a single local all night. And my best tool had just reduced my night to ashes rather than helped me puff my way to popularity.

It started raining when I got to the hill at the base of Favoretto's house, soaking me and worsening my mood. But I knew feeling sorry for myself wasn't going to get me anywhere. I needed to rise to the challenges I encountered during my journey. What would the best of the best do? They wouldn't have given up, that's for sure. Michael Jordan wouldn't have thrown away his Lucky Strikes if he had just lived through the same experience I had. He would have picked himself right back up and given it another go. MJ would have forced himself to smoke cigarettes all night until they stopped making him vomit. I was going to Michael Jordan this problem.

I pulled another cigarette out of my pocket and entered the next bar I saw, a dirty dive that consisted of little more than a metal counter behind a pull-down metal garage door. I walked up to a group of guys and once again pantomimed a request for a light.

"Injiun?" asked the first responder, who looked like Basquiat.

"Yes. I'm Indian."

He responded with some broken English that I couldn't understand, then started laughing. His friends joined him. Wanting to fit in, I laughed, too.

A tall white woman in her thirties turned around and asked Basquiat a question in Portuguese. He repeated himself. Then she started laughing. I laughed again. This time, a little bit harder. It looked like they were starting to accept me.

"Do you understand what he said?" she asked.

"Nope."

"He said that you need to be very careful because you have just run into the most dangerous gangsters in Rio."

I took a long drag off my cigarette and exhaled dramatically. I wanted these guys to think I might be dangerous also. I probably should have exhibited other devil-may-care behaviors, but not-vomiting required the rest of my concentration.

Could these guys really be dangerous gangsters? I studied them with my expert journalist senses.

- ☛ Smell: gunpowder odor noticeably absent—Not Gangster-Like.
- ☛ Hearing: was explicitly told they were gangsters—Gangster-Like.
- ☛ Taste: unable to determine.
- ☛ Touch: smooth skin—Not Gangster-Like.
- ☛ Sight: several visible tattoos—Gangster-Like.

So my journalistic senses left me with two Not Gangster-Likes, two Gangster-Likes, and one unable-to-determine. I really needed to taste these guys to break the tie, but I couldn't come up with an organic way to lick one of them. I suppose that's one of the skill gaps preventing me from becoming a Pulitzer Prize–winning journalist. Bob Woodward would have been licking those guys in a heartbeat.

"Where are you from, Injiun?" Basquiat asked, handing me a beer.

"Los Angeles."

"America?"

"America."

I was in. For the rest of the night, we communicated surprisingly well using only broken English and exaggerated gestures. I soon learned his name was Gais and that he and his friends made up a Rio graffiti gang.

Cigarettes had led me to a Rio graffiti gang!

I thought about all the wonderful experiences I had missed out on because I hadn't smoked for the first twenty-six years of my life. I vowed not to let my son repeat my mistake. He'll start smoking the day his first pube comes in.

I lit another cigarette and ordered a round of beers for everyone. I wanted to get to know these guys and nothing forges friendships faster than drinking. Accidental drunkenness, simply having one too many, doesn't have the same effect. The drunkenness must be chased and deliberate.

Agreeing to get drunk with someone is like saying, "In an hour or so I might start crying about something I don't really care about. I understand you might do the same. Let's not judge." You need to really trust someone to enter a contract like that. That's the secret to the Old White Men's Club. I challenge you to let another man watch you cry while reminiscing about how carefully your father ironed his shirts, then *not* award his company the contract to install all of the toilets on the aircraft carriers you make. Booze is the keystone holding together the fat cat WASP network. When everyone else figures that out, their stranglehold on money and power will be doomed.

The drinking worked. Within twenty minutes I was showing the gang photos of the jetpack in Mexico and performing imitations of the crooners I saw in the honky tonks of Nashville. Within an hour, we were ranking our favorite Bob Dylan and Morrissey songs.

There was absolutely nothing dangerous about the gang. They were a terrific group of guys. I would have betrothed my unborn daughters to them. In fact, I probably did.

Gais appeared to be the unofficial leader of the group. He had a tattoo of a train car that took up his entire forearm, celebrating his distinction of being the first person in Rio to successfully tag a train car. Then there was Chico, a happy Friar John type, who showed me pictures of his son on his cell phone. And Braga, a tall lanky guy who wore all black. He spoke perfect English, which he taught himself in order to learn Flash animation. Other members of the group came and went, their names lost under the clinking of one-liter Antarctica beer bottles against each other.

When my night ended, several hours later, we had collectively emptied my pack of cigarettes and over a dozen liters of beer—nothing crazy, but enough to forge the friendship I had hoped for. We agreed to meet up at 2:00 p.m. the following day so we could all go tagging together.

I arrived at the meeting place at the agreed-upon time, but a hard rain had ruined my plans to decorate the walls of Rio with smiley faces and rainbows. So Gais took me to the studio where the gang hung out and planned their work.

The studio looked like a more authentic version of the workspace every hip Silicon Valley startup aspires to. It housed three computers with Internet access atop a folding table, a wall where the graffiti artists practiced their tags, and a couple of skateboarding and alternative art magazines from around the world. Add a whiteboard, a refrigerator stocked with Red Bull, a couple of nerds and a dweeb and you'd have the offices of PurpleMittens Internet Solutions.

Gais showed me photos of his work. My favorite was probably one of his less technically challenging tags—a huge boulder on which he'd painted fierce eyes and round teeth, turning it into a dragon's head.

We tried to talk but found sober communication surprisingly difficult. Based on our conversations from the night before I knew Gais was actually pretty good with English. But without the booze to keep his self-consciousness at bay, he couldn't get a full sentence out.

Gais lit up a joint. And a few minutes later we were talking again.

Around five p.m., the rest of the gang began filtering in. Somebody opened a new YouTube clip of Rio cops driving armored cars into the favela Gais had grown up in, recklessly shooting everything in their path.

Gais muttered something in Portuguese.

"Yeah, fuck the police," I, in my polo shirt, absentmindedly concurred.

STEVE: A Bad Night in Erlian

All I wanted to do between Beijing and Ulaanbaatar was sleep.

You will recall, Reader, that I'd spent the previous evening disgorging myself of a meal of duck webs. After befouling dozens of Beijing alleys, storefronts, and trash cans, I'd retired for fitful minutes of sleep punctuated by violent stomach-based eruptions that did considerable damage to Room 311 of the Beijing Hebei Guest House and which led to the forced abandonment of three pairs of previously unscathed Fruit of the Loom boxer shorts.

In the morning, exhausted but cleansed, I thanked Amy for her heroic efforts and willed myself onto the Beijing-Ulaanbaatar train. I shook hands with my courteous Mongolian compartment mate, who removed his boater hat and allowed himself a slight loosening of his tie. He and I made conversation until every combination of his twenty words of English and my three of Chinese were exhausted. Mostly he would say something incomprehensible to which I'd reply "shi shi" ("thank you"). I congratulated him on what I understood to be the success of his daughter. He looked confused. We shook hands again.

I could've gone to sleep then. Our first-class train car was downright frilly—the fold-down table was excessively doilied, the windows had lacy curtains, and on my bench-bed there was a gold velour pillow waiting to be drooled upon. The whole effect reminded me of the den of my boyhood neighbor, an eighty-something woman who insisted on being called Auntie Norma, and who was always inviting me over to stuff me with mints and hard candy. I could've sprawled out and in seconds been transported back to Massachusetts in a minty dream.

But we were heading to Inner Mongolia.

As it would so often on this trip, geographical curiosity trumped bodily necessity. My eyes were actually aching from tiredness, as if they'd been scrubbed with steel wool, but I couldn't close them. What if, years later, I was at an intimate cocktail party, recounting my adventures, and a charming guest clutched my forearm and asked me to tell her what Inner Mongolia was like.

"Well, I slept through it," I'd have to say. She would let out a feeble "Oh."

"I can tell you about *Outer* Mongolia," I'd offer.

"Mmm," she'd say, staring into the distance with a look of disappointment.

Sleeping was out of the question.

If you stare out the window on a Beijing to Mongolia train, you will spend a decent portion of your trip in a puzzled trance. On a stretch of grassy farm, for example, I saw a frustrated farmer goading an enormous pig along a canal.

After that I probably couldn't have gone to sleep even if I'd tried, because this pig was as big as a Toyota Corolla and I couldn't stop thinking about it. What kind of relationship do you have with a pig like that? The pig seemed—even from a moving train car a hundred yards away—to be kind of surly, and from the farmer's slouched walk you could tell he'd just about had it with this pig. But while the pig kept growing more pork, the farmer had to keep chasing him along the canal, slave to a surly pig master, although someday he gets to eat him. Who really has the upper hand?

It doesn't take long north of Beijing before the desert starts, and there the visual puzzles grow even more challenging. An enormous fan blade, for instance, abandoned out in the roadless middle of the dustiest, emptiest emptiness that I'd ever seen. I couldn't go to sleep after I saw that, because I was launched into a mental game of "How Did That Get There?"

By the time the sun finally went down, and the sky shifted from solid desert blue to dirty sunset orange to decent suitcoat brown to black, I was absolutely mentally depleted. And physically tired as well. You'd think that sitting on a padded, florally decorated bench wouldn't require much physical exertion. But, since the compartment was narrow, constant jockeying was required so that the Proud Mongolian Father and I could avoid the kind of gentle passing gaze that would force both of us to avert our eyes.

So when we finally pulled the curtain closed on the Gobi night, I was as eager as I've ever been to go to sleep. I laid down and within seconds I was drooling on the gold pillow.

Now, I knew that at some point that night we'd cross the Chinese-Mongolian border. Due to stubborn engineering decisions, when this happened the train would have to stop for several hours to have its wheels changed to fit the Mongolian gauge.

While that happened, there'd be a border inspection. The

Mongolians could care less about this, there not being much to steal or spy on in Mongolia, but the Chinese would want to stamp my passport.

I came up with a terrific plan for sleeping through all this: I left my passport jutting out under my pillow.

I'm not sure what I expected. Ideally the Chinese border guard would tiptoe into the compartment, slip out my passport, turn its pages as quietly as possible, stamp it, slip it back under my pillow, gently pull my blanket up under my chin, whisper a wish for pleasant dreams, and give me a soft kiss on the forehead.

That is not what happened.

The border guard woke me up with a vigorous shoulder shake. He was a young guy but with huge saggy bags under his eyes, so you'd think he might've sympathized with my sleepy face. He did not. He had the grim expression of a notorious non-sympathizer.

I offered up my passport.

The border guard kept flipping back and forth between my Chinese visa, in the front, and the stamps in the back.

Then he looked at me and said, "Comewidth."

I looked over at the Proud Mongolian Father, hoping that we were all in this together. We weren't. He looked away at the night nothingness out the window.

"Comewidth," the guard said again.

What no one knew but me was that I was naked under my knit blanket, save for my pair of Never-Wash underwear, which I had obligingly never washed. The border guard stood firm. I was reduced to the indignity of lowering my blanket, futzing about and then awkwardly shimmying into my pants, and scouring the car for my shirt, which the Proud Mongolian Father kindly found and handed to me under the unamused eyes of my captor.

We were in Erlian, China. Best as I could tell in the blackness, the border central station was the only building around. It was the kind of drab, squat government HQ that I knew one should avoid going into in China. I was the only person being led away.

A thing that did not soothe me in the least was the eerily bland classical music being piped in from out-of-tune speakers along the train tracks, the kind of soothing music they play for people who are about to be victims of war crimes.

Inside I was taken to a desk in a little cubicle, which didn't seem so bad. But as my guard and the desk guard got to talking I could tell that my problem was unusual. Without speaking Chinese my best sense was that the desk guard kept saying, "He has what?!" and my guard kept saying, "Look, I dunno, you deal with it," and then he left.

The desk guard scrutinized my passport for a while, as though it were an unusually challenging Sudoku. He looked up at me.

"Fiankichu?" he said. Or something to that effect (the effect being my not understanding).

He flipped a few pages in my passport.

"MYANkichu!" he said with a vigorous point.

"I'm very tired."

Finally he got up, pointed at the ground where my feet were as if to indicate that's where they should stay, and wandered off.

In a few minutes he came back with a fellow guard, a young woman with a ponytail and too-big glasses. She could've played the nerdy Chinese American friend on an '80s sitcom. Only now she was NOT complaining about how her superstrict mom wouldn't let her wear lip gloss.

"Fiankichu," he said to her, and showed her my passport.

"Ah, myankichu." She looked up at me, worried. Then she smiled a really unconvincing smile and said, "It's no problem, it's no problem!"

She looked at her associate and they kept talking as though it were a really big problem.

Slowly I was bumped up the Chinese border-guard food chain. Each increasingly higher-ranked guard tried to solve the Fiankichu situation, with no help from me. From time to time they'd call over the It's No Problem girl to deliver her line.

I pointed out to her that since it wasn't a problem maybe I could go back to sleep. To which she shook her head sadly.

In China it is bad news to be alone in a government office, and the one they led me to looked like especially bad news. It was huge, for one thing, but the hugeness was compounded by its near barrenness. There was a filing cabinet, with an old classroom-style globe on top. There was a simple metal desk, with a chair in front of it, where I was deposited. That was it—the rest was just huge emptiness.

"It's no problem," the girl said sadly. Then she left.

Alone in the office I had time to speculate on what might, in fact, be the problem.

1. *There was something wrong with my visa.* Unlikely—it had gotten me into China okay.
2. *There was something wrong with my passport.* That seemed unlikely, too—I'd certainly checked it neurotically enough times.
3. *Vali had rigged it.* Not likely, given his general level of competence.
4. *I'd committed a crime in China.* Possible. I hadn't registered as a journalist, and I'd vomited all over a cultural landmark and then fled the scene.
5. *The government had decided I was a spy.* Also possible—I was carrying lots of spy stuff like notebooks and Never-Wash underwear.
6. *The government had decided to keep me in China.* Also possible—I have a lot to offer any country.
7. *There'd been some bizarre Communist confusion.* Perhaps most likely, and most worrisome. Was I about to be executed because a Steve Haly had smuggled in some heroin back in the '70s?

At this point, an unbelievable thing happened. Reader, if I were in your place, I would not believe it. But it really happened, so I set it down: The piped-in classical music switched. Over the speakers the theme song to *The Benny Hill Show* began to play.

So it was when an official came in carrying my passport.

My best reason for hope was that he seemed as tired as me. He sat down at his desk and let out a great, whining sigh. At me, presumably, and at the Fiankichu situation, and at Erlian, and at the poster shortage that left his office barren. And at the phone call he was about to make. This phone call did not go smoothly, because when he was done he let out an even worse sigh.

Then he took out from his desk an enormous, aging leather binder. It looked like an arcane volume of obscure baseball rules or magic spells. But after a few minutes of flipping, he slammed it shut, leaned back in his chair, and let out the greatest, deepest "Why am I stuck working in Erlian in this crappy office with this ignorant, incompetent white spy?" sigh of all.

After a moment's post-sigh relaxation, it suddenly dawned on him.

"Work!" he said.

"Uh . . . okay."

"Work! Work!"

Not knowing quite what kind of work, I remained motionless and semigrinning. In case making me do mental work was what he was after, I tried to do some trigonometry in my head. The official opened my passport and pointed to the Chinese stamp I'd gotten four days ago in Shanghai harbor.

"Work!"

It occurred to me suddenly what had happened.

STEVE: What Had Happened

This is how I got off *Hanjin Athens* in Shanghai. The captain had called me up to his office, where two Chinese guys who looked about twenty were waiting.

"If you want to get off this ship, a fast way would be to pay these men one hundred American dollars," the captain said.

"Okay . . . are they immigration officials or something?"

The captain shrugged. "They can get it done."

So that's what I did. I gave them a hundred dollars and an hour later they gave me back my passport, stamped.

No wonder everyone had been so confused—they hadn't known how to deal with an escaped merchant seaman trying to sneak out of the country in a first-class train car.

"No! No work!" I declared. As evidence I held up my thin, puny arms. "Look!"

He nodded at my valid counterargument but continued to point at my passport. "Work."

Probably, I realized, I was just supposed to bribe the guy, but instead I stood up and grabbed the only prop in the room—the globe.

There followed an impressive mime-and-globe show by me, in which I attempted to explain the terms of the Ridiculous Race. I'd point at the ocean and mime a ship. The official would countermime an airplane, and I'd mime myself being bored at sea. He'd mime me swabbing the deck, and I'd mime my reading and sleeping. I'd mime my proceeding to Mongolia, and he'd mime my staying in China and going back to Shanghai to work some more on another ship.

Finally, exasperated, I held up my lily white, unblemished palms.

"NO WORK!"

He stared at my workless hands. He shrugged. He sat back down, took out a set of stamps, did an impressive series of stampings and restampings in the back of my passport, and waved me out.

"See!" the girl official said as I slunked past her desk. "No problem!"

When I finally got back on the train, back to the frilly compartment, I was as eager to go to sleep as any human has ever been.

But out the window the sun started to come up over the impossible moon-man landscape of the Gobi Desert. We were in Mongolia now, real Mongolia, Outer Mongolia.

Across the tan sands I saw a man riding a horse, on no

visible trail, toward no visible anything. He was riding frantically as if pursued by wolves, but there was nothing else alive within the whole miles-long hemisphere of the horizon. *Where is* that *guy going?* I wondered.

And I knew I'd never get to sleep.

VALI: Down and Out in London

From Rio, I flew to Heathrow airport in London. By the time my flight landed, I was sick as a dog. (And I'm not talking about one of those healthy dogs.)

I needed to rest until I was healthy again. But I couldn't stomach the idea of wasting even one second of the Ridiculous Race. (Doing nothing for days on end is more Steve's thing.) So I resorted to a time-tested problem solver: drugs. I took my second Provigil of the trip and called a friend who helped me explore London's poorer Indian and Pakistani neighborhoods.

The Provigil kept me awake but didn't prevent me from feeling like garbage. My friend did a lot of pointing and saying of things while I focused all my energy on not collapsing. As a result all I remember about London is the sidewalks looked like they could inflict considerable damage to my head.

I awoke the next morning feeling slightly better and made my way to Cambridge University for a leisurely stroll. The campus is so old, there are grooves worn into the walkways from where the earliest students used to drag their knuckles. Eventually Cambridge developed into a storied institution of scientific thought. It was where Newton "discovered" gravity, Watson and Crick "discovered" the double-helix structure of DNA, and I "discovered" that you should use three examples if you really want to drive a point home.

England was pleasant, but it wasn't really that exotic. I wanted to work my way through western Europe as quickly as possible so I could have some real adventures.

But before that I had to check Paris off my to-do list.

VALI: Things That Feel Stupid When You're Home Somehow Feel Less Stupid When You're on Vacation

On the Eurostar train from London to Paris, I noticed my fellow passengers looked stereotypically French. They were long, svelte, and elegant. Like baguettes.

Paris is arranged into twenty districts called arrondissements originating in the center of the city and spiraling clockwise outward. So the 1st arrondissement is in the center of the city, the 2nd bends a little southeast of that, and so on. Parisians consider this logical. Perhaps because they do not know what *logical* means. Could one, through the application of logic, postulate that the 13th arrondissement neighbors the 5th, just on separate rings of the spiral? The answer is no. Rigorous logicians like myself are constantly lost in Paris. The city's layout is a cruel insult to the country that produced Descartes.

When I finally got my bearings, I went to the 13th arrondissement to meet Leila, whom close readers will remember as the wonderful young lady who gifted me with cigarettes before I left Los Angeles. But Leila is more than just a great gift giver. She is also a five-foot-four one-hundred-ten-pound vegetarian from Portland, Oregon, whose sweetness is matched only by her enthusiasm for bourbon. Leila has the incredible ability to go drink for drink with the fattest, most carefree, and most self-hating drunks in the country . . . for about two hours. Then she will fall asleep, no matter where she is located. Usually a floor.

By the time I arrived, Leila had already found a party for us to attend on a Monday night in Paris. It was at a nightclub off the Champs-Elysées. Going out to a nightclub was not the sort of thing I normally did. But, as the saying goes, "When in Paris, act like a douchebag."

Within seconds of entering Club Madame, Leila was accosted by a never-ending string of aggressive Parisian men. Later in the night she told me men were approaching her, saying hello, then immediately kissing her on the mouth. Seconds later I watched that exact scenario unfold.

I realized I really needed to step up my game if I was going to smooch a girl in this town. French ladies were accustomed to a high level of aggressiveness. They probably thought I was gay because my pants were still on when I approached them.

VALI: Meeting the Best Bartender in the World

Leila, a tenacious go-getter, came to Paris with one and only one goal in mind: to get the greatest bartender in the world to invent a new cocktail especially for her.

On my second day in Paris, after an hour of wardrobe and makeup deliberations, Leila and I took a taxi across the Seine to the Right Bank where the Ritz Paris is located. Leila wore a black dress with a light blue and black shawl. And I wore the same blue jeans I had worn every day for the past eighteen days.

Once at the Ritz, an incredibly luxurious hotel that makes all other luxurious hotels I've ever seen look like urine-stained cardboard boxes, we made our way to Bar Hemingway where the man we were hoping to meet, Colin Field, is head bartender.

Bar Hemingway is small, but not so small that, like a coffin, it induced claustrophobia. Nor is it so large that, like a graveyard, it made visitors feel unimportant. It is a fitting office for the best bartender in the world but, to be honest, it isn't the type of establishment I imagined Hemingway spending time in. I always thought alcoholics drank at bars where men drank alone, staring out of their faces. Bar Hemingway seemed too nice.

But we know that Hemingway frequented the bar at the Ritz Paris and that it was as classy then as it is now. We also know, thanks to *A Moveable Feast*, Hemingway's account of Lost Generation life in Paris, that Ernest had money troubles. As I looked over the menu of thirty-dollar cocktails at the bar within the incredibly ornate interior of the Ritz Paris—all marble, dark lustrous woods, massive chandeliers, and rich fabrics—I wondered if maybe Hemingway should have drank someplace cheaper. Maybe Hem wasn't so poor after all. Maybe he was simply an idiot when it came to money management. Hey Hemingway, just buy some beers at the supermarket and drink them in your apartment.

Leila and I sat down at the bar. Almost immediately, Colin Field greeted us in a handsome white jacket and black tie and asked if we'd like a drink. Not wanting me to embarrass her, Leila had prepped me on what to order.

"I'll have a French Seventy-Five," I told Colin. Leila followed suit.

Over the next few minutes, I sipped my mix of lemon juice, gin, sugar, and champagne and saw what separated Colin from other bartenders.

First, he had an encyclopedic knowledge of cocktails and their histories. He is a walking, talking cocktail book.

Second, Colin considered the selection, mixing, and serving of a cocktail to be acts of expression by both the bartender and bar patron. In the "Garniture" chapter of his book, *The Cocktails of the Ritz Paris*, Colin wrote, "I like to think that, for perhaps just a few seconds, as the bartender delicately places the glass in front of the lady, the cocktail becomes part of her jewelry." It's difficult for a patron not to feel wonderful when the bartender puts so much care and consideration into every choice.

Third, Colin is the best conversationalist I have ever met. He could speak intelligently on any topic without ever saying anything that could offend anyone's sensibilities or politics. He keeps up to date on current events, business, and sports by going through three newspapers in different languages every morning. And on days he is not working, he reads novels and books on topics that interest his clients. On this night, Colin was able to participate in a brainstorming session on how to give Steve dysentery the next time I saw him.

Colin's incredible skills as a bartender boil down to selflessness taken to the point of mysteriousness. One leaves the

Ritz Paris having had a fantastic time, having bonded with one's friends and fellow patrons, but without any knowledge of Colin Field as a person.

"Are you married, Colin?" I asked.

"Yes. But not always on duty," he charmingly replied.

Everyone laughed. None of us actually thought Colin did or would cheat on his wife. He was just telling a joke, one he might have told before to a different crowd of mostly foreign businessmen. Colin deflected the question about himself by giving everyone at the bar a laugh. Then he was off to greet a couple who had just entered the bar.

Colin never gave us any information that would allow us to size up his character. His focus on service prevented us from having to know him and might explain why everybody loves him.

As the evening marched forward, I made my way through the French 75, and then the wonderfully named Serendipity, Lutter III Horse's Neck, Brandy Old Fashioned, and a Wait and Sea. Well greased with the oil of conversation, my painstakingly legible notes indicate that I made fast friends with everyone sitting at the bar. I apparently made plans to meet a young Japanese man who ran a tractor-engine manufacturing plant for a drink in Memphis in exactly one year's time and, for some reason, wrote down the names and e-mail addresses of a couple from Wisconsin along with the note "need to contact their daughter."

Just before the night ended at two a.m., five hours after entering Bar Hemingway, I ordered a glass of cognac that was bottled in 1830. Why? Who knows. Trying to divine the motivations of a drunk is an unrivaled waste of time. I wish I could describe anything about it to you, but my notes and memory are blank on this subject. All I can faithfully report is that the cognac didn't sober me up.

When we left Bar Hemingway, Leila and I were both far down drunk street. She had more difficulty walking than me, so I draped her across my shoulders and slowly made my way toward the exit of the Ritz Paris. Each time I saw a hotel employee, I pointed to Leila and explained: "Don't worry.

She's just a friend of mine. We came together. I'm not going to rape her."

A few days later, after I had left Paris, Leila messaged me with triumphant news: Colin Field had invented a new cocktail for her. As of this book's publication, they had not yet settled on a name. I refer to it as the Vicious Vali. Please ask Colin for it, should you find yourself at the Bar Hemingway while he is working.

VALI: Paris, I Love You So Much It Makes Me Angry

Paris is so beautiful it's stupid. Everything I had heard about the city, all positive, turned out to be true. Every meal became a two-hour-long wine-drinking exercise and every walk involved several stops to enjoy absurd views or curious shops.

At one point I decided to see how long I could walk in a straight line without seeing anything great. (Other people might know this experiment as "justification for being lost.") Within two minutes I found myself in the insanely pleasant Luxembourg Gardens. The garden's wide statue- and tree-lined pathways led to a massive fish pond surrounded by hundreds of French people sitting in chairs, taking in the sun, listening to music, reading, chatting, kissing, and having a generally terrific time.

Beneath my awestruck face my blood boiled. I was furious Paris was not overrated.

I had always thought modern Europe was coasting on its past accomplishments. During Europe's heyday, the sun never set on the British empire. Nowadays the sun sets on the empire sometime between five p.m. and nine p.m., depending on the time of year. At the time of my visit, France was even worse off than her age-old rival. Unemployment was high, more than double the United States' rate. Anecdotally, I heard anti-Semitism was, for the first time since World War II, increasing. And the car-burning 2005 riots in the suburbs of Paris showcased the nation's problems with multiculturalism. Europe was finished, I thought. The future, the excitement, the growth is all in the Americas and Asia. Who cares about the past?

Apparently I did. I was as surprised as anyone at this.

I was scheduled to take a train to Amsterdam the next day but didn't want to go. I desperately needed an excuse to stay.

That's why I started pretending to care about the French presidential election.

Sarko or Ségo?! It was the question on everyone's mind. The election was three days away and both candidates were locked in a neck-and-neck race.

Sarko referred to Nicholas Sarkozy, the right-of-center Gaullist candidate who is as handsome as a man can be while still looking a little monstrous. Something about his mouth and teeth made me always imagine him with his face buried in a gazelle carcass, chomping away.

Sarkozy was a complicated conservative. He wanted to reform France's thirty-five-hour workweek system but didn't go so far as saying that the market should set labor demand. His critics claimed his plan to create a ministry of immigration and national identity would suppress multiculturalism. Meanwhile, Sarkozy was pro affirmative action. By United States standards, Sarkozy's politics were barely conservative. In France, I heard several people refer to him as a fascist.

Ségo referred to Ségolène Royal, the socialist candidate, who was running mostly on the "anything but Sarkozy" platform. She was the first woman with a serious shot at France's presidency, and, as everyone was unafraid to note, a woman who somehow made even pantsuits look sexy. She could make any kind of suit look sexy. Even a fat suit.

The main difference between the candidates, it seemed to me, boiled down to Sarkozy wanting to Americanize France and Royal wanting to protect the country's Frenchness. In other words, the press claimed it was a culture war. The whole ordeal brought back painful memories from the 2004 Bush v. Kerry U.S. presidential election. But the pain was worthwhile if it gave me an excuse to stay in Paris.

VALI: The Vali Guide to Meeting Parisian Girls Two Days Before an Election

Armed with my new fake-interest in French politics, I took to the streets of Paris. Eighty-four percent of eligible voters voted in the primary election, significantly higher than the turnout in the 2004 United States presidential primaries. It was the highest voter turnout in forty years and the final round between Sarkozy and Royal was running excitingly tight. As a result, everyone in Paris had an opinion on the election. And cute French girls were a subset of everyone.

I left my hotel room in the morning with the explicit goal to talk to as many pretty French girls as possible under the pretense of being an American journalist. It wasn't a lie, it wasn't the whole truth, and, admittedly, it was more lie than truth. But what isn't these days?

Café culture greatly aided my quest. Paris was bursting with smartly dressed cute girls sitting alone at streetside café tables drinking coffee and smoking cigarettes. They were prime targets for this smiling idiot.

Through trial and error, I improved my lady-charming skills. For example, I quickly learned my story worked better if I appeared more "journalist-like" and took notes during conversation instead of just suggestively raising and lowering my eyebrows at the end of every question. Another failed tactic was, after spotting a cute girl, slightly raising my sunglasses and loudly screaming, "Wow!" I made mistakes so you don't have to, folks.

Eventually I developed the following foolproof Vali Method of Meeting French Girls During the Days Approaching an Election™:

Step One: Spot a cute girl sitting in a café.

Step Two: Sit at table next to cute girl.

Step Three: Order coffee then spend a few minutes smiling and typing fake e-mails on your Blackberry, establishing yourself as a man of wealth, taste, and enviable finger dexterity.

Step Four: Pull out a copy of the *International Herald Tribune* and thoughtfully underline random sentences in an article about French election.
Step Five: Lean over and ask girl which candidate the popular left-leaning *Le Monde* newspaper endorsed.
Step Six: Change topic from French election, which you do not care about, to anything else—preferably how you are an awesome dude writing a book about racing your friend around the world.
Step Seven: Suggestively raise and lower eyebrows.

Many cute girls incorrectly answered the question posed in Step Five. (*Le Monde* endorsed Ségolène Royal.) Receiving incorrect information is one of the journalistic drawbacks of exclusively interviewing attractive twenty-something girls. On the other hand, looking at ugly people is one of the drawbacks of good journalism.

In my limited sample, most of the girls supported Ségo and hated Sarkozy and the right-wing policies he stood for. When I pointed out that, in my opinion, Sarkozy did not seem very right wing, especially when compared to the right wing of the U.S.'s Republican Party, the girls told me that I did not understand France.

And they were right. The police feared car-burning riots if Sarkozy won the election. If every voter in America rioted we wouldn't be able to put a single Denny's out of commission. The Americans, the French girls said, only care about money. Somehow drawn into this debate, I was about to respond that a stable and strong economy provides the foundation for a stable and strong society, when my American-ness hit me. I had always thought of myself as an open-minded, serious social liberal. But even with that open mind, I could see other societies only as more functional or less functional versions of American society. My understanding of the world is handicapped by my personal experience.

Claiming that a visit to Paris has opened your eyes is a great way to meet French girls.

VALI: The Stupidest Way to See Paris

I arrived at the south leg of the Eiffel tower and quickly found my tour guide in the crowd. He stood out.

My first night in Paris, I had spotted a pamphlet advertising a Segway tour. It seemed like the stupidest way to see one of the world's greatest cities. Obviously, I had no choice in the matter; I booked a tour with the Fat Tire Tour Company.

It's impossible to see someone standing with a Segway and not think he's an idiot. From afar I saw my guide attract sad head shakes from almost every passerby. By the time of this book's publication in the summer of 2008, Segways will probably be the preferred mode of transport in every corner of the civilized world. However, back in May of 2007 only attention-craving jerks rode them.

After introducing myself to the guide, who in the interest of identity protection I will henceforth refer to as NotVali, we made our way to company headquarters for a brief hands-on tutorial on how to maneuver a Segway.

NotVali, a perfectly nice guy, had recently graduated from the University of Texas. He had come to Paris a few months before to be a tour guide for the Texas-based Fat Tire Tour Company. So Fat Tire Tours was an American company employing American tour guides who had lived in Paris for less than six months. NotVali did not speak French and had not studied anything about France before becoming a guide. Having been in Paris for three days myself, *I* could have charged *him* for an equally informative tour of the city. The only thing NotVali had over me was access to Segways.

At Fat Tire HQ, six other tourists joined us. The group consisted of four men—in town to attend a conference of Ramada hotel managers—and two of their wives. They were all American—hailing from one of Dallas, Tulsa, or Harrisburg—and they were extremely fresh to Paris; they had come straight from the airport. With only two days for sightseeing before the activity-packed Ramada conference began, the Americans didn't want to waste any time. It would've been easy to brand them hicks, but they were good polite people who just wanted a fun vacation. In the spirit of goodwill, I chose to like them.

The Segways were shockingly simple to use. The machine reacts to pressure from the feet, making it almost impossible to fall. Lean forward and the machine accelerates. Lean back and the machine slows down. No matter what you do, the Segway moves to stay under you.

In a matter of minutes, all of us felt comfortable with the machines. Also within a matter of minutes, I started hating my fellow Segway tourist Bob. Bob was the type of Ugly American I used to think existed only in movies. He wore a loud yellow T-shirt tucked into blue jeans that crawled into his crevices. And he had more crevices on the lower half of his body than most people have in their entire extended families. He spoke loudly and delivered every sentence with the cadence of a joke, yet never said anything funny. When I commented about how foolish all of us were going to look while riding Segways around Paris, Bob responded, "Eh. I'm never going to see these people again." He was probably correct, since Bob planned to spend the free time remaining between his Segway tour and the Ramada conference widening his perspective at EuroDisney.

To complain in detail about the quality of tour information is unfair since the real point was to have fun while riding a Segway. And the tour delivered on that front. Anyone who would claim to not enjoy whizzing through the legs of the Eiffel Tower, zipping down the banks of the Seine, and gliding past the glass pyramid in the Louvre courtyard on a Segway is a liar. It was so much fun I thought I might forget I was on a ridiculous vehicle after a few minutes. This never happened.

Toward the end of the tour, we needed to cross a bridge through rush-hour traffic. NotVali, who made up for his lack of Paris knowledge with his commitment to safety, waited for an opportune moment for the entire group to cross. After a minute of waiting, Bob became antsy and annoyed that his fellow American, NotVali, was backing down from what appeared to be an easily surmountable challenge. He turned to the group.

"Everyone who likes to take risks in their life, raise their hand," Bob commanded.

Apparently risk taking in Bob's life involved flying to Paris with just enough time to see the city by Segway before going to EuroDisney. Was he serious? The hands of every man in the group, except me, shot into the air. The two wives and I kept our hands firmly wrapped around the handlebars.

Nobody made a big deal of giving me a macho stare or asking me if my vagina hurt. However, at that moment, I knew I would never be anything more than the weird effete coat-and-tie-wearing Indian kid in every story those guys told about their Paris vacation.

Two minutes later, Bob fell off his Segway. I am ashamed to say I was delighted. When the tour ended, Bob was one of only two people to fall off his or her Segway (I was not one of them) and the only person to fall off twice. I guess that's what happens when one loves risk so much he forgets to watch out for curbs.

VALI: Why Dick Clark Should Announce the Election Results in France

Outside the National Assembly building, two massive TV screens flanked a stage where a band set up. A crowd gathered, one of several around the city, to wait for the election results, which were to be announced live at 8:00 p.m. The event more closely resembled a New Year's Eve party than any election night I had ever seen.

Exactly at 8:00, the jumbo television declared Nicholas Sarkozy the new president of France. Approximately 53 percent of the crowd cheered and sang. They ran into the streets as their new president drove by on his way to officially accept his victory. The rest stared into the middle distance. It was a look I recognized from the faces of many Democratic voters on the evening of November 2, 2004, after George W. Bush was handily reelected president of the United States. It was a look that said, "I do not know my country."

It was painful to watch. All of a sudden, 46 percent of the French population felt like outsiders in their homeland. They shuffled slowly away like zombies.

The result was not surprising. Sarkozy's lead had been growing in the days leading up to the election as centrist voters slowly decided in his favor. Sarkozy won on the promise of change. Nobody knows if his reforms will help France as much as he promised. But the majority seemed to agree that a Royal presidency would mean more of the same—the same unemployment, the same lackluster growth, and the same problem of talented individuals leaving France.

"I'm disgusted. This means it will be a France of everyone for themselves. It is the France of the rich now," a voter told the *International Herald Tribune.* The subtext of her message was clear: France was going to become more like America. Half of the country thought this was a horrible fate.

While walking around after the results were announced, I saw two children, probably around four and five years old, happily singing out pro-Sarkozy slogans on their balcony. Sad-eyed Royal supporters walked by, trying to hold their tongues. A few couldn't do it and screamed up at the tiny children who really had no idea what they were saying. A kind Parisian translated a few of the exclamations for me:

"Shut up, you idiots!"

"You have no idea what is going to happen to your futures!"

"I feel sorry for the France you will grow up in!"

"Your parents are fascists!"

To understand the Royal supporters' rage one needs to understand how seriously the French take Frenchness. They have an almost four-hundred-year-old institution, the Académie Française, whose primary task is protecting the purity of the French language. Protecting it, mostly, from English. Recent attacks on French have included the words *computer* and *e-mail,* which have been Frenchified to *l'ordinateur* and *courriel.* I thought the matter of language protection was a bit silly until I learned that the forty members of the Academie are called immortals. Apparently no one else is bothered by the irony when an immortal of the institute of language dies.

These people didn't want to say "e-mail" and now they were facing mass Americanization of their culture.

It was time for me to get out of there.

STEVE: Gamesmanship

When Vali and I had concocted this "race" scheme, I'd envisioned a lot of beg-borrow-steal-type scenarios. I assumed I'd have to do things like sleep in chicken coops and hitch rides with Gypsy caravans and talk my way onto convoys of Russian tanks. One of those old-timey hand-car railway things would be my conveyance for, I estimated, a solid third of the trip.

As it turned out, it was much easier. On May 6, for instance, nineteen days after I left Los Angeles, I was in Mongolia on a train that was headed all the way to Moscow.

I could've doped myself with sleeping pills, laid back, and slept for seven days as we rattled through the taiga. From Moscow a few changes of trains could've taken me to any of the busy ports of Europe, where I could've found a ship. A boat ride and a final dash across North America, and I'd be clutching the Victory Scotch. All I had to do to win the Ridiculous Race was stay on the train.

I didn't. Here was my thinking:

- ☛ It was hard enough getting on a ship in Long Beach, where I spoke the language and was fortified with pie.
- ☛ When Vali reaches the western edge of the Pacific, he will be disheveled, exhausted, missing his passport, his eyes bloodshot. Very possibly his face will be withered from syphilis.
- ☛ There's no way he will have booked a ship in advance. If he booked anything farther east than Nevada I'd be stunned.

- ☛ Vali will check into the nearest Sheraton and spend several days crying before giving up.
- ☛ Of course, it's possible he's out-thought me. He may even have thought that I'd be thinking this right now. Or, perhaps, knowing I'm thinking this, he knows that I won't be worried about him, and will therefore be too casual in his own planning, because he knows my thinking about his thinking will cause me to slow down. Or, maybe he assumes *that's* what I'm thinking.

The point of all this was (1) it's very easy to go insane while sitting in a train car in the Gobi Desert and (2) I could probably spare a day or two to do some exploring and still win the race.

We were deep into Mongolia, where the national beverage is fermented mare's milk. *Fermented mare's milk.* Was I really going to pass through here without finding out what that tasted like? If there was one kind of fermented milk I wanted to taste, it was mare's.

But the real reason I wanted to check out Mongolia is that I'm a huge Genghis Khan fan.

STEVE: Hurray for Genghis Khan!, or, The History of Pants

In eight hundred years, Mongolia has produced exactly one famous person. If you're only going to produce one, you could do much worse than Genghis Khan. He may not have been the best person who ever lived, but Genghis Khan has an indisputable claim on the title of "most kickass dude in world history." Consider:

He was born in a tent and at least once during his childhood his father accidentally forgot him while packing up camp. As a young man his own wife was once kidnapped from him. This was a bad move by the kidnappers, because Genghis chased them down and killed them.

Perhaps this incident made him see the need for some order on the Mongolian steppe. Genghis somehow managed to unite all the Mongols, impose a much-needed law against wife-kidnapping, organize the various tribes into a gigantic, disciplined army, and conquer an area four times the size of the Roman empire.

It appears that part of Genghis's success stemmed from being much *less* cruel than his competitor conquerors, who did things like fling captured children in catapults and boil people alive. The Mongolians preferred "smothering under heavy carpets" as a form of execution because it was bloodless. A thin technicality, but at least they were trying.

After Genghis died, his sons and grandsons tended to be either alcoholics or awesome conquerors, with the latter group continuing on until they'd conquered China, Persia, Russia, and much of Turkey. Their empire stretched from Vietnam to the gates of Vienna. The Mongols managed to subdue both what's now Afghanistan and what's now Iraq. (I encourage you at this point to arch your eyebrows with an unspoken ironic remark. If you insist on saying something, two suggestions: Liberals may wish to remark that Genghis Khan was a better administrator than George W. Bush; conservatives may want to note that we could probably subdue Iraq, too, if we were allowed to smother anybody we wanted.)

In managing all this, the Mongols developed paper money, spread crops, built bridges, fostered scholarly and diplomatic exchange, and more or less invented global commerce. The Mongols had all kinds of great ideas. They forced captured criminals to form an auxiliary police force, for instance. I hereby claim this idea for a TV show (a hard-hitting drama on FX about ex–drug dealers forced to be police deputies on the gritty streets of modern-day Pittsburgh).

In his terrific book *Genghis Khan and the Making of the Modern World*, Jack Weatherford credits the Mongols with introducing their battle cry "hurray" into English and teaching tunic-wearing Europeans about pants, two solid and lasting achievements. Five minutes of Internet research has left me unable to confirm Weatherford's claims. But until someone gives me a better explanation for why I'm wearing pants, I'm giving GK the credit.

Perhaps the single best indicator that Genghis Khan was a kickass dude is this: The guy may have fathered somewhere in the region of a thousand children. The implications of this are boggling. Geneticists have found that something like 8 percent of the men in Central Asia are descended directly from Genghis Khan. The guy has sixteen million living descendants. For comparison, the apparent runner-up, a fifth-century Irish warlord named Niall of the Nine Hostages, has a mere three million living people who can count him as an ancestor. (Imagine what he could've done if he'd had, say, *twelve* hostages.)

The Mongolians know how cool Genghis is—a giant statue squats outside their Parliament building, and there are at least (by my count) twenty vodka brands named after him. Which makes ordering vodka in Mongolia an Abbott and Costello routine but remembering your heritage easy.

Everyone knows a dude who hit his stride in high school and has sort of just been hanging around ever since, reminiscing about when he took the team to States, and never accomplishing much past graduation.

World-historical-wise, that's what Mongolia is like. Mongolia reached its high point around 1220, and it's been downhill ever since. You can't walk around Mongolia without wondering, "What would Genghis Khan think of this place *now*?"

Take, for example, Mongolia's capital "city."

STEVE: Ulaanbaatar: A City for People Who Hate Cities

Looming over Ulaanbaatar is a giant white portrait of Genghis, painted onto a mountainside, with the Khan staring down. A fun game as you stroll the city is to imagine Genghis rolling his eyes at the various things going on beneath him, and wondering when somebody's going to get smothered.

Ulaanbaatar (apparently pronounced "ooo-lawn batter,"

like what you would mix up if you were making a batch of ooo-lawn cookies) looks like old photographs of American Depression–era shantytowns. It's the only city I've been to where the outskirts consist of tents, white felt circles called gers. I'd seen tents like these dotting the landscape here and there out the train window; they're the traditional homes of Mongolia's nomads, who form about half the country's population. Recent years of horrible winters and frozen livestock have forced many of these nomads to give up on raising camels, sheep, cows, and horses, pitch their tents in the city, and patch together work.

The "building" options in Ulaanbaatar don't seem much better. Beyond the tents, rows of rickety shacks line dirt alleys. My greatest fear is being bitten by a rabid dog, and this seemed like prime territory for that to come to pass. But the only dog I encountered was a ludicrously scruffy mutt rooting about in some trash. This was by far the mangiest dog I would encounter on a world tour not unmarked by mangy dogs. The poor guy appeared far too exhausted and indifferent to bite me. He was kind of a sheepish, incompetent dog, doing his best to act fearsome. I named him Vali.

The actual, for-real buildings tend to be bleak Soviet-era apartment rectangles. As I walked past one of these a gentleman barked at me in his native Mongolian. This is harsh, guttural, and consonant-happy language, so what he said sounded like "Charglish blarsh klarg blarg tarcho," but as he said it he shook an empty can of beer at me, and so I understood him to mean "How about you buy some beers and then I drink the beers?"

I declined with the only word I knew in Mongolia, *baayalalaa* ("thank you," pronounced "bye-are-[RETCHING NOISE]-la"), and kept going until I found the Hotel Ulaanbaatar. It's fronted by a statue of Lenin, whose feet were at that moment (around three in the afternoon) being used as a napping spot by two drunk guys. I checked in and was suitably impressed by the hotel's ghostly, dilapidated, Communist-era grandeur—the dusty billiard room, for example, clearly haunted by the ghosts of visiting Soviet bureaucrats, who appear at night to fill out spectral paperwork.

STEVE: A Conversation That I Imagine Must Have Occurred Somewhere in Ulaanbaatar on the Night of May 6, 2007, Following My Attempt to Eat Lunch

Starring Tishgilit and Borte, two Mongolian girls.

TISHGILIT: 'Sup, Borte.

BORTE: Hey, Tishgilit.

TISHGILIT: Hey, how was work today at Yochin Booye?

BORTE: Just another day at "Mongolian national fast food." Oh, the craziest thing happened today.

TISHGILIT: Really? What?

BORTE: Well, this lanky American guy came in—at least I think he was American. He had, like, a huge backpack on, and his hair was all crazy and he was totally sweaty and everything. So he walked up to the counter and started saying stuff in English.

TISHGILIT: What'd you do?

BORTE: So, I was like, "I don't understand," but of course he didn't speak Mongolian, so that didn't help. So he starts pointing randomly at the menu, and going like this. *(She pantomimes eating.)* And I was like, "Okay, I get it, asshole, I'm not an idiot. You want some food. What do you want?"

TISHGILIT: And he of course keeps babbling.

BORTE: Of course. So, finally, a guy, a Mongolian guy, in the restaurant comes up and says he speaks French and maybe he can translate. So he and the American guy start speaking French. Except that it's pretty obvious this American guy can't speak French very well, so this takes, like, ten minutes. During which the American guy keeps making the "eating" gesture. Finally the

Mongolian guy is like, "He says he just wants whatever's good." So, I'm like, "Okay."

TISHGILIT: So you give him the sauced fat lump?

BORTE: Right, exactly, I give him sauced fat lump with a fried egg on it and some salty tea.

TISHGILIT: Salt tea, good call.

BORTE: Right, a totally delicious meal. And of course it takes him forever to figure out the money.

TISHGILIT: God, he couldn't figure out the togrog? What an idiot.

BORTE: So that takes him forever, and he acts really grateful. But then he sits down with his sauced fat—which is totally good, by the way—and sort of picks at it.

TISHGILIT: Huh. Was there something wrong with it? Was it beige?

BORTE: Of course it was beige! I gave him like the beigest piece we had! And he *still* didn't like it!

TISHGILIT: Weird. What about the salt tea?

BORTE: Oh, he tastes the salt tea, and it's, like, this dude has never tasted salted tea before. 'Cause he's all, like, surprised when he tastes it.

TISHGILIT: Ugh.

BORTE: I know. And I'd made it extra salty, just for him! But then he tries to pretend that he really likes it, and keeps looking at me and smiling. Meanwhile he's, like, picking at the sauced fat. And I'm just staring at him, and thinking, "Dude, I don't know how you got here, or what you're doing, but if you don't like *beige fat* with *fried egg*, you're gonna have a hard time in Mongolia, man."

TISHGILIT: True that. Anyway. Only one way to relax after a day like that.

BORTE, TISHGILIT (*simultaneously*): Fermented mare's milk!

They pour themselves two big glasses of fermented mare's milk and high-five.

STEVE: Cultural Wonders of Ulaanbaatar

There are only three things in Ulaanbaatar worth seeing. One is the Winter Palace of the Bogd Khan, which, according to my guidebook, has "an extraordinary array of stuffed animals." I did not visit it. I can see stuffed animals in Vali's bedroom.

Second is the Museum of Natural History. The dry air of the Gobi Desert is good for preserving fossils, so this museum had its pick of dinosaur skeletons. It's totally awesome. Probably. I can't say for sure, because it was closed when I went. I tried the old "but I'm a famous paleontologist from the prestigious United States Institute of Dinosaurs who has traveled all the way here to see the dinosaur skeletons but am only here for one day!" routine, but the guard understood me just enough not to believe me.

The third thing to see in UB is the Gandantegchilin (or you can get away with just "Gandan") monastery. This is the only one to which I can give my wholehearted personal endorsement.

While I was at the Gandan monastery, I saw two American hippie kids in expensive sweat-stained T-shirts making a huge show of how moved they were by the place, which struck me as really phony and lame, and I was rolling my eyes with thick syrupy irony until I walked inside and had my eyes promptly unrolled.

The experience of walking into Gandan monastery should be musically scored like this: *cheery unimpressed whistling SMASH TO BASSY MYSTICAL CHORAL CHANT.* The eighty-seven-foot-high Gandan Buddha is not one of these pudgy-and-smiley Buddhas. It is a serious, four-armed, no-nonsense Buddha that looks more likely to smite you than to offer you a flower. It has vivid, scary eyes that you're afraid to look into. Birds fluttered above in the rafters as I walked around it and spun the prayer wheels. Ordinarily I would've prayed for a swift victory for myself and a hilarious demise for Vali, but this Buddha looked like it might come alive and eat me if I didn't keep my prayers unselfish.

During the 1930s, a Communist crackdown on Buddhism led to the destruction of many of Mongolia's monasteries. The current Buddha statue is a replica of the original, which was hauled away in 1937 by the Soviets. No one seems to know what happened to it, but a prevailing rumor is that it was melted down to make artillery shells, which sounds like a joke from the world's most ham-handed black comedy. And yet here were devoted monks maintaining a place whose name, translated, means "the great place of complete joy."

STEVE: Battle of the Birdseed!

Leaving the Gandan monastery, you can't help but scatter the crowd of pigeons that gather outside. You also can't help but be solicited by street children who try to sell you birdseed.

The first kid that came up to me was a girl who couldn't have been more than seven, and she practically clamped herself to my thighs as she chased me with a plastic baggie of birdseed. The pigeons looked downright stuffed, so I didn't think I needed to help. Politely as I could I told her I didn't need any birdseed right then. She apparently decided that the deal was if she could get birdseed into my possession, I'd have to pay her. So she started flipping the bag of birdseed at me with remarkable wrist athleticism. And after about five tries, in a nearly impossible act of physical dexterity, she managed to fling a bag of birdseed into the pocket of my windbreaker, a feat roughly akin to throwing a beanbag into a vagina and getting it to stay there.

So I gave her an American dollar, which was the best I could muster without exposing too wide of a pocket to further flingings. This of course only incited the other street kids. I was thus chased away from the Gandan monastery by a gaggle of deft-wristed children side-arming bags of birdseed at me as I fled, spewing dollar bills.

Now, this little girl and all the other street kids had smudges of dirt on their faces, like extras from a 1930s movie version of *Oliver Twist*. And ever since then I've wondered if the dirt was accidental or deliberately pity-inducing. If it's the latter, fair enough, I can respect tradecraft. But whether these kids are running around Ulaanbaatar with naturally dirt-smudged faces, or whether they're smudging their own faces with dirt as part of the birdseed sell, I can't get the image out of my head.

I felt sad for these kids, but I didn't know what I could do for them that wouldn't involve me getting saddled with pounds and pounds of needless birdseed. If it wouldn't have seemed creepy, I'd have taken them out to dinner.

So I ended up, alone, at Bandidos, a Mexican/Indian restaurant. I sighed as soon as I saw it. It was going to be terrible. But as the perceptive reader my have surmised by now, I'm not the kind of guy who's capable of walking past a Mexican-slash-Indian restaurant in Mongolia without eating there. So that's where I ate. One of the walls was decorated with pictures of bullfights and mariachi, and the opposite wall had pictures of elephants and the Taj.

On the way home I stopped at several bars, once again trying and failing to get fermented mare's milk, and settling for Chinggis Khan beer. In my now somewhat-buzzed state, I concluded that Ulaanbaatar has got to be one of the worst cities in the world. It might not be as dangerous as, say, Port Moresby, New Guinea, where I hear gangs of marauding rapists rule the streets. It may not be as poor as, say, Lagos, Nigeria, where people live on floating shacks above a chemically spoiled lake.* But Ulaanbaatar is a makeshift city inhabited by nomadic herdsmen who hate buildings.

The next train to Moscow was leaving in two days. Before I boarded it, my plan was to go out to the countryside and try to find the real Mongolia, the Genghis Khan Mongolia. Hopefully that Mongolia would be within the limits of a day trip.

One sight cheered me up as I walked back to my hotel around midnight. On wide-open Sukhbaatar Square, in front of the Parliament building, I came across a bunch of kids

*If any curious party wants to pay for my airfare, I will happily go to both Port Moresby and Lagos and see if I can sort out the Worst City title. helphely@gmail.com

rollerblading to music from a boom box. I don't know if Mongolians have not yet heard of skateboards, or if they have simply decided to stick with rollerblades. They weren't even very good at it. It wasn't like they were jumping barrels; the boldest move I saw attempted was "skating around in a circle." One way or another, beneath the watching stone eyes of a giant statue of GK himself was a full-on impromptu roller disco.

If you would like to have a near-mystical experience, travel the long way to Mongolia and stand at midnight in the middle of an Ulaanbaatar roller disco.

No city that boasts impromptu open-air roller discos can be that bad. So that's good news for Ulaanbaatar. And bad news for Port Moresby and Lagos.

STEVE: Nomads!

I'd like to here advertise a vacation experience, primarily aimed I think at Japanese tourists.

Dude Lifestyle Immersion

> On your next vacation to Los Angeles, USA, live the twenty-something bachelor lifestyle through an interpretive visit with an authentic American guy in his one-bedroom apartment! Try such "typical" activities as drinking Coronas, playing PlayStation, and watching *The Shawshank Redemption* on TBS. Your Host Guy will answer your questions about his rich culture, such as "Why aren't you wearing pants?" and "What are these stains on your rug?" When your busy day of Dude Living is through, you may experience an evening of traditional storytelling, as your Host Guy regales you with such tales as "My Old Roommate Boyland and His Mustache." At night, you will be provided with accommodation on the couch. The next morning, awaken to the smells of reheated pizza for breakfast! Price: $300, includes ride in an authentic scratched-up '98 Camry, two beers, one pack-

age of chicken-flavor Maruchan ramen, and some Kettle chips.

I'm not above stealing business ideas from the nomads of Mongolia. This is a good one. Some nomadic families supplement their yak-based incomes by taking in foreign guests and forcing them to perform livestock-related chores under the guise of "interpreting their way of life." Probably the best day ever for nomad children is when a family of chubby Germans shows up and pays Mom and Dad to let them take over the goat milking for an afternoon.

"The commoditization of culture et cetera!" I thought when I first heard about this. "This seems like an intriguing opportunity for me, an intrepid and insightful journalist, to explore the interactions between traditional Mongolian life and modern adaptations to a globalized economy," I told myself when I signed up. But really I just think nomads are weird and cool and I wanted to hang out with them.

My guides to the nomads were Amgalan and Baadai. If you would like to picture these gentlemen, imagine the opposite of what you might expect Mongolian guides to look like. Baadai was chubby and drowsy-eyed, and Amgalan had a side job as a computer programmer. I was heading out into ferocious horde country and my guides looked like office IT guys.

Baadai could speak perfect German, but as this was of little use to anybody at the moment, his role was to drive and take naps. Amgalan did the talking. Knowing that I would be unable later to re-create his patterns of English speech, I frantically scrawled down in my notebook two excerpts, and reproduce them here:

It is, ah, just only, ah, in the northern area, it is some people are building a camp because, ah, that is a place where they are, to have, a camp for having and also to have the camp.

It is I think, ah, a not bad, ah, thing, to have, because it is, the two, ah, groups are making each the other, to have, ah, not as much in the sort of problems, and, ah, crime and that type of thing.

The latter part, I believe, is from when he was explaining how Mongolia's Parliament tends to be half-Communist, half-other. As for the former sentence I could not then and cannot now understand it.

It was an ugly morning when we drove out of the city, the Eternal Blue Sky at the moment more of a Dirty Couch Gray. Heading south we went through a town, or at least a tent-and-shack assemblage on the side of a hill, which Amgalan said was a coal-mining town. The only images I can compare this place to were faded sepia photographs of western mining camps from the 1880s, complete with rutted mud roads and flimsy board fences. Had his English been just a shade better I bet I could've persuaded Amgalan to pretend along with me that our Toyota was a time machine.

My advice to visitors to Mongolia is to get outside of Ulaanbaatar as quickly as possible, because suddenly you'll realize that for all its swaths of bleakness the country has patches of beauty to rival the finest car-commercial backgrounds and IMAX movies you've ever seen. We made a stop at Turtle Rock, a giant formation so called because it looks nothing like a turtle and is some rocks. Amgalan gleefully encouraged me to wedge myself through various crevices, each of which seemed to have a history to him of some previous guidee who'd gotten stuck. Climbing up near the top, we could see across a brown grass rug of valley to a mist-shrouded rise. Amgalan pointed out an otherworldly white building wedged in a crevice between dwarfing boulders, hundreds of feet up—a Buddhist monastery. To my eternal shame, the first thought that entered my brain was *Wow! That looks like where Batman trains in* Batman Begins*!* As clouds made its walls shimmer, I thought, *Wait, it looks* cooler *than the place where Batman trains!*

Just to keep me from getting lost in some kind of transcendent meditation, Amgalan pointed to the monastery with the lit end of a Kent Ultra Menthol.

We had another hour's drive along butt-jostling dirt ruts during which Baadai's drowsiness caused a number of near-misses with various wandering livestock, but my spirits couldn't have been higher. It wasn't just because of Amgalan's Muppet cackle at each dodged cow. We were going to hang out with *nomads*, people who still camp out and walk the Earth. Amgalan mentioned that it was okay to take pictures of this particular family; some nomadic people he'd heard of were animists who didn't necessarily *believe* that a camera might capture their soul, but weren't willing to risk it.

Try to picture your own family living together in a tent: the kids gathering manure to burn, Mom stitching your clothes, Dad entertaining everyone in the evenings on his horsehead fiddle, and at every change of season you strap everything you own to horses and head off for better grass. Imagine, say, the Clintons doing this. Or the Spearses.

My own nomad host family had some surprises. The son, for instance, who was about twenty-five, was not wearing still-bloodied yak skin. He was wearing a manufactured fleece and a sort of cool-guy, hipster white cap. On this cap was the following, printed in English block letters, which I copied down but for which I cannot provide explanation: DEFEND THE EARTH. THE DEMON XIAND HAS INVADED JUPITER. I asked Amgalan about this troubling warning. He asked Nomad Son in Mongolian and came back with the answer "It is, ah, his *hat*."

Nomad Mom was also wearing synthetic clothes, which in an odd way comforted me. I'd been worried the nomads they take you to are fake, just-for-tourists show-nomads. These guys weren't trying too hard to show off how nomadic they were. They lived in a tent, yeah, and raised horses in a log barn, but they'd seen rayon. I'd just seen the urban Mongolian alternative, and living out here, in a wedge in the rocks, didn't seem so bad.

Amgalan, Baadai, and I sat down in the ger for a snack of salt tea and crackers, and it seems as if the best way to summarize the life of a Mongolian nomad, circa 2007, is to list the things inside:

- ☛ Horsehead fiddle
- ☛ Small altar to ancestors topped with framed photographs

- Buddhist bell
- Sandstone statue of camel
- Unopened DVD player in box
- Handmade wooden couch with blanket featuring two horses nuzzling each other
- Hand-painted orange and green cabinet with plastic dishes
- Refrigerator
- Wooden sink
- Super Wash machine with smiley seal on the logo
- Poster of shirtless Mongolian actress with nipples obscured by flowers.

I suspect some but not all of these things were in the tent where Genghis Khan was born.

I didn't have any specific goals in visiting these nomads, except to drink fermented mare's milk, a point which I'd made so frequently to Amgalan that he said he was worried "you will like our, ah, *airag* with too much and you will drink many too many glasses and sing and, ah, fall asleep and those type of thing." So I was very disappointed to learn that this particular family had none, as making it is a seasonal process involving leaving a barrel of mare's milk buried for several months. Nomad Mom didn't have any chores that needed doing, either.

"Maybe," Amgalan suggested, "you would, ah, meaning it would be enjoyable to learn to ride a horse?"

STEVE: Horse-Buzz

In Genghis Khan's day riding a horse was basically part of the deal of being a man, so had I been born in Mongolia, AD 1200, I would've very quickly been smothered for incompetence.

I'll say that what I was lacking wasn't bravery. I'm willing to risk great physical injury to avoid even minor shame, which is what society calls "bravery."

When a long speech in Mongolian about my horse was

translated back to me by Amgalan as "this horse is, ah, it is crazy," I still gamely mounted her, because I didn't want the nameless nomads whom I'd just met to look down on me. It was suggested that my horse might not care for my smell ("unwashed white guy who recently ate at Bandidos"), but I was sure I could persuade her to be cool.

This was incorrect. My horse, a tiny brown pony with her own wacky ideas about speed and direction, immediately darted off as I gripped my saddle in one hand, the reins in the other. Our gallop ended only when my pony decided to drink some oil she found in a gulley.

After chasing us down on his own horse, Nomad Son, disappointed in me (and perhaps also offended by my smell), grabbed my reins and said a few sentences in Mongolian. I wasn't sure whether these words were for me or the horse. If for me they probably meant, "Look, just try and keep it together," and if for the horse they probably meant, "Yeah, sorry about all this."

So Nomad Son took my horse's reins along with those of his own and led me along in a two-pony caravan across the grasslands. I felt sort of embarrassed in this humble, submissive position, but, *Hey,* I thought, *who am I gonna run into on the steppes of Mongolia? In what ludicrous scenario will I see someone I know out here in the middle of Central Asia, almost literally the middle of nowhere?!*

There was an unfortunate answer to this question.

Across the grass, framed against a ridge, we spotted four other riders. Two of them were Mongolian guides. But the other two I recognized. I became the first man in world history to look across the Mongolian steppe and be horrified that the two riders approaching were Swedish girls.

They were two eighteen-year-old friends I'd met on the train the day before. Swedish women are on my mind a lot, for obvious reasons, and had been on my mind even more recently for reasons that will soon become clear. These particular girls had been on my mind still more, because they were charming as I ate with them in the dining car, and because they were lithe, athletic-looking, and had several times expressed a life philosophy based on how willing they were to "try anything once."

In the chaos of the Ulaanbaatar train station they'd been swept up by a guide and I'd lost them. Now Fortune had delivered them to me, not two hundred yards away. And they were about to see me on a horse I had obviously been unable to manage, being led by my guide, meek as a kidnapped bride.

This was too unmanly. As quickly as possible I managed to persuade Nomad Son to toss me back my reins. He reluctantly did. To my horse I said a sound I'd heard Nomad Son say many times—"Choo! Choo!"—as I smacked the reins against her muscular backside.

Possible meanings of "Choo" in Mongolian horse talk: (1) "Do whatever you want!" (2) "Hey, go nuts!" (3) "I trust your horse judgment completely." (4) "Are you ready to ROCK?!" (5) "Show me what you got, bitch!"

So it was that I experienced the mind-blowing rush of being shot across the plains on the back of a frenzied pony, the Mongol Experience of a full-on one-man cavalry charge as I barely managed to stay upright, gripping the back of my steed, in the all-consuming effort to keep my spine unmangled as my deranged pony tore up the earth, heedless of how all this might look to the Swedish girls.

And in between flashes of paralysis panic and new washes

of adrenaline flooding my every cell, it occurred to me that this is what it must've felt like to ride with Genghis Khan.

Forget any historical interpretation of why the Mongols kept conquering. They did it because riding full speed on a pony as they attacked Samarkand or wherever must've felt incredible. And they wanted to keep the buzz going.

I'm not saying this was a better thrill than anything two eighteen-year-old Swedish adventuresses might've offered, but it was pretty awesome.

Moot point anyway, because when my insane horse finally cooled off, we were a valley away from the Swedes, and I barely remembered waving at them as I passed in a blur of man-animal motion-meld. Nomad Son was trying to catch up, and when he finally caught me he said a number of things in Mongolian, all in a tone of astonished relief that my skull was still intact. Without regret I handed over the reins.

As we rode back I thought very seriously about trying to get across the rest of Asia by horse. There were some pros and cons to this.

> **Pros**: Feel dreamy rhythm of earth beneath hooves, constant adrenaline rush, see the unpaved portion of the world, untoppable travel story to tell in the future at parties.
> **Cons**: Slow. Vali would beat me in the race, probably by several years. Lyme disease. Poop smell. Resulting book would be boring meditations on the tender relationship between man and animal, putting us at one with the slow patterns of nature, et cetera. Nobody reads those.

So I decided against it, but I made the most of riding around for the rest of the afternoon. By the time we got back to camp, Nomad Son and I had worked out a comedy routine, where I was supposed to pretend to say "Choo! Choo!" and he would pretend to freak out and go "Ahh!" and pantomime chasing after me. He thought this material was terrific and kept making me repeat the bit. I have never had a better comedy audience.

When I tell people that "I camped out with nomads in Mongolia" (which I do whenever I can weasel it into the conversation), I make it sound really hard and earthy, like I was really *living*. The truth is Amgalan, Baadai, and I slept nearby, in a special set of tourist gers, and at three in the morning while I was nuzzled under a pile of cozy blankets a girl came in to make sure my fire was still going. In the middle of the night I heard Amgalan outside talking on his cell phone, and in between Mongolian syllables I heard him say "extended drive." When I asked him about it the next morning, he explained he'd been giving tech support to a friend trying to install a new computer.

Before leaving the next day, Amgalan took me to the Zaisan Memorial, a circular mural/sculpture on a hill overlooking Ulaanbaatar. Built by the Soviets, the mural shows the history of Communist Russia and Communist Mongolia as some kind of expressionistic Arthurian romance of chiseled men and round-breasted lady heroes launching rockets and stomping on the Japanese. But down below are the ugly blocks of the capital, with a few smokestacks in the distance along a riverbend. I asked about a particular building I saw nearby and Amgalan explained, "That is, ah, a children's, it is a children's prison."

On the giant mountainside sketch of Genghis Khan, a kind of Mongolian Hollywood sign, his feline whiskers stretch out and he looks down as if to say, "Hey, c'mon, Mongolia! It's your great-great-and-so-on-grandfather here! We were amazing once, and we could be again! Now let those kids out of prison—at least the ones who are descended from me."

In Mongolia, I am told, there's a river that stays frozen year-round. In western Mongolia, people go hunting with trained *eagles*, and there are hillsides that throb from the movement of thousands of wild hamsters.

In retrospect, it seems sort of stupid that I decided winning the race was more important than heading out west to watch a leather-faced nomad fling forth his eagle and to see it soar back with a mangled hamster clenched in its talons.

But I'd done enough toward the Awesomeness Contest and I was still absorbed with winning the race.

There was just enough time to accomplish one last goal.

STEVE: Fermented Mare's Milk: What It Tastes Like

The desperate minutes before my train left for Moscow were spent with Amgalan at the State Department Store, named with typical charm by the Communists. There, to my immense relief, we found a bottle of airag, fermented mare's milk, to take with me on the train.

Reader, I invite you to share with me the airag experience. No worries if your local Stop & Shop doesn't stock it. Here's an easy substitute to approximate airag's distinct taste: Get some half-and-half and a can of warm Sprite. Mix the two in a glass. Let sit for a few days on top of your radiator.

Airag is fizzy, and curdled, and just altogether awful. I would take a sip, then spend about fifteen minutes contorting my face as I forced it down my throat. For half an hour I would muse on how that was absolutely, definitely, the worst thing I'd ever tasted, just unbelievably awful. Then thirty more minutes would pass, during which I'd think, *Well, the Mongolians like it. Genghis drank it. Maybe I just need to acquire the taste. Besides, it wasn't* that *bad.* I would take, another sip and the face-contortion cycle would begin again.

Two days later I discovered the bottle—which is meant to be refrigerated—stored under my train bed. I took it to the bathroom to dispose of it, and as I opened it I was the victim of an explosion of the vilest-smelling, most noxious white liquid I've ever encountered. In horrific slow motion I protected my face as the blast splattered all over my shirt and pants.

This accident, and the resulting ongoing smell, considerably diminished my enjoyment of my trip on the Trans-Siberian Railroad.

VALI: Me, a Ninja Turtle, and a Ghostbuster

After a week in Paris, I was anxious to get on with my journey. The City of Lights was pleasant, but there wasn't much in the way of adventure there. It had become too easy to amble around drunk, happy to be alive.

My train ride to Berlin was a stereotypical trip on a Eurorail pass. I shared a cabin with an American theater student from Los Angeles who sported a wild head of hair that approximated a lion's mane. His name was Raphael. I was thrilled to meet someone with the same name as my favorite Teenage Mutant Ninja turtle. *This is fortuitous,* I thought. Then Raphael produced a Coca-Cola bottle filled with whiskey. *This is extremely fortuitous,* I thought.

We made our way to the dining car to purchase some actual Coca-Cola to mix with the whiskey. There we met a nineteen-year-old Canadian named Egon. *Hot damn!* I thought. On a train to Berlin with a Ninja Turtle and a Ghostbuster! What were the chances?

"I think you misheard me," said the Canadian. "My name is Keegan."

I pretended not to hear him.

Egon had worked as a cook back in Toronto. After he had saved enough money to travel for three weeks he "gave the boss the finger" and bought an airplane ticket.

"Where you guys staying in Berlin?" Egon asked. He didn't wait for an answer. "You should stay at the same hostel I'm staying at. It has a pool table and the highest party rating in my book of European hostels." Later he listed the price of a joint in different European cities.

Looking back, I think Egon was on crystal meth. At the time, in my increasingly drunken stupor, he seemed pretty worldly. He had a way of imparting information that made it seem like he learned it firsthand. (". . . the thing about tear gas is that it sticks to your clothes.")

I told Egon about the Ridiculous Race and soon he was regaling me with advice and suggestions for the rest of my journey.

"Where are you going after Berlin?" he asked.

"Moscow. I'm hoping to meet up with Steve there."

"Dude, what are you doing?" Egon asked. He gave me the serious look he had used earlier when explaining how pot in London is really expensive. "I've heard in Russia, they shoot minorities on sight."

This statement caused me some discomfort. I didn't believe it, but I also didn't like it even existing as rumor. The fear and booze mixed in my stomach, aided by the motion of the train. Teetering on the edge of functionality, I decided it was time to go to bed.

WALL: Berlin, Where East Meets West to Form More West

The wall that famously separated Berlin into East and West sections until 1989 has been almost completely torn down. I was eight years old when it happened and couldn't understand what all the hoopla was about. *So they tore down a wall,* I thought. *Who cares? Wake me when the Transformers get involved.*

Now that I was in Berlin, I figured I'd atone for my youthful ignorance with a visit to one of the remaining pieces of the wall. The most noteworthy section, the East Side Gallery, stands near the center of Berlin. It is about one kilometer long and covered in murals. One would expect these to be some of the finest examples of political and revolutionary art in the Western world. And at one point they were. The original East Side Gallery showcased awesome paintings of a car with a shadowy driver crashing through the wall, hoards of oval-faced East Berliners pushing through the border into the West, and a bushy-eyebrowed Soviet premier making out with a green-faced East German premier. Today most of the murals have been either defaced with less artful graffiti or completely painted over with much lamer images, like a sunset, cartooney grim reaper, or, inexplicably, a man and woman clutching each other while sliding down some living room draperies. It's sad when graffiti ruins graffiti.

From the East Side Gallery, I just started randomly wandering around, occasionally stopping in bars hoping to be the first person to order a beer that morning. I never was.

In most parts of the city, one can easily tell which side of the wall's ghost he is on. In the West the buildings are classical and European. They all looked like important libraries. In the East most of the buildings looked like giant cement computer processors. Those that didn't looked worse. The most famous East German landmark, the TV tower, looks like a cement toothpick skewering a metal ball. A Freudian wouldn't have to stretch too hard to see sexual undertones in the design. (To non-Freudians: It looked like a penis skewering a vagina.) If the tower's primary function was to make everything nearby appear soul-crushingly sad, it worked. A building near the tower bore the sign RISTORANTE ROMANTICA PIZZERIA. It had the ambience of a gas station.

Modern Berliners are doing their best to perk up the old East. New construction has turned sections of the East into an überWest. The Mitte neighborhood, located just east of Checkpoint Charlie—the storied crossing point between the Soviet Zone and the American Zone—now boasts a Burberry and several other Fifth Avenue–style thousand-dollar-plus-for-a-sweater emporiums. It's a fine example of capitalism twisting the knife of victory into communism's back. The next step is erecting a statue of Ayn Rand beating Karl Marx to death with a polo mallet.

New construction hasn't been limited to the former East. They've been building and repairing all over Berlin like gangbusters since the British bombed the bejesus out of the city on a nightly basis during World War II. My favorite structure was the Kaiser-Wilhelm-Gedächtniskirche, known to the non-Germanic savages of the world as the Kaiser Wilhelm Memorial Church. It's actually two churches. The original church was almost completely destroyed in 1943, and the Germans have left it as an antiwar memorial. All that remains is a charred tower with its spire broken off and stained glass all gone. Next door a new church has been constructed. It's a rectangular prism, only as tall as the broken tower, and covered with tiny, dark stained glass windows. From the outside the new church looks like a miniature skyscraper. On the inside . . . oooh boy. It's amazing.

Sunlight shining through the thousands of stained glass panes bathes the small, intimate space with bluish light. An emaciated golden Jesus floats above the altar. The cross is thick behind his arms, thin behind his body, and ends before his dangling feet. It looks like a sculpture commemorating the time Jesus jumped on a trampoline.

Another wonderful structure was the Parliament building. It had a giant walk-through glass dome added to the top of the building in 1999. The guidebook said that visiting the dome feels like walking inside a glass beehive. Thanks, guidebook! Now I don't have to go inside, since I could just reminisce about the time I walked through a beehive—a thing humans do all the time. Also, there was an hour-long line and nobody near the end wanted to talk about the beehive analogy so I left.

VALI: The Worst Deal in Berlin

After leaving the Parliament building I came across one Berlin attraction with no line: the Kennedy Museum. Located next to the spot where JFK delivered his famous "Ich bin ein Berliner" speech, the museum showcased a rarely seen blend of crappiness and high entrance fee (Seven euros for a room the size of my apartment). I'll save readers of this book the annoyance of a visit and list everything one can learn at the museum: (1) JFK was photogenic and (2) JFK carried a briefcase during his presidency.

On the other hand everyone seems to know that the museum stinks, so it's nearly empty and very quiet. It's probably a great place to meditate about the great sandwich you *could* have bought with seven euros.

VALI: Are the Germans Sorry?

Anyone familiar with Academy Award–winning films knows that during World War II, the Nazi party oversaw the murder of up to eleven million humans, approximately six million of whom were Jewish.

What affect does this history have on Germans of my generation? For starters they are not allowed to wear the clothing emblazoned with the stylish swastikas that Steve favors.* In fact, any and all anti-Semitic activity and speech are now illegal in Germany.

So, perhaps not surprisingly, modern Germany is ashamed of her World War II behavior. To ensure that the atrocities are never forgotten, several physical reminders have been built.

Berlin's most impressive meditation on the Holocaust is a memorial designed by Peter Eisenman. It is a field of over 2,700 concrete stelae, uniform in all dimensions except height. They stand, arranged in a grid pattern, on slightly uneven, hilly ground. When I walked through the field, I rarely saw any of the dozen or so other tourists there with me. The rolling ground and gently rising and falling tops of the stelae are intended to create an uneasy and confusing atmosphere, like when the Germans tried to eliminate an entire race of humans.

Even after visiting the memorial, the question still remained: How does the Holocaust affect Germans my age? One night, I met a group of well-educated young Berliners at an indie rock concert and went with them to a nearby bar. The group, a former investment banker and two graduate students, was friendly and after an appropriate number of empty Pilsner Urquell bottles had accumulated at our table, I asked what the Holocaust meant to young Germans. The answer: almost nothing.

*To readers who, thus far, have maintained a positive opinion of Steve: Please spend a moment with your conscience and decide if you can continue supporting such a man. As you consider, please allow me, Vali, to note that I think you look great today.

I was shocked. Was sixty-some years of contrition enough for the slaughter of eleven million humans—more than the entire population of Los Angeles County?

"The Holocaust was an unforgivable wrong," one of the graduate students said. "That's why I would have never participated in it. And that is why I don't feel guilty."

"But your grandparents' generation participated in ethnic cleansing," I shot back.

"Do your white friends feel guilty about slavery?" asked the former investment banker.

I wanted to say yes but felt obligated to tell the truth. "No."

"Does that mean your generation of Americans agrees with slavery or with the people who spit at black students as they tried to go to white schools?"

That shut me up pretty quickly.

VALI: Warsaw and a Nap in Five Hours

After two days in Berlin I boarded an overnight train to Warsaw. I shared a cabin with a Polish computer consultant named Klaus who, immediately upon departure, locked our door then sprawled out across the bottom bunk in his underwear. In an effort not to seem too touristy, I also stripped down to my boxer briefs. There was definitely something slightly off about Klaus, but he seemed harmless. "Slightly off, but seemed harmless" is also how serial killers are often described by their neighbors once their crimes are made public. I did not sleep that night.

I arrived in Poland the following morning at 6:30 a.m. Immediately, I realized that I had finally left the West. Berlin's train station was an ultramodern glass and metal temple to design. Warsaw's was a concrete bunker. Outside, the view didn't improve much. The city appeared to be little more than concrete, smokestacks, and soot stains.

I had five hours to kill before catching my next train. So bleary-eyed, tired, and cranky I walked down a stark road in search of a hot shower and a bed.

I went to every hotel within walking distance of the train station. "Walking distance" started at a few hundred feet and eventually became a mile and a half. The receptionist at each hotel looked at me, a dirty, unshaven, brown backpacker, and told me no rooms were available.

"I can pay," I assured them. "I'm a journalist on assignment." I showed them the vague letter of introduction my editor had given me. Then the receptionists stopped thinking of me as a dirty backpacker. Now I seemed more like a crazy homeless person who had found stationery in the Dumpster behind a major NYC publishing house. Still no rooms, I was told. Was it really possible that every hotel in Warsaw was booked? Who comes to Warsaw? Generous people who wouldn't mind me borrowing their hotel room for a few hours while they go off to work? No.

Eventually I gave up and went to breakfast at a nice hotel restaurant. It had white tablecloths, a lot of fish in the breakfast buffet, and a nice view of the city, which was more picturesque than I first gave it credit for. There I discovered that an hour is about the longest you can nap on a restaurant table without being asked to leave.

Newly refreshed and with another two hours left to kill before my train departed, I decided to do a quick walking tour of Warsaw's Old Town.

During World War II (one of the rare sequels that lives up to the original), Old Town Warsaw was almost completely destroyed. After the war ended, the area was painstakingly reconstructed from photographs. If I had been around during this process, I would have submitted a lot of Photoshopped pictures of town squares featuring statues of me performing difficult slam dunks. Then I'd have no problem getting a motel room in this town.

Walking through the reconstruction was surprisingly fun. I meandered down narrow cobbled streets, crossed quaint brick roads, and leaned against shoe repair stores that looked like gingerbread houses. It was like walking around in a fairy tale, except there were fewer talking animals.

Afterward, I headed back to the crumbling old station to catch a train to Moscow, where I hoped to meet up with Steve.

STEVE: How I Trans'd Siberia

The Trans-Siberian Railroad! It's practically a synonym for the epic and exotic. The name alone summons up visions of decommissioned soldiers swilling vodka, babushkas selling *omul* and swilling vodka, swaddled Eurasian babies crying for more vodka! Whispered train car intrigues and hypnotic landscapes mesmerizing the vodka-blurred eye!

"Siberia" is the huge eastern chunk of the country of Russia, everything between the Ural Mountains and the Pacific Ocean. I mean *huge*. Really, really huge. Since you insist on not recognizing how huge Siberia is, I'll tell you: You could fit all of the continental United States into it. Then you could put in Alaska. After that, you could squash in all of Europe (minus Russia, smartass). Once you'd done this, you would have three hundred thousand spare square miles of Siberia left over.*

The excuse to take the Trans-Siberian Railroad was part of why I'd agreed to this whole race thing. Once you rule out airplanes, it's the fastest way to cross the most land. Longitude-wise, it'd make up about 20 percent of the whole race.

There's a small but magnificent minority of romantics who, from the first time they hear about the Trans-Siberian Railroad, know they'll never get the idea out of their craw until they've ridden the thing.

Count me among these weirdos! Surely this would be the grandest journey I'd ever take. I'd trade on the stories for years! Dark glances exchanged along rattling compartments, rumors of the Russian mob and the KGB recounted over pots of tea and salted meats and pastries. Smoke rising over chessboards as an elderly Moscow ballerina, her glory now hidden by dense Soviet wrinkles, told me filthy stories about Gorbachev, and a

*So said George Kennan in *Siberia and the Exile System*, but I've looked at a globe and it seems implausible.

Siberian geologist recounted a macabre mining accident seen under the Arctic sky, and an Orthodox monk showed me the gnarled hands he'd used to wrestle with Satan, and a Chinese defector gave me a coded map to a stash of stolen uranium.

I have a pretty active imagination.

This is not what my trip on the Trans-Siberian Railroad was like.

Then, too, there were my baser illusions about the Trans-Sib (as your more casual travel guides call it). Before leaving, I'd heard some stories from my friend Kruggie, who'd recently attended the wedding of two English people who'd met on the legendary train.

"Oh, it's wild," he told me. "Think about it—drinking, traveling, everybody's away from home, the motion of the train, cramped quarters, crazy backpacker chicks from New Zealand."

I'm no idiot, I could do the math here.

"Oh yeah," said Kruggie, "the Trans-Siberian Railroad is a fuckfest."

STEVE: How It Turned Out

It's true that there were some interesting characters aboard the train. I started to meet them as we rolled out of Ulaanbaatar. Two compartments down from me was a pair of Australian homosexuals heading all the way to Murmansk, a shipping port above the Arctic Circle famous for being suicidally depressing.

"Why would anyone go to Murmansk?" I asked.

"Oh, don't get into it, John," said Peter.

"I *will* get into it," said John. "They're a hardy lot up there in Murmansk."

"I don't doubt it," I said. "But . . . still . . . Murmansk?"

From his bed Peter looked up at me and gave me a look that begged me to *please* not get John worked up about Murmansk, not again. Too late.

"They're a hardy lot indeed!" said John, his eyes inflamed

with a passion I could now identify as Murmansk-love. He told me the following story. When the Russian navy sub *Kursk* sank in an accident in 2000, Vladimir Putin's government handled the whole thing terribly. At a press conference, one mother of a dead sailor stood up and gave some naval officials an earful, at which point some guys in white showed up, injected her with something, and dragged her away. This villainous comic-book trick didn't stop the mother, because she did the same thing again at another press conference, mouthing off about the government's incompetence and generally proving to be the awesome sort of righteous, brassy mom Sally Field might play in a TV movie.

"She's a hero, in my opinion," said John. He took out an ornate turquoise pendant. "We're going to Murmansk to try and find her, so I can shake her hand and give her this pendant, and tell her to keep fighting the good fight."

How they intended to find her was not revealed. These guys were going all the way from Sydney to Murmansk (something like nine thousand miles) to present jewelry to a woman they'd never met, which seemed at the very least eccentric, but then again I was competing in a race around the world without the use of airplanes for a bottle of Scotch. So, fair enough.

The Australian guys were at least making a few stops along the way. At Irkutsk they, and almost everybody else, got off.

Irkutsk—which claims, with wacky boldness, to be "the Paris of Siberia"—is a gateway to mighty Lake Baikal, the deepest lake in the world, holding 20 percent of the Earth's unfrozen freshwater. It is also the "oldest lake in the world." I have no idea how or why anybody sorts out which hole has had water in it the longest, but I assure the credulous Reader that I confirmed this fact on various scientific-looking Internet sites.

Lake Baikal is also home to the world's only freshwater seal, a species adorably known as the "nerpa." Judging from the various dried creatures on offer at the station, it's also home to a number of other odd aquatic beasts, none of which look especially appetizing when dried out, salted, put in a plastic bag, and waved through a train window by the hairy arm of a grizzled hunchback.

Despite these enticements, all I saw of Lake Baikal was ominous water out the window. There was still plenty of Siberia to cross, and no time to lose in Irkutsk. I gave my earnest best wishes to the Australian Murmansk enthusiasts and settled in for a very long ride on a now almost empty train.

I would travel from Irkutsk to Moscow in the company of a Canadian industrial chemist, her smartass twelve-year-old son, a family of traveling Mongolian denim salesmen, an orange-haired conductress who strutted about in three-inch heels, and her bald-headed boss, who one day waved me down, led me to the window, put his sinewy arm around my shoulder, pointed out at the vast birchy beyond, and declared, "This . . . SIBERIA!"

There would be no fuckfest.

STEVE: What That Blob on Your World Map in Between Europe and the Pacific Looks Like Up Close

First, there was more Mongolia. One glance at Darkhan, Mongolia's second-largest city, explained why nomads were sticking it out. Darkhan looked as though it were designed by the world's worst urban planner, who then gave his plans to an assistant, who spilled coffee on them and copied them upside down. It is a splotchy disaster of grimy industry.

Darkhan's sister city: Irving, Texas. I've never been to Irving but let me advise her mayor: trade up.

Most of the towns we passed were so insignificant that I could scout them in their entirety during the twenty-minute stops, taking existential strolls down the dirt roads to the point where "town" ended and "nothingness" started, passing nobody. Sometimes these towns would have one really desperate landmark going for them, like a sculpture of a silver rocket on a stick.

We crossed the Russian border at night. The scene would've looked corny if you saw it in a James Bond movie: a soldier smoking, steam rising off the train, ghostly birch trees, a dour lady clutching two sacks of beets. I had no passport problems, but I *was* chased around the station by a surly and fat-backed lady attendant after failing to pay the requisite thirty kopeks to use the bathroom.

Then we were in Siberia.

Imagine a violent outbreak of zombie-disease infects half the world's population. These zombies gather weapons and start attacking us for our brains. Humans and zombies fight a horrific all-out war for ten years. Now the zombies have just barely been defeated (or have they?). On the ravaged earth, traumatized humans begin to rebuild the shattered fragments of a civilization.

Earth, ten years after the Zombie Wars. That's what Siberia looks like: rusted-out boats, abandoned railway boxcars, gutted factories, meaningless concrete walls with rebar sticking out of them, and tiny clusters of huts built of scrap iron, with bent iron pipes for chimneys and faded clothes hanging from tree branches.

You can't go far in Siberia without seeing some guy doing the zigzagging, addled, shuffle-walk of a serious, paint-thinner-level drunk. Sometimes at, like, seven in the morning.

In Siberia I swear to high heaven that I saw a goat eating a tin can, a thing that I'd thought goats did only in cartoons. Lots of sights in Siberia seemed to come from some kind of tragic cartoon. I saw two men standing knee-deep in water, holding an argument over the open hood of a car. Maybe they were arguing about what was wrong with the car. From where I was the problem appeared to be that the car was in the middle of a river. Perhaps they were arguing over whose fault this was or who had dibs on the sunken car.

Soviet planners have a bad reputation. They deserve a way, way worse reputation. Imagine some central building committee planner looking out over, say, an unspoiled bend along a tranquil river and declaring, "Hey, you see that unspoiled bend along that tranquil river? Let's put some kind of horrible munitions plant there. Don't spend too much of the People's money on, you know, windows. If you have any giant lumps of twisted iron, just go ahead and strew those around anywhere." That's the only way to explain much of Siberia's architecture.

More than anything, there's forest. Not the cutesy, Shady Glade air freshener Smurfs-and-Bambi kind of forest, Grimm-Brothers-in-the-original-German, wolves-eating-you type of forest.

Often in these forests I'd see log cabins. But not tidy Abe-Lincoln-commemorative-plate log cabins. I'm talking about hard-core witch-cooking-stray-orphans-in-a-cauldron log cabins.

It's possible I'm being hard on Siberia, because most of it

I observed through a dirty window. And there were some lovely spots, villages where quaint wood houses had old-lady flourishes of blue fringe and rippled carvings, and monumental bridges over black rivers. I got out at every stop I could, and the stations, even the bleakest Soviet ones, had a foreboding grandeur. In fact, I'd say that Trans-Siberian train stations pretty much define "foreboding grandeur." Novosibirsk is a particular must-see for the foreboding grandeur enthusiast.

It wasn't all misery. At one stop, the bald-headed boss and I got matching chocolate and vanilla ice cream treats. He saw me, nodded, and said "good," and together we stood on the platform happily licking away as we watched the Mongolian family hawk jeans to waiting Russians for whom Mongolian jeans were the height of fashion.

STEVE: The Restaurant Car

I bought most of my food at station stops, mostly ramen noodles, bananas, assorted bizarre crackers, and meat pies whenever I could find one that looked like it had an under 50 percent chance of giving me violent diarrhea. This is because I was afraid of the restaurant car.

The employees of the restaurant car: SMUSHBUTT, a lumpy woman who would not have been unattractive except that she insisted on wearing pink sweatpants that were like three sizes too small and thus highlighted in detail the topography of her rear; SMOKEFACE, a hideous gorgon so called because her features were mercifully hidden behind a perpetually lit cigarette; and RIZZO, the rodentine cook. For him, just go ahead and picture the man you'd least like handling your food.

Clearly these three thought they had a good scam going, where they could sit around all day making what I assumed were very unkind remarks about the pictures of celebrities in Russian magazines, closing arbitrarily, and trusting would-be diners to be too repulsed by them to eat.

The Canadian industrial chemist was having none of it; she and her son told me they were too afraid to go in there.

Well, I wasn't going to let them get away with it. Eating at the restaurant became a profound necessity for me. I had a point to prove! I wasn't quite sure what that point was, but I was 80 percent sure it was there.

At first, when I summoned up the courage to go in for dinner, they tried to call my bluff. I pointed one by one at items on the menu, and one by one Smokeface said "nyet." But then Smushbutt said something in Russian and Rizzo got to work.

You may not think it's possible for food to be sarcastic. I didn't think so, either, until Smokeface presented me with a chicken dish. At least I think it was chicken. It was some kind of once-winged animal, now a knot of gnarled cartilage. It was served with peas that looked like tiny yellow suns on the verge of supernova, and a cup of coffee glazed over with a sick viscous film, like the wastewater outside an oil refinery.

They knew what they were doing. They'd made a joke of it, decorating the chicken with an ever-so-elegant touch of parsley. Smokeface even made a big show of unfurling my napkin for me. The joke to all this being, "Oh, you want to insist on making us be a restaurant? Fine! Look what a magnificent feast we've prepared for you, Your Majesty!" All conveyed snarkily in Russian by Smushbutt. At least, I assume that's what she said. It made Smokeface cackle, whatever it was.

It was terrible, of course, mouth-curdlingly bad. But clearing my plate of their mockery-food was a grand moral victory. I think.

STEVE: A Story About How Empty Siberia Is

In 1908, either a meteor, a comet, or an alien spacecraft (scientists are still arguing) exploded over northern Siberia. The blast blew down something like eighty million trees, flattening an area of 830 square miles. This explosion—the Tunguska event—was so huge that if it had happened in New York it would've annihilated Manhattan and blown out windows in Boston and Washington. But because it happened in

Siberia, nobody paid much attention.* No one even bothered trekking to the explosion site for thirteen years. When they got there, they concluded, "Man, good thing this happened in Siberia!" and trekked back home.

STEVE: How I Entertained Myself, Part One: A Capitalist Triumph

At one end of my train car was a samovar of boiling water, and at the other end was a bathroom where you could watch your waste being plopped directly onto the whizzing tracks below. That and the window is all the Trans-Siberian offers in the way of entertainment.

Here and there someone would get on, a sad-faced soldier or a gang in tracksuits. But before I knew it they'd be gone again. I never even got a roommate in my compartment. The Mongolian jean-salesmen family seemed to be having a good time, eating weird cheeses and excitedly getting jeans ready to sell at each stop. But no matter how much I paced in front of their door, they never invited me in.

That left me with the fifty-ish Canadian industrial chemist and her twelve-year-old kid. These two were on the last leg of a huge world tour. You would think these kinds of experiences would be very broadening, but that did not seem to be the case. For example, I asked this pair where the best meal they had in the world was, and they both agreed it was at the Chili's in Lima, Peru.

"We love Chili's," said the mom. "We don't have one in Halifax, so imagine how excited we were in Lima!"

I've never been to Lima, Peru, so maybe these folks knew something I didn't.

I don't want to say anything too bad about the kid. I was hardly at my best, either—I hadn't taken a shower since before the nomad camp, and the closest I'd come in three days

*There are some great conspiracy theories floating around about the Tunguska explosion, by the way, my personal favorite being that it was caused by Nikola Tesla testing a mysterious electric superweapon that could shoot through the Earth.

of horseback riding and train sitting was to shake some Gold Bond medicated powder over those of my fleshy crevices that I considered most moisture-prone. And I'd caught this kid at an awkward age, after nine months on the road with his mother. I'm sure he'll grow into a solid, happy, Liberal-voting Canadian man who coaches his kids' pee-wee hockey team, makes trenchant remarks at his book club, is beloved by a doting wife and admired by his many friends and associates.

But at the moment he was a weaselly little wiseass who rolled his eyes at everything, and every time I asked him to clarify some troubling detail he told me about his screwed-up life he'd make a joke of talking really slowly like I was stupid, and I wanted to kick him in the teeth.

So when he challenged me to a game of Monopoly on his laptop, I whipped out my multiplug adapter.

Somewhere between Bogotol and Mariinsk, we sat on the floor by the outlet. He was boot (rookie mistake) and I was racecar.

The kid was not a bad player. He bought smartly; he built aggressively. When I'd offer him sucker deals like Waterworks and a "Get out of jail free" card for B&O Railroad, he'd turn them down. In fact, he'd make a big show of scoffing and go, "Uh, no, I don't *think* I'm going to do *that*."

Which is why what followed gave me so much pleasure.

The poor bastard overexpanded. Started putting up hotels at a rate that would make Trump blush, slapped down houses until Indiana Avenue was as crowded as Tokyo. He was one of these Johnny Dreamers who thinks you can build up Mediterranean into a second Boardwalk. Meanwhile, a few lucky rolls and flips of the Community Chest kept me out of trouble, and he stopped winning ten dollars in beauty contests and started getting income-tax assessed. Before long he was in serious trouble.

(Periodically, by the way, I would look out the window at the gray birch forests, just to confirm that I was in fact playing Monopoly on a laptop with a twelve-year-old as I zipped through Siberia.)

"Okay, um . . ." he said, staring at a very serious rent bill for a three-housed St. James Place. "How about I trade you . . . Atlantic Avenue and we call it even?"

"Atlantic Avenue is mortgaged. That's not an advantageous trade for me."

"C'mon!"

"I'm sorry you're facing misfortune. I assure you it's not personal. This is just business."

"Um, I don't think I have the money."

"If you don't have the money, the game is concluded. You are bankrupt. I have won."

This may have been the most satisfying sentence I ever said.

As we were playing, the bald-headed boss walked through, smiled at us, and said, "Good!"

I suspect what he was really thinking was, *In Russia, we play chess by age two. And here is a twenty-seven-year-old American taking obvious pleasure in beating a poor kid at this game of Capitalist Money Exchange Squares. And we lost the Cold War.*

STEVE: How I Entertained Myself, Part Two: Mustache, Tracksuit, Vodka

Before leaving the United States I'd read that de rigueur fashion on a Russian train is a vintage tracksuit. So I bought a vintage Adidas tracksuit on eBay. I wore it most days on the Trans-Siberian Railroad. I looked terrific. Also on the Trans-Siberian Railroad, I grew a mustache. I also thought this looked terrific. It may not have. I had a bottle of Chinggis Khan vodka I'd bought in Mongolia, and at one point I offered to split it with a soldier I met on the train. But in what must be a first for Russian soldiers, he waved me off and continued staring out the window. That's when I got to thinking that perhaps my mustache made me look "creepy." You be the judge.

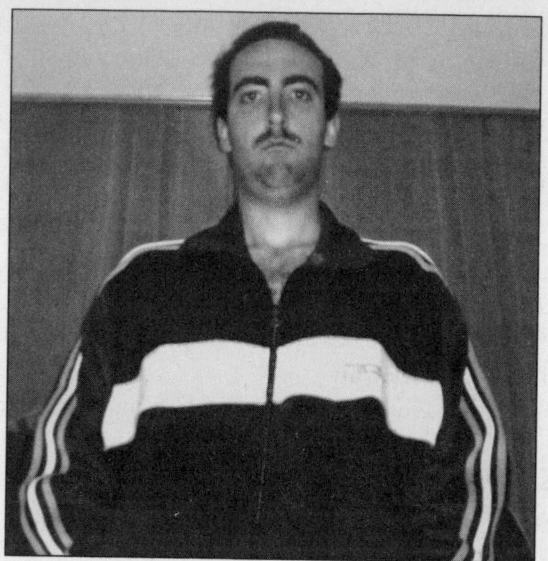

Anyway, I drank the Chinggis myself.

I thought it might be an interesting experiment to write down what I saw out the window as I drank a bottle of Mongolian vodka. Here's the only section I can still make out:

Power Station.
Town of wood houses, ~ 200,
Muddy Pond
[Here there's a crude drawing of the pond.]
Such that the town is thusly.
Pile of uneven wood.
Semi-paved rode U
Pine forest, birch fringe.
Very rough road.
Thing people don't hide from trains: laundry

Then my notes descend into some kind of indecipherable code. Possibly Chinggis vodka contains a chemical that teaches one Mayan hieroglyphics? Scholars can sort it out at the Steve Hely Archives. The hieroglyphics section ends with a drool stain.

So it was that I journeyed on to Moscow.

VALI: To MOCKBA

Moscow was the only place I was actually afraid to visit during my trip. In the weeks before leaving Los Angeles I obsessively read about racist activity in Russia. Highlights included: "Girl killed by Russia 'racists'"—a story about a nine-year-old girl who was stabbed to death by a gang of skinheads; "Student Murder in Russia 'Racist'"—a story about a black student who was shot upon leaving a nightclub; and an Amnesty International report stating that racist killings in Russia were "out of control."

I called a lawyer friend who travels to Russia frequently for work.

"I'm terrified that I'm going to get beat up in Russia by a gang of neo-nazis," I told him.

"I'm not going to say that won't happen," he replied.

Those were not the words I'd hoped to hear.

My friend continued: "However, if you are chased by a gang of neo-nazis, they will most likely be drunk so you'll be able to outrun them."

Great. So not only did I have to be on the lookout for racist gangs, I also couldn't get super drunk. Russia and I were not getting off on the right foot.

While waiting for my train in Warsaw, I eyed the other passengers, searching for a friend for the twenty-four-hour journey. There was no obvious choice. Everyone was staring at the floor and looked like they might have been born without the muscles required to smile. The friendliest face belonged to a homeless man who was asleep on the train tracks.

I smiled at a broad-shouldered man sitting on his suitcase and innocently asked, "Is this where I board the train to Moscow?"

"Moscow," he responded without looking up.

Once on the train, I tried again with the Russian woman inhabiting the cabin next to mine. I decided to break the ice with the old Can I Have a Light for My Cigarette Trick. It worked! Emboldened by my success, I followed up with the old Ask a Simple Question Even If You Know the Answer to It Trick.

"Do you know if we need to change trains on the way to Moscow?"

She responded with hand gestures indicating she didn't understand me and retired to her cabin.

By the time the train started moving, everyone in my train car had entered their cabin and closed the door.

No matter, I thought. I had great luck meeting people in the dining car during all my other train rides. I'll just go down there, buy a sandwich, and see who comes in.

Then the old Russian man who curated my train car informed me that there was no dining car. He would soon become my primary source of human interaction until I got to Moscow. Our communication was constrained by the limitations of pidgin English so I never got his official title. He wore the sort of red bellboy's uniform that one normally sees only in movies where a monkey works at a fancy hotel. He was also tremendously nice. Not long into the trip I wanted a cup of coffee but didn't have any Polish or Russian currency. When I asked if he would accept euros, he waved his hand and gave me a free cup of coffee. "Souvenir!" he explained.

Before too long, we crossed out of Poland and into Belarus. Out the window the scene oscillated between quaint and bucolic. The most frequent image was a pile of logs. My expectation that Belarus would be one long nude beach was apparently based on misinformation. Within an hour I was bored out of my skull.

Once again I thought about how awful it would have been to race without cheating. I couldn't imagine tolerating this level of dullness for a week while crossing Russia on the Trans-Siberian Railroad. It would have reduced my brain to a stinking gray paste.

VALI: Let Me Guess. I Don't Have the Proper Documents

At some point Russian customs officials boarded the train, which I assumed meant we had left Belarus and were entering Russia.

A stark woman took my passport and asked me to fill out an immigration card. A few moments later I heard someone say something in Russian, followed by "the American." I was pretty sure they weren't saying anything along the lines of "The American has great skin," so I grew alarmed. On the other hand, calling me "the American" was better than the Slavic racial slurs I assumed everyone else had been using around me the whole ride.

Before I could make sense of anything, a large man, a solid cube of a human, entered my cabin and swiped my passport through a machine. I smiled politely. He then said some words in Russian, pointed into the distance, and pantomimed sleeping. I widened my smile. After a few more seconds of performing to my dumbstruck face, he pointed to the Russian visa dates in my passport: May 11–May 14. It was then May 10. He was trying to tell me that I should have spent one more night in Warsaw.

I tried to explain my situation. Since the train did not arrive in Moscow until May 11, I hadn't thought to start my visa until that date. I had not accounted for crossing the Belarussian-Russian border on the tenth. This information was very difficult to convey using only hand gestures. The only really solid hand gestures I know are the thumbs-up and the middle finger. I thought I did an excellent job with what I had, but the border guard either didn't follow or feigned misunderstanding. He motioned for me to exit my cabin with him.

I walked with the guard to the space between the cars, where passengers can enter and exit the train. He repeated the speech he gave me in my cabin. I repeated the blank stare and wide smile. At this point, I was more confused than scared. What was he going to do? Send me back to Poland for one day? I figured he'd eventually get annoyed with my ignorance and let me go.

I was half right. He eventually got annoyed with my ignorance and just blurted out, "Dollars." Oh, right. I had gotten so wrapped up in my fear of hate crimes that I forgot the art of the bribe.

"Euros," I responded as I reached for my wallet.

Suddenly the guard panicked. He grabbed my shoulder and pulled me behind him, away from the open train door. Then he whispered something that I understood to mean, "Be discreet, you idiot." The corrupt activity, clearly commonplace, still had the theater of a backroom deal. I handed the guard a twenty-euro note. He smiled, slapped me on the back, and warmly said, "Everything is fine."

Hours later we stopped in Minsk, the capital of Belarus. We hadn't crossed the Russian border yet and probably wouldn't before midnight.

I spent the remainder of the day drafting a letter to the Belarussian embassy in Washington, D.C., requesting my twenty euros back.

VALI: Chandrasekaran Men and Russia

The Chandrasekarans* have been Russian enthusiasts since the birth of the U.S.S.R. My grandfather, a peanut and sugarcane farmer, was active in the Communist Party of his small Indian village. Through the party, my grandfather, whose formal education ended somewhere in grade school, became familiar with the history of class struggle and the society-improving mechanisms of violent revolution and war. And via this educational Communist propaganda, my grandfather was introduced to Napoleon Bonaparte.

I can't imagine that the Communists had anything nice to say about Napoleon. After all, he watched Moscow burn

*I use "Chandrasekarans" for simplicity's sake. As I'll explain in a moment, the name does not really cover my entire family line.

from the Kremlin. So my grandfather must have read between the lines—seeing a strong character in the short stout general who escaped imprisonment from the island of Elba, returned to France with a rebuilt army, and took back his position as emperor—because he became quite taken with Napoleon.

His obsession with the famous general grew so strong that he wanted to name his first son, my father, Napoleon. To fully grasp the impact of this decision, one must know that in Tamil Nadu, the Indian state where my parents are from, people often go by only one name. Official documents do not ask for a first name and last name, they ask for a given name and a father's given name. When my parents immigrated to the United States, my father gave his birth name as his family's last name.

As history played out, my grandmother ended up putting the kibosh on my grandfather's plan. So my father was named Chandrasekaran, after a star of some astrological importance. Had my grandmother not intervened, instead of Vali Chandrasekaran, I would today be Vali Napoleon.

My father grew up to be a bright young man. His goal, at the time, was to become a university professor. So he was understandably excited when, after finishing his PhD, he received a fellowship position in Russia. However, the excitement was short-lived. He was eventually informed that the position was open only to PhD candidates, not those who had already completed their doctorate.

After the fellowship was revoked, my father went with his backup plan and applied to postdoctoral positions in the United States. Soon after he got one, he and his new wife, my mother, moved to Chapel Hill, North Carolina. Less than one year later, I was born and my parents decided to stay in America.

Now, twenty-six years after the first attempt, the Chandrasekarans had finally made it to Russia. I'm not sure it was worth the wait.

When I arrived in Moscow the weather was cold, drizzly, and overcast. Hundreds of people walked through the streets, never smiling. The average Russian brow was well lined from near-constant furrowing.

And everything was expensive. Moscow had recently unseated Tokyo, capturing the Most Expensive City in the World title. Price increases were driven by a small group of Russian superelite. They walk around draped in designer clothing, wearing sunglasses with some luxury brand name proudly engraved onto each arm and driving cars I had previously seen only in magazines. My mortal mind can't even imagine something the Russian superelite would deride as ostentatious. If someone charged a lot for mink-fur-lined drinking straws, the Russian superelite would buy them. It is as if they are making up for the years of consumerism lost under Communist rule.

I was sure Russia had its charms, but for the time being I was thrilled that my father's Russian fellowship had fallen through.

VALI: Finding Love in Russia— An Aborted Plan

My initial plan for Moscow was to go to a Russian mail-order bride service and see if I could negotiate a discount if I picked up my bride in person. I know what you're thinking: Vali, as a businessman, you are unrivaled. *Thank you.*

Selecting a service is the biggest challenge facing a potential mail-order-bride customer. A Google search for "Russian mail-order brides" yields over fifteen million results. Most of the companies I researched seemed equally disreputable, though some like hotrussianbrides.com classed it up a tad for customers looking for a little courtship before sealing the deal. From its Web site:

> Browse through thousands of profiles of exceptionally beautiful, sexy Russian girls, and get ready to correspond with your match! You can chat with them, watch them live via streaming video, watch their personal profile video, or

just be amazed at how beautiful their profile pictures are. Be prepared, though, a "mail-order bride" site we are definitely NOT!

So, in conclusion, the folks at a company called Hot Russian Brides want you to know their service is completely on the up and up. Also, I'm interested to see the statistics on how many hotrussianbrides.com members joined just to be amazed at how beautiful the profile pictures are.

If you're wondering how quickly thinking about mail-order brides goes from being funny to being sad, the answer is: less than one minute. As I clicked through the Web sites looking at amazingly beautiful profile pictures, I started to wonder why these women put themselves in such danger. How can Russia house both the most expensive city in the world and a sizable population of women who are willing to abandon their families to live in a faraway place with a stranger who spends all day sitting in a rocking chair, drinking beers he opened up with a shotgun blast?

According to a 1999 report on International Matchmaking Organizations by the office of United States Citizenship and Immigration Services, approximately 200 mail-order-bride companies arrange between 4,000 and 6,000 marriages each year. I'm sure I'll hear this figure later in life, when Steve tries to justify his marriage as "not that uncommon."

The International Matchmaking Organizations do their best to silence critics worried about the safety of the girls. They claim: "The fact that the male customer is a U.S. citizen or lawful permanent resident makes him more attractive to a foreign-born bride, who may come from a society in which women are pressured to take steps that are not beneficial to them as individuals (e.g., to become a prostitute, overseas domestic worker, or mail-order bride)." If I read the last sentence correctly, it purports that becoming a mail-order bride might be attractive to a woman who wants to avoid becoming a mail-order bride.

The USCIS report takes care to acknowledge the other side of the proverbial coin: men victimized by their mail-order brides. That is to say, men who marry foreign women familiar with the nuances of U.S. immigration law and who, once in the United States, manipulate their spouse into paying for and assisting in the immigration of their family members.

It's tough not to find the above scenario incredibly hysterical. Especially when I cast Steve as the henpecked man.

After about an hour of reading and thinking, I decided I couldn't go through with my mail-order-bride stunt. I wouldn't be able to make light of the sadness and then just walk away from it. Also, the issue of safety crossed my mind. The type of guy who didn't have a problem with women-trafficking probably wouldn't have a problem responding to my jokes by stapling uncooked steaks to my chest and tossing me into his shark tank.

If I was going to meet my bride in Russia, it would have to be the old-fashioned way.

VALI: The Kremlin, a Great Place to Be Scared of Children

The word *kremlin* generally refers to a town's fortified stronghold. If a city came under attack, its citizens would hole up in the kremlin until the invaders, hopefully, gave up and left. We don't have similar strongholds in American cities, probably because a conventional army hasn't attacked us on our soil since the Revolutionary War. Our closest analogs are sports stadiums. If a Mongol horde surrounded Los Angeles next week, we'd probably all go to the Staples Center.

The most famous kremlin in Russia is Moscow's, where the government has operated for most of Russian history. It has been the source of political violence since it was built in the 1150s. It was where Ivan became the Terrible, Stalin crushed his rivals, and Putin decides whom to poison to death with polonium. The place has some seriously bad mojo.

The Kremlin is difficult to access even today. I walked around the sprawling triangular redbrick complex for almost an hour trying to cross a multilane street packed with cars. I went down stairs only to come up other stairs on the same side of the street. I walked through tunnels that took me halfway, but not all the way, across the street. Nothing seemed to work. Any army generals reading this book who are serious about sacking Moscow should either (1) have a detailed street map handy, (2) not rely too heavily on foot soldiers, or (3) hire a guide like the one I sneakily followed across the street.

By the time I made it to the Kremlin side of the street, it was too late to actually enter the stronghold. So I walked through Alexandrovsky Garden, a colorful and beautiful space that I wouldn't have associated with the Communists. There were lovely fountains, beds of flowers, and Russians sitting around, holding hands and even—gasp—smiling. At the edge of the garden is the Tomb of the Unknown Soldier. I stood there for a few minutes telling everyone who passed by, "I know who's buried here. It's my friend Bob. Don't tell anyone."

Red Square, which contains St. Basil's Cathedral, is located just outside the garden gates. The cathedral, with its multiple, uniquely textured and brightly colored Hershey Kiss–shaped domes, looked more like a cake than I expected.

Adjacent to Red Square is a high-end shopping mall where Muscovites can purchase all the Gucci and Louis Vuitton they need. It's probably where Stalin bought all his pashminas.

After my walk, I decided to pay a visit to the Kremlin's armory. I paid the two-hundred-year-old Russian woman working the ticket booth and made my way toward the entrance. As I got into line, I saw a group of fourteen-year-old boys ahead of me. I had seen them earlier while walking through Alexandrovsky Garden. They had given me strange looks, pointed at me, and mumbled to each other in Russian. Now they were doing the same thing. In my head, I imagined snippets of their conversation: "Check out the nigger!" "What the fuck is he doing here?"

People come from all over to visit the Kremlin museums

just as people from all over visit Washington, D.C. For all I knew these kids were from Bumblecreekovich, Russia, and had never seen a brown person in their entire lives.*

As I approached the entrance, I imagined what might happen inside. What if one of the punks openly said something to me or "accidentally" dropped an ice cream cone on me? Then what could I do? It would be demeaning and emasculating to ignore the act. But yelling at them in English wouldn't accomplish anything. They would just laugh while I looked crazy and petty. So a diplomatic solution wouldn't be an option. And I couldn't punch a fourteen-year-old in the face. Cops can be real jerks in situations like that. So a military solution also wouldn't be an option. And, oh god, even worse: What if some adults saw the kids taunting me and didn't say or do anything about it, thereby implicitly insulting me themselves?

Maybe I was reading too much into the teenagers' actions. If I was, I had my reasons. I was alone in Moscow and nobody was friendly and the nation's racist beliefs are well documented and I felt vulnerable.

I threw away my ticket and walked back to my hotel, feeling stupid that a group of children had upset me so badly.

The following day I went back to the Kremlin and saw the impressive palaces and cathedrals. But I never felt totally comfortable again, until I left Russia. Moscow was the only place I visited during the trip that I feel no desire to ever visit again.

VALI: Preparing for Truce Day with Steve

During the early days of the Ridiculous Race, Steve and I tried to arrange a meeting point roughly halfway around the world. The idea was to meet up for one day of truce, where we would put the race on hold and have some fun and adventure together.

*This didn't seem impossible since, after one full day spent wandering Moscow, I'd seen only one person with skin darker than a milky cup of tea.

After some back and forth we tentatively agreed on Moscow and the incredibly vague time frame of "May." We decided to arrange a more specific time by text message as we both approached Moscow. This was much easier than it sounds since I was committed to flying whenever necessary and thus could meet Steve in Moscow anytime he wanted. Whenever Steve texted me about the meeting I would respond with a cryptic message designed to make him wish he was where I was ("The women in this country are beautiful and love pretentious poseurs.") and imply that I was slightly closer to Moscow that he was. Finally we arrived on a date: May 13.

After thirty days on the road and in the air, most of it spent alone, I was looking forward to seeing Steve again. Partly because I felt like I'd be less of an assault target in Moscow if I was walking around with a white guy.

More important, I wanted to check in with Steve and make sure I was really as far ahead in the Awesomeness Contest as I thought I was. I mean, I had strapped on a jetpack, hung out with a Brazilian graffiti gang, and watched the political tide change in France. Could he have had more interesting experiences during his last four weeks on a boat and train? I didn't think so. But the possibility, however unlikely, drove me in sane. Sussing out who was winning the Awesomeness Contest would involve a little rhetorical footwork. Neither of us could talk about any of the specific places we had been. And I had to be especially careful not to mention things like the great movie I saw on the airplane. Steve was so upset by the simple handcuffing incident at the beginning of the race that I expected him to go insane as soon he heard the word *airplane* waft from my lips. I planned on having a knife drawn to protect myself.

To keep myself occupied in the time I had before Steve arrived in Moscow, I planned an appropriate welcome experience for him.

"Could you assist me in getting a large burlap sack and a nonpoisonous snake?" I asked my hotel concierge.

She had a little difficulty following my English. "A sack?" she asked.

"Yes. I need a big cloth bag. Something large enough to fit a two-meter-tall man."

"And a snake?"

"Yes. But the snake doesn't need to be that big, so don't go enlarging the bag on account of the snake." Silence. "And did I already say I don't want the snake to be poisonous? Well, either way, I'll say it again. I don't want to hurt the guy."

The concierge didn't know anyone who could help me. "This is a very unusual request," she explained. The stonewalling continued even after I relaxed my constraints to include mildly poisonous snakes. This plan hit a dead end very quickly. Luckily I had set up another plan a few weeks in advance . . .

An Oral History of Truce Day in Moscow

On May 13, 2007, the authors met in Moscow. Neither trusted the other to write a description of the events of this day. After a violent argument, they decided the only solution was to bring in an impartial interviewer to take separate oral histories in an effort to reconstruct the events.

STEVE: Vali and I had a very clear plan, which was to meet at one p.m. in front of the Sanduny Baths. I'd confirmed it by text message a few days before on the train.

VALI: By May 13 I had not heard from Steve in several days. He had not responded to any of my text messages or e-mails. I actually started to worry about his safety. By eleven a.m. I was certain Steve was dead, which saddened me but also meant I'd be able to keep the Victory Scotch.

STEVE: I arrived in Moscow a night early and went about trying to find a driver who could kidnap Vali. My plan was to have Vali driven out to the very outskirts of Moscow and then dropped off with a note that said, "You're out of the range of the Moscow public transportation system and your first challenge is to get back." But this required a cabdriver to follow some complicated instructions, and I couldn't find anyone that I trusted who wouldn't turn it into an actual kidnapping.

Then I got some text messages from people in LA, saying that Vali thought I'd died. So I called Vali and told him, "Look, I'm in Moscow. I'm not dead. It's okay. I'll just see you at the meeting place." And he said, "What meeting place? What are you talking about?"

VALI: No. There was no meeting time or location. Steve totally made that up while going insane on the Trans-Siberian Railroad. I finally heard from Steve around 11:30 a.m. He sent a text message telling me to go to the bar at the Peter the Great Hotel where further instructions would await me. While I was legitimately worried about his safety, Steve was planning some sort of insanely stupid scavenger hunt.

STEVE: The Peter the Great Hotel seemed like a good place to try some spy stuff. I tried the trick of holding up the newspaper and seeing if he would just walk by me. I had a thin, very elegant Cary Grant mustache.

VALI: As soon as I entered, I saw Steve sitting in the lobby with this huge grin and a pedophile-type mustache on his face.

STEVE: We started drinking. Vali was super excited about this gift he bought me, an attaché case. I remember saying, "Oh, Vali, what a nice gesture. That's so touching." Meanwhile Vali was struggling to suppress a giggle.

VALI: It was black leather with his initials monogrammed in gold leaf on the inside flap. And Steve was really appreciative, because he knows that the ladies like men with accessories. I don't have to explain this to readers. Ladies like the accessories.

STEVE: So I opened the case, and inside was a flash drive with a note that read, "Look at the contents of this as soon as possible." So I thanked Vali and said, "Oh yeah,

I definitely will." But Vali couldn't contain himself. He wanted to look at it right away. So we go to the hotel business center and pop the flash drive into the computer. It's pictures of tattooed, disgusting men inside my apartment. They were making out on my bed, trying on my clothes. . . . Just revolting images. One of the dudes was using my hairbrush in a way he shouldn't have.

VALI: The photos were all taken the previous day at Steve's apartment back in Los Angeles. They were wonderful. As soon as Steve saw the photos he turned to me with his eyes ignited to the color of hot coals and asked, "Who betrayed me?"

After I stopped laughing we went out to brunch. I did a little research and found the best brunch in Moscow. Excellent borscht, tasty caviar, fresh blinis. Steve never thanked me for finding that spot.

STEVE: Vali insisted we go to brunch at his hotel, the Sheraton. Everyone there was American. And all the food was like lasagna and ham and cheese sandwiches and it cost seventy dollars.

But we were just happy to see each other. All we wanted to do was talk about the adventures we'd had, but of course we couldn't. We didn't know what to do instead, but we agreed that to do Truce Day properly we would need suits. So we went to this big Moscow department store. I bought a suit jacket off the rack, but Vali like fell under the sway of this hypnotic salesman who kept bringing out more and more expensive, incredibly tacky Russian-guy suits.

VALI: At the department store I bought an incredibly well cut blue blazer. It was so well cut that after returning to Los Angeles, I took the only suit I own to a tailor and asked him to match the cut. Steve, on the other hand, bought this sleazy shimmering gray blazer. He looked like a jackass at a nightclub. As he was trying it on, I saw one of the Russian salesgirls look at Steve and shake her head no, no. He looked ridiculous. For that reason, I wanted him to buy the jacket. So I never told him about the Russian salesgirl.

STEVE: After he bought his suit, Vali kept checking his calculator watch—did you know he wears a calculator watch, like an eight-year-old?—because he couldn't believe how much he'd paid.

Anyway, now looking great, we went to a Siberian theme restaurant called Expedition. It is to Siberia what Outback Steakhouse is to Australia. It's just terrible. Vali demanded we be seated next to the stuffed polar bear.

I wrote down what we had that evening. We started with some horseradish vodka. Then we had the "Meat Delicacies from the North" platter, which was: uncooked smoked reindeer, boiled reindeer tongues, reindeer heart, mild duck roll, reindeer sausage, reindeer liver pâté, colt meat, marinated partridge, and cranberries. I think the only thing that I was able to eat were the cranberries.

VALI: It might have been the worst meal of my life. Though I'm reluctant to declare Siberian cuisine as a whole to be terrible. It's not like we were eating farm-fresh baby horse meat. I think the stuff we were eating was horse meat that had been frozen and thawed out. A drop in taste quality is unavoidable in that situation.

After dinner Steve and I asked a driver to take us to the "coolest club in Moscow." The driver looked at us and ten minutes later we were dropped off at the front door of a gay bar.

STEVE: After that we went back to the driver and said, "Take us to the next coolest club in Moscow and it's okay if it's not a gay bar." So he took us to a smoothie bar. There I got into a conversation with a girl at the bar. I thought it was going well until she told me I looked like Borat.

VALI: We returned to my hotel room around three a.m. I

had a flight to catch at five a.m. but, of course, I couldn't tell Steve that. I just grabbed my stuff and told Steve I was going to the train station.

STEVE: By the time we got back to Vali's hotel, he was so drunk that he was talking in a Hunter S. Thompson accent. No idea why. He kept repeating, "If I were staying in Moscow, I would definitely explore the political situation."

The next morning I woke up in Vali's hotel room and I wanted to drive up his bill. So I ordered a bunch of porn movies, plus *John Tucker Must Die*. I called and ordered two cheeseburgers, one I told them to smother in caviar. Then I opened the minibar, dumped everything in the sink, scheduled a massage, and left.

STEVE: Moscow—In Which I Explore the Political Situation

As I finished my caviar burger in the Moscow Sheraton, I considered the circumstances.

I was ahead in the race. Not stupidly far. Not I-should-stay-in-Moscow-and-get-a-job-for-a-couple-weeks-to-pay-for-all-this ahead. But longitude-wise, Moscow was 13 percent farther for me than it was for him.

Rattling in my head was Vali's Hunter S. Thompson impression as he repeated, over and over again, "If I were staying in Moscow, I would explore the political situation." This was bluster—if he were staying in Moscow, he would've explored the nap situation.

But his was an interesting, if stupid, idea.

Winston Churchill famously said, "Russia is a riddle wrapped in a mystery wrapped in an enigma."* Bullshit. I

* He also said, "I hate Indians. They are a beastly people." Churchill would've retracted this statement and apologized had he met Vali's lovely parents. Then he would've reinstated it after meeting Vali.

decided to spend an extra day and a half in Moscow, and by the end of it I'd solved the Russian Riddle (Mystery [Enigma]).

VALI: The Kindness of Strangers

I knew leaving Steve alone in my Moscow hotel room made me vulnerable to attack. He could have made hour-long international phone calls, extended my stay by a week, filled the bathtub and toilets with cement, covered the bed with dildos slathered in strawberry jam, posted flyers around town and thrown a huge party in my room, or performed any number of other acts with the goal of running up my credit card bill and soiling my sterling reputation with the Starwood Hotels Group. But I wasn't particularly concerned. I knew Steve's simple mind would never think beyond the most obvious prank. He would empty out my minibar, order some room service, and sit pleased with his devilishness. I could handle that.

I realized all this just before leaving my hotel room. Then I figured if I was going to be paying for all the booze no matter what, I might as well have some of it myself. So I grabbed all the scotch and bourbon bottles out of the minibar and shoved them in my bag.

"These are for the train," I barked toward Steve, who was now crumpled into an armchair. The combination of his shiny gray suit, pedophile mustache, and boozy middle-distance stare was frightening. No children should be allowed within five hundred yards of that man.

Downstairs I celebrated entering a cab with a nip of Johnnie Walker Red. It was about four a.m.

By five-thirty I was at the airport, where my new best friend, Kan-Yan, a six-foot-tall cowboy-boot-wearing Harvard Law School–attending Asian from Texas, and I had finished all the whiskey. We then spent the rest of our Russian currency at a vending machine that sold beer.

My last truly solid memory of the morning was trying to fill my fountain pen* with ink so I could take notes on what was happening. This lasted about two seconds before I dropped my glass inkwell to the ground, smashing it to pieces and splashing ink onto my pants and shoes. After that, my memory was reduced to a few snapshots: Kan-Yan carrying me to my seat on the plane; Kan-Yan helping me up off the floor in the Milan airport and telling me what gate I needed to go to; eating an egg McMuffin. All I know for certain is that I somehow made my connection from Milan to Cairo.

When I finally sobered up, I noticed Kan-Yan had left me a parting gift: a postcard featuring a painting of a well-dressed young Russian man refusing another glass of wine at dinner.

If there is any justice in this world, Kan-Yan will one day sit on the United States Supreme Court.

STEVE: Russia Solved with Six Clues

CLUE ONE: Krasnye Oktabr chocolate factory. This is a gigantic candy plant on an island in the Moscow River, and its smokestacks fill the air from Gorky Park to the Kremlin with a hint of rich, chocolaty aroma. If we'd known during the Cold War that much of Moscow smells like chocolate we would've been less worried.

I spent a day and a half trying to get in there. My friend Liz had visited Moscow on a high school exchange and was taken on a tour. She described a Willy Wonka wonderland where you could eat as much chocolate as you wanted, right off the assembly line.

Unfortunately, all my efforts of calling and poking around the factory and talking to security guards in bulletproof vests did not bring this about.

*Short story, still not worth it.

LESSON I TOOK AWAY ABOUT RUSSIA. None. In fact, left with an additional question, "Why does a chocolate factory need guards with bulletproof vests?"

CLUE TWO: The Museum of the Great Patriotic War. In Moscow you can see a giant panoramic painting of the Battle of Borodino, an outdoor event that took place in 1812 when Russian soldiers and invading Frenchmen under Napoleon met on a field and killed each other for a while. In the Borodino panorama, it's sunny and everybody's in cool costumes and horses are absorbing most of the bullets. It makes war look sort of fun.

Not so the nearby Museum of the Great Patriotic War. This commemorates the war that broke out the next time somebody (Hitler, as it turned out) invaded Russia. It makes war look really, really not fun. The Great Patriotic War is what the Russians call World War II, and it should convince you that the Russians should be allowed to call it whatever the hell they want.

The main exhibits here are also paintings, but they are way less fun than the Borodino panorama. In fact, as war museums go, they are stunningly frank. In the mural of the Battle of Stalingrad, there's a pale man sitting on the ground, head in his hands, obviously shell-shocked, mangled bodies in the ruins around him. In the mural of the Siege of Leningrad, there's a frozen corpse and some parents burying an infant. The mural of the battle of Kursk is just a mess of flaming metal death cars and exploding tanks.

If you get too down in the mural section, you can always wander through the Hall of Memory and Sorrow, or past the exhibited skull with its teeth ripped out.

The Great Patriotic War transcends depressing. It was fought between the armies of Hitler and Stalin, so you can't even root for anybody. Something like thirty million Russian people died, which is about a hundred times the number of Americans who died in World War II.

On the day I visited the Museum of the Great Patriotic War, there was some kind of conference going on in an auditorium, featuring weathered veterans, men and women. It was all in Russian, so I couldn't understand their stories. But I sat in the back and watched them anyway, because even without words they conveyed this message very clearly: *We are some tough-ass dudes who went through some serious shit the likes of which you can't possibly understand. All you can do is not forget it.*

I won't.

LESSON I TOOK AWAY ABOUT RUSSIA: We in comfy America can't possibly wrap our brains around how bad Russia's bad times have been.

CLUE THREE: The Sanduny Baths. The Sanduny Bathhouse is an ornate, intricately tiled, high-arched palace designed so that Russian men can sit in incredibly hot saunas as they whack their own and other backsides with birch branches. Women are allowed, too, but as women tend to be less inclined to do stupid stuff like sit in incredibly hot saunas whacking their backsides with birch branches, it's clear which gender is the target market. This place is a Moscow institution, founded in the 1790s* and famous as a location for deal making. This makes sense, because a very good negotiating tactic is to force your opponent to sit in an extremely hot sauna. I can tell you from personal experience that it greatly weakens the mind.

Reading this at home, you may think that the Sanduny Baths sounds (1) extremely unpleasant and (2) pretty gay. As to your second point, shame on you for having such a close-minded opinion, and let me tell you you're completely wrong. Because I thought that, too. But there's no place in the world as full of naked dudes and as free of homosexual tension as the Sanduny Baths. I'VE CHECKED.

As for the idea that the Sanduny Baths are unpleasant, wrong again. After arriving and being presented with a towel, you change in an elegant room lined with leather couches, and you can order traditional Russian sauna (or "banya")

* I'm learning this from the English-language section of its Web site, which is a masterpiece of prose comedy: http://www.sanduny.ru/.

snacks, like pickles and vodka. I had a beer, because the waiter took one look at my American visage and brought me a beer.

The procedure, then, is to sit on a bench in a dry, hot box full of hairy uncircumcised monsters until you're ready to pass out, which for me took about five minutes. As you do this, you should batter your limbs with wet birch branches. If you appear to be slacking off in self-flagellation, one of the monsters will offer to do it for you, and believe me, they will show no mercy. Then, it's suggested, you should plunge yourself into a wooden bathtub full of ice cold water, or pull a string so that a wooden bucket of ice cold water dumps on your steaming head. Repeat, five to ten times.

I know it sounds crazy. I don't know how to explain it. I was skeptical walking in. But visiting the Sanduny Baths left me with the greatest feeling of physical relaxation I have ever had.

LESSON I TOOK AWAY ABOUT RUSSIA: The Russians have come up with some very pleasant ways to take the edge off the bad times.

CLUE FOUR: Lenin's Tomb. Lenin's preserved corpse looks terrible, his skin resembling a melted yellow crayon. If he happened to come to life, stand up, and walk outside his tomb, the first thing he would see would be a poster advertising Chanel Rouge Allure outside a mall that includes a Sbarro.

LESSON I TOOK AWAY ABOUT RUSSIA: Capitalism not only won, it's an obnoxious winner.

CLUE FIVE: The Kremlin Wall. Leaving Lenin's tomb, I heard two Americans, an Indian guy and a blond woman, both about thirty, getting a tour in English from their Russian friend about the monuments to Communist heroes that line the Kremlin wall. They kindly let me tag along, which was an interesting experience.

"Oh yeah, this guy—he was a real asshole," said the Russian

guy, pointing to some hero of the 1917 Communist Revolution. "This guy, too. He was an asshole."

Huh, that's interesting, I thought. *I'm certainly getting an insight into Russian—*

"And a Jew," said the Russian.

Welp, here we go, said my brain, as the Americans looked at each other, mutual discomfort spilling out our ears.

"Yeah, this guy," said the Russian friend, "he was another Jew." The Russian guy laughed. "In fact, we have a joke in Russia. It goes, 'The revolution was started by German Jews.' "

LESSON I TOOK AWAY ABOUT RUSSIA: Some Russian people have troubling, angry theories about their own past. And tell jokes that aren't very funny.

CLUE SIX: The Museum of Soviet Arcade Machines. I was the first American to visit the Museum of Soviet Arcade Machines, and I'm proud of this accomplishment. The MSAM is housed in a basement of Building One of MAMI State Technical University, so finding it was the equivalent of finding the laundry room of Livingston Hall at Columbia University if you've just arrived in New York and don't speak English. Only one of the proprietors speaks any English and that at such a primitive and uncomprehending level that he would be hard-pressed to parse an episode of *Dora the Explorer*.

If we'd known how inferior Soviet arcade games were to ours, we would've felt like bullies in the Cold War and generously offered to let them surrender in exchange for a few Pac-Man and Galaga machines. Their games—Sub Commander, Tank Commander, and the Mysterious Game of Guessing Traffic Signs—were manufactured in secret army factories, and are total unfun garbage. At the time when the Americans and Japanese were developing elaborate backstories for pixilated Italian plumber-heroes, the Soviets were making games that relied on wedges of cardboard moving in synch.

The three curators of MSAM were curly-haired nerds. Alexsander was the one who did the talking.

"Always when I am boy I am asking mother if I can ride,

and she is saying no and I am much crying, but now, I am never again crying!" This said as he bounced along in a child-size rocking-boat ride after feeding it one kopek.

The four of us drank Uzbekistani tea and played Sniper. I was very good at it, and I assume word will filter back to Putin not to mess with America and her sharpshooters.

The curators were all of a type I thought existed only in America: the ironically nostalgic nerd. They loved their Soviet arcade games the way Americans their age love *Flintstones* cartoons and *Hungry Hungry Hippoes*. They spoke with the innocent good humor of geeks everywhere. When a Russian-language version of *The Simpsons* hits the airwaves, these guys are going to go nuts.

LESSON I TOOK AWAY ABOUT RUSSIA: The generation born in the Cold War has come so far as to find the whole business pretty silly. Maybe that'll keep us from doing it again.

These six clues have enabled me to come to the following definitive solution to the mystery of Russia:

Russia is a complicated land with a textured history, a resilient people, and many pleasures and wonders.

This may not be the most insightful take. But compare it to Vali's conclusion that Moscow is "scary and bad."

On with the race!

VALI: Baksheesh

The impact of my airplane hitting the runway jolted me awake. A fierce hangover combined with general confusion regarding my whereabouts produced a strange panic that didn't let up when I finally realized I had landed in Cairo. I had no place to stay and had yet to open a guidebook.

Fortunately, the airport was filled with Egyptians eager to help tourists find accommodations and book sightseeing tours. Within a matter of minutes, I had withdrawn a bunch of Egyptian pounds from an ATM, booked a hotel room, and secured myself a ride there.

Before jumping into the car, the tout who had taken me to the in-airport travel agency asked me for some *baksheesh*, a tip. I gave him ten Egyptian pounds. The ride itself was short and not particularly scenic. The Cairo streets were choked with small, boxy cars. The pollution and dust tinctured the landscape with sepia, giving it the look of a 1970s photograph. But it smelled great, a combination of people, fresh flowers, and diesel fuel that, ever since my childhood trips to India, I fondly associated with third world metropolises. When the driver dropped me off, I gave him a E£10 tip.

Once in the hotel I gave E£20 to the bellboy, who, despite my objections, carried my backpack up to my room for me. He was friendly and recommended several fine restaurants in the area. *Service in this country is great*, I thought.

Two minutes after he left, another hotel employee came with a "welcome gift" of a package of biscuits and a bottle of water. He waited for an uncomfortably long amount of time after I said "thank you." Getting the hint, I gave him a E£10 tip as well.

Something was clearly wrong. I had done so little research on Egypt, I didn't even know what the exchange rate was. I searched through my guidebook and learned the standard tip is E£1 or E£2. I also learned I was charged 10X the normal rate for my taxi ride.

Knock-knock. Word must have spread downstairs about the rube in room 648. I opened the door to find a smiling Egyptian man bearing a bottle of water and a second robe, just in case I had already worn through the robe that came with the room. I'm not even sure this guy was a hotel employee. He might have just been another guest who wanted in on the action. I accepted the goods and closed the door without giving a tip.

A minute later there was another knock at the door. I realize this is starting to sound unbelievably absurd, but I'm honestly reporting everything as it happened.

"Welcome gift," called an Egyptian voice through the door. I didn't move.

Knock-knock.

"I'm sleeping! Go away!" I screamed.

Thus began my war with the hustlers of Cairo.

VALI: Islamic Cairo

Cairo has a lot to offer. Ancient trophies from the time of the pharaohs stand just outside the city. Christian churches and convents, built by the Romans in the second century for the ancient fortress of Babylon, still stand today in Coptic Cairo. But in my opinion the coolest part of town is Islamic Cairo.

Describing a part of Cairo as Islamic is a bit like describing part of a lake as wet. About 90 percent of Egyptians are Muslim. And Cairo is covered from end to end, top to bottom, with mosques, minarets, Mecca arrows, and other things that begin with M. Islamic Cairo refers to the section of town where the most important mosque, the Al-Azhar Mosque, is located.

The official Egyptian government name for the region is Fatimid Cairo, referring to the people who built the Al-Azhar Mosque. They might as well have called the region "Hey, white people, please don't think about suicide bombers. Just come spend money over here."

The mosque itself is pretty awe-inspiring. For starters, it is over one thousand years old. It was built by the Fatimids, who I can only assume were both fat and timid, so the fact that they built anything other than a machine that politely requests more cake is impressive. The mosque, built in AD 988, also functions as a university, which claims to be the oldest still existing educational institution in the world. So I guess they haven't heard of a little something called the University of Phoenix Online.

I walked up to the Al-Azhar entrance and removed my shoes. This was not my first visit to a mosque, but with all the recent overt and covert anti-Muslim hysteria, even I had forgotten what peaceful places they are.

In the first room I entered, hundreds of men lounged. Some chatted, others prayed, a few read the Koran, many slept. All took advantage of the cool covered space, a respite from the ferocious Egyptian sun. A walkway led to the main courtyard of Al-Azhar, which gleamed impressively for a thousand-year-old building. The mosque must have had an abnormally dedicated building super. Around the perimeter of the courtyard, more men sat, read, and caught up with friends. An ornate latticework ran around the roof. Each entryway and every space between pillars looked like the silhouette of a pointy-topped grain silo, a sight I've associated with Arab architecture since the movie *Aladdin*.

The actual prayer room was less social. It was filled with brown bodies, beards, and a noticeable lack of broads. Men and women had different entrances and never interacted inside the mosque.

"The women and men are kept separate because the sight of women in prayer position—a raised buttocks and forehead touching the floor—would distract the men," a local explained to me.

"That makes sense," I lied. I lied because the statement invoked questions that I felt too uncomfortable to ask. They were as follows:

☛ Really?
☛ Are you sure you aren't just rationalizing a baseless practice?
☛ Do Muslim men really find the sight of a woman prostrate in a burka particularly distracting? If so, what *don't* they find distracting?
☛ If I wore a burka and prayed would men find me sexy?
☛ Does asking these questions place me in any physical danger?
☛ You think I'm an asshole, don't you?

I was too scared to ask any of these questions based on what I had heard about Islam in general, not based on what I saw at Azhar. The mosque-goers were contemplative and sociable. It's hard to imagine anyone who frequented a place like this being capable of mass violence. I suppose that's what makes violence performed in the name of religion so chilling.

After Al-Azhar I crossed the street and entered the enormous Kahn al-Kahlili bazaar. The wide lanes of the bazaar featured hundreds of small shops, each focused on a very particular need. One store sold only plastic combs, another only batteries and a selection of electrical switches. The lanes were crowded with people walking in both directions, people standing around, and people engaged in some sort of dirt road repair. A ringing bell approached from behind, then a bicyclist carrying a crate of ten thousand multicolored flexible drinking straws passed by. I should have flagged the rider down and gotten some straws at wholesale prices, but I didn't think of it at the time. I'll curse my slow mind every time I overpay for straws for the rest of my life.

The nicer shops, selling things like brassware and jewelry, and coffee shops with chairs were located in a narrow lane of the bazaar. The guidebook promised shops that sold books of magic spells but despite hours of searching I never found one. It's like they wanted readers to be disappointed.

Down alleyways, men sat on blankets in outdoor cafés smoking apple-soaked tobacco out of *sheesha* and drinking tea.

Kahn al-Kahlili has existed for about six hundred years. And probably every major tour of Cairo from the early 1800s to today has stopped at the bazaar. This has allowed the touts and shopkeepers a lot of practice and helped them elevate hustling to an art form. Not long after I got to the bazaar, a tour bus made a stop. You could find the group by following the shouts of "Hello, my friend" and "Look for free, sir" and "Where you from, young lady?" These guys knew how to give the hard sell. I, on the other hand, wasn't getting harassed at all. After receiving a few questions in Arabic, I realized it was because people thought I was Egyptian. With my short hair, white short-sleeve button-down shirt, and blue jeans I looked like a Nubian college student. It was one of the few times in my life I thought, *Life would be so much worse right now if I was white.*

Then it all came crashing down. I was following a hundred meters behind the tour group, laughing to myself at the difficulties they were having, when the shopkeeper of a perfume store noticed all the other shopkeepers were ignoring me. He looked at me carefully, then yelled, "He's Indian!"

"Namaste!" yelled one shopkeeper. "Come see my store, my friend!" yelled another. "I sell sandals like Gandhi's!" yelled a third.

My cover was blown.

VALI: Pickin' up Ladies in the Middle East

When I was in western Europe, a twenty-two-year-old solo female traveler told me stories of how difficult she found traveling in Egypt. Egyptian men, she said, constantly and lewdly propositioned her in the street. I also met a British woman who told me that a few of her older single friends went to Egypt every year because they enjoyed the attention they received while there. As everyone knows, there are two sides to every coin. (The tricky part is that most things aren't coins.)

In general, Egyptian men have little close interaction with women before marriage. And a lot of their "knowledge" on what Western women want comes from movies. One taxi driver, upon learning I was from the United States, told me that his girlfriend lived in the United States. He then went on to describe himself sexually harassing some poor girl from Minneapolis. Even in his telling of the story, nothing remotely romantic happened. His "girlfriend" was a woman who he had given a cab ride to, very aggressively requested contact information from (she refused at first), then called several times despite her never answering. Some who have heard this story argue that the taxi driver was harmless and merely misunderstood the term *girlfriend*. To them I ask: Did he think "girlfriend" means "person you annoy"?

Of course, you shouldn't judge a culture by its cabdrivers. If you did, you'd think everyone in the country drove cabs for a living. You also probably shouldn't judge a country after spending only a few days within its borders. But informed opinions take time to form and I'm a busy guy.

Cairo, like any major city, is a bit more progressive than

the surrounding areas. There, in the heart of the Middle East, dating took place. I saw very Western-looking couples in cafés near the University of Cairo. Both the boys and girls were dressed in clothes that looked like they were from the GAP and drank lattes. Also, just like Western couples on dates, they appeared uneasy with this correspondent staring at them from the next table while taking notes.

Most interesting were the dates I saw at Al-Azhar Park. For the first time in my life I saw girls in burkas, only their eyes peeking out of their *hijabs*, on dates, holding hands with guys dressed like me in T-shirts and jeans. The couples flirted as if everything was normal. I guess it was. There were other Egyptian girls on dates at the park dressed completely in Western clothing. So if the burka girls wanted to take off their veils while hidden from their parents, they could have comfortably done so. Nobody had seen anything beyond the eyes of these girls since they were adolescents. These girls could use their regular faces as disguises. But they had either chosen not to or not chosen to. If I could've forgotten all of my preconceived notions, I would've thought they looked happy.

VALI: The Pyramids, Part I

The Pyramids of Giza and the nearby Sphinx have been luring travelers to Egypt for over four thousand years. Every travel writer worth his salt has dutifully written on the sights. Each has had to invent a new way to describe how big the pyramids are. "The Pyramids looked as if they would wear out the air, boring holes in it all day long," wrote Florence Nightingale. She was an accomplished woman, but clearly her expertise did not cover How Air Works.

There are three main pyramids on the Giza plateau. All are pyramid-shaped, just like in the photographs, and the tallest, the Great Pyramid of Khufu, is forty-five stories tall. Careful examiners of photographs will know that the sides of the pyramids are stepped rather than smooth. In person, the steps are surprisingly large. Some were taller than me and even the smallest would require some serious thigh flexibility to climb. Until a few decades ago, scaling the pyramids was standard practice for European and continental tourists. Then a couple of suits in the Egyptian government decided too many people were falling to their deaths and banned the practice. These days, killing yourself at the pyramids is nearly impossible.

The pyramids are crazily awesome to behold. They're amazing. And hordes of Egyptian hustlers do their best to ruin the experience.

The hustling begins early. As I walked up a hill toward the pyramids ticket stand, two Egyptian men approached me.

"Hello, my friend!"

I ignored them.

"Stop. Stop. I am trying to help you. You need to buy tickets to see the pyramids."

"I know. I'm walking to the ticket stand," I told them, pointing to the stand at the top of the hill.

"That ticket stand is closed." I could plainly see that it was not. "Don't worry, I will not cheat you. I work for government. I work for government."

Having never before seen a government official wear a tight purple bootleg Diesel T-shirt and stonewashed jeans, I was suspicious of this guy's claim. What this hustler lacked in official stature, he made up for in persistence. His mouth didn't stop emitting syllables until I reached the open ticket stand. Then he abruptly stopped talking, spun around on his heels, and raced back down the hill. In the distance I heard him scream to an unseen tourist, "Ticket office is closed!"

Thrilled to have avoided the scam, I paid for my ticket and was led toward the pyramids.

"Where you from, my friend?" the ticket seller asked. Suddenly, I realized I hadn't given my money to a ticket booth worker. I had given it to a conniving official-acting hustler.

"Thirty pounds for full tour including camel ride," he told me. I grew furious. The official ticket booth workers and tourist police had just watched this fraud accept my money, purchase the ticket on my behalf, put *my* ticket in *his* pocket, then proceed to fleece me. And nobody did anything to stop it. The official pyramids staff and security did nothing as I screamed at the beady-eyed jerk to give my ticket to me. "I will hold ticket for you, my friend," he calmly kept repeating. Never have I wanted to kick somebody in the face so badly.

"These pyramids were built for the pharaohs," he said, starting the tour I had repeatedly said I didn't want. He was determined to wear me down. I could already hear the absurd requests for *baksheesh* that would come at the end of the tour. I grabbed his arm and demanded my ticket back.

"Maybe we see the Sphinx first," he suggested through a smile. I grabbed his face and threatened to report him. Upon hearing the words *tourist police* his demeanor immediately changed. He pulled my ticket out of thin air, like a sleight-of-hand artist, handed it to me, and scurried off.

Finally free from hassle, I walked toward the Pyramid of Khufu. Over two million creamy limestone blocks, all arranged by hand, towered over me and disappeared at a point deep into the sky. My anger instantly melted away.

Looking at marvelous things makes me dangerously prone to foolish reflection. As I stared I became overwhelmed by the power and audacity of man. The ancient Egyptians, I thought, must have used the same part of the brain to conceive the pyramids that modern man used when he decided to launch satellites into space so consumers could watch every NFL game from any part of the country. If man could build the pyramids without cranes or trucks or hard hats, is there anything we couldn't do? I didn't think so. In that moment I thought I could breath underwater.

Then I felt something touch my head. It was a red and white checkered *keffiyah*, placed there by a new smiling Egyptian man.

"Hello, my friend," he said.

"I am *not* your fucking friend!" I barked back.

STEVE: St. Petersburg—Russia Further Solved, Plus Deformed Animals

The city of Leningrad suffered more deaths during World War II than did the United States and Britain combined. With the Nazis surrounding the city, people ate paste, wallpaper, sawdust, lipstick, their pets, and each other. The only supplies came in on trucks driven over a frozen lake. Finally the siege ended, and the Nazis were driven away. To celebrate, Stalin had most of Leningrad's leaders secretly executed.

It is perhaps no surprise that Vladimir Putin, whose brother died in the siege, seems to think of the United States as a bunch of pesky, spoiled, adorably naive infants. Putin was an officer in the KGB, already practicing silencing his enemies, while George W. Bush was doing cocaine* and mismanaging a baseball team.

The story of Leningrad has a happy ending, kind of. These days, "Leningrad"—now restored to its former name, St. Petersburg—is beautiful, one of the coolest cities I saw during a high-speed sampling of cool cities. It has some of the world's most impressive architecture, grandest avenues, and canaliest canals. It is home to the Hermitage, arguably the finest art museum in the world.

None of that is what I wanted to see.

STEVE: The Great St. Petersburg Gamble

I knew now that Vali was somewhere east of Moscow. I knew also that there wasn't much between Moscow and the Pacific, at least not the sort of glittery easy-to-understand stuff that might attract my simpleminded opponent.

My best hope was that he wouldn't be able to resist his ancestral subcontinent now dangling just south of him. Vali

* Allegedly.

has a weakness for Indian food and a weak man's tendency to follow his weaknesses. He's pretty much a giant wad of human weakness.

That was hardly a guarantee—I might be ahead, but the race was far from over.

Still, I had a long-scheduled appointment in Scandinavia. All the trains headed that way from Moscow pulled through St. Petersburg. There was a site in St. Petersburg that had haunted my dreams since I'd first heard about it. It was a gamble, but I decided to allow myself one day's stop to see the Kunstkamera in the city built by Peter the Great.

STEVE: Peter the Great

Peter the Great was a crazy giant with an enormous head and huge hands who became tsar of Russia in 1682. Determined to revolutionize his nation, he took a tour of Europe, where he did a number of remarkable things, not limited to: demanding to be pushed around in a wheelbarrow, vandalizing houses, learning shipbuilding, studying medicine, and biting a chunk off a cadaver to demonstrate science somehow. When he came back to Russia he decided to Westernize things, build a navy, and impose a "beard tax." Peter enjoyed mathematics, anatomy, and watching dwarfs do things, and he hated cockroaches and his own son, whom he certainly tortured and possibly executed.

Perhaps Peter's greatest monument is St. Petersburg itself, which is technically named for St. Peter but, c'mon, who are we kidding? In Peter the Great's day this spot was a fetid swamp, but he liked the looks of it on the map so he decreed that a new capital be built there. He hired the best European architects, put to work the toughest serfs, and then forced people to move there.

And in this magnificent city that Peter the Great willed into existence, he opened a museum called the Kunstkamera, first contender in Hely's Contest for Craziest Museum in Europe.

STEVE: The Museum of Horrifying Fetuses

Much of the Kunstkamera is made up of dusty, old-school anthropology exhibits. You can decide for yourself how much time you need to spend pretending to look at the Eskimo furs and dioramas of Japanese Noh theaters. Personally I considered ten minutes to be more than enough before proceeding upstairs to examine the anatomical oddities.

Peter the Great bought, collected, and demanded delivery of all manner of freaky fauna. He had a special interest in deformed fetuses. At the Kunstkamera, the amateur scientist can see, preserved in jars:

- ☛ dried Siamese twins
- ☛ a fetus with a "double face"
- ☛ a four-legged hen
- ☛ five fetuses on a single placenta (this looks like some kind of fetus Ferris wheel)
- ☛ the "malformed fetus of an unknown animal"

This last is—surprisingly—quite cute. They should make kids' plush toys based on it. The rest of it may sound disgusting. It is. It is really, really disgusting. But crude as it was, the Kunstkamera was also an early attempt at unfrightened scientific observation of biology, and as such represents a leap forward in man's quest for knowledge.

Or whatever. That was my justification; if you're the kind of person who can't not look at mutated animals, you're welcome to adopt it as your own.

If you don't believe me about Peter the Great's head and hands, by the way, you can compare wax casts of them to your own at the Kunstkamera. You will come up wanting.

Before leaving St. Petersburg I also visited the Hermitage, housed in the former Winter Palace. At that point I was so exhausted it was all I could do to count how many paintings of guys with sideburns there were in the Hall of Paintings of Guys with Sideburns. There were 268.

STEVE: Across the Invisible Line

When you cross the Russian border into Finland, everything immediately gets better. The signs on train stations are cleaner and use better fonts. The dogs are less mangy.

My trip from St. Petersburg to Finland was delightful—my only companion in the four-person train car was a Russian lady who'd cracked her first beer at 9:30 in the morning before launching into a pidgin English monologue about skiing.

I'd gone from Shanghai to Helsinki overland, and I'd done it at a decent clip, too. An undistracted hard charger who'd timed it down to jumps between moving train cars could've done it in nine days. Including shenanigans, explorations, and a truce day with Vali, it had taken me fifteen.

With me I had a list of freighters—leaving Antwerp, Le Havre, and Liverpool—that could get me across the Atlantic. I figured I now knew something about container ships, and I had the number of the *Hanjin Athens* captain in my pocket, so maybe he could help me out, and surely I could get on to something. Maybe by now the sheikh of Dubai had loosened up.

I wasn't looking forward to the ten-day trip across the stormy north Atlantic, ending with me on a dock in someplace like Chester, Maryland, waiting for a Greyhound.

Luckily, between me and that was Scandinavia, where I would ensure my victory over Vali in the Awesomeness Contest.

STEVE: Finland in Six Hours

In Helsinki, the capital of Finland, I had six hours between getting off a train and getting on a ship to cross the Baltic Sea. I didn't know of anything to see in Helsinki—a quick glance at a tour book in the train station suggested that 90 percent of the city's sites were monuments to the composer Sibelius. *How silly!* I thought. *The only true monument to Sibelius are his orchestral works, which I have never listened to!*

To spend my day, I came up with the following game: I would walk into the first bar I saw. I would order a shot of the local liquor and a pint of the local beer. I'd explain to the bartender my situation and ask what was the one thing to see in Helsinki. I'd get directions and head toward it.

The catch was, every time I passed another bar, I'd have to go inside and repeat.

So I kept getting new directions, and worse at following them, and I never got anywhere, but I had a ramble that grew increasingly cheery. It was some kind of national holiday in Finland, although no one could explain to me what the holiday was.* It wasn't because they couldn't speak English. Everyone in Finland speaks perfect English. Talk to a foul-smelling wino curled up in a corner of a Helsinki dive, and he'll say, "I'm sorry, you must pardon me, my English is not—what is the word?—mellifluous."

Somehow I crossed a park and ended up in front of the U.S. embassy, where a protest was going on. In a jolly mood, I thought, *Hey! My first anti-American protest!* It made me almost homesick. I went up to a dreadlocked Finn and asked him why he was stomping so vigorously on Old Glory.

Specifically, he told me, he was mad about our treatment of convicted murderer Mumia Abu-Jamal, and, generally, he was mad about "markets."

I promised to spread the word.

"What do you guys think of the government here in Finland?" I asked.

"Well, what can you say?" scoffed the lead protester.

"What can you say, indeed!" I replied. Personally I could say nothing because I'm completely ignorant about the government of Finland.

The main thing I took away from his protest is that I'd like to be appointed ambassador to Finland. The U.S. ambassador gets to live in a beautiful house along a park overlooking

*I'd learn later that it was Ascension Day, when Finland celebrates Jesus ascending to Heaven. The reason no one could tell me about it is that everyone in Finland is both godless and sensible, so they think this holiday is kind of silly but don't ask questions about a free day off.

the harbor, and the protesters are well behaved, if a little shaggy. I hereby offer my endorsement to any semi-serious candidate who pledges to appoint me to this position.* Once appointed, I swear to learn at least the basics about the government of Finland.

STEVE: The Silja Ferry

Telling a Scandinavian you're going on the overnight Baltic Sea ferry is like telling an American you're going to a bachelor party in Vegas. They wink and nudge you and say, "Have a good time! But not *too* good!" then they laugh hearty Scandinavian laughs.

"Oh, you're going on the Silja ferry?" asked my cabdriver, in mellifluous English. "Yes, that one's quite a party. But the *really* trashy one is Viking. That tends to be more of the

* Our ambassador as of this writing is a woman named Marilyn Ware, who, intriguingly, has donated lots of money to George Bush and the Republican Party.

'teenagers throwing up from having too much to drink' ferry."

Immediately I attempted to change my ticket and get on the Viking line. It was too late.

Not to worry—the Silja line ferry to Stockholm is a plenty ridiculous way to cross a few hundred miles. Aboard, there's a casino, an English pub, several stores, a nightclub, an arcade, conference rooms, regular performances by acrobats, a spa including a Finnish steam bath, all the meatballs, smoked herring, and caviar you can eat, a waterslide, and a thousand of the loudest, drunkest Scandinavians you'll ever encounter. Start drinking in Helsinki at 5:30, stuff yourself at the buffet, gamble, marvel, pass out, and you'll be in Stockholm in the morning.

You would think that such a trip would be fun, but for me it was not, because my travels so far had taught me that it's illuminating to snoop around in the history of a place. When you're floating on the Baltic Sea, that's not a great idea, because the tragedies feel awfully close.

What follows is depressing, so skip it if you must.

The *Estonia*

852 people drowned when the *Estonia*—a Baltic Sea ship not unlike this one, a car-and-people ferry with a resort flare—sank in a storm between Tallinn and Stockholm in 1994.

I heard a story about it from the bartender at the Silja Serenade spa, as I sat in a bathrobe drinking a Lapin Kulta beer after visiting the Finnish steam bath about a hundred miles out on the ocean.

"I was working that night on another ship, and we were the first ones there." The bartender was a middle-aged woman who spoke with long drags on her words, like a friendly vampire. "We picked up only six people, all of them young, strong. They had managed to cling on. It was so hard to keep still, the waves were fifteen meters. We saw the ring, a ring of lights, from the tankers as they started to come and help. It was . . ." she paused—the first time I'd seen a Finnish person search for a word—"like a night . . . dream." An odd thing, she said, was that the next morning the sea was calm. "As though, 'I took my offering. I am quiet.'"

At this point I thought she was going to cry. To change the subject I asked about her dog.

It's hard to party too much or eat too many meatballs after hearing a firsthand account of one of the worst maritime tragedies of the past fifty years.

I spent the rest of the night standing alone at the nightclub bar, topping off my already overfilled liver with a series of gin and tonics as drunken Swedes karaoked "Maggie May" and "Dancing Queen" a few yards behind my left eardrum.

I'm not a smoker, but with me I had a pack of Lucky Strike cigarettes Leila had given me as trading material for my trip. At 2:30 in the morning it seemed like a good idea to smoke some, so I did, standing at the railing, staring at the black Baltic.

As we arrived in Stockholm five hours later, I woke up in my cabin, stinking of gin and tobacco, my mouth a dried-up chalk mine, my body still exhausted.

It was the beginning of the greatest weekend of my life.

STEVE: Stockholm Syndrome

On May 18, 2007, I decided to win a Nobel Prize. If you win the Nobel Prize, they throw you a party in Stockholm. Only a Nobel Prize Party Weekend could possibly be a more fun weekend than the one I'd already had in Stockholm.

You could claim my weekend could be topped, by some Caligulan frenzy of strippers, Gulfstreams, pharmaceuticals, and winning the Super Bowl and an Oscar on the same day. I'd argue that's like claiming that eating a thousand M&Ms is better than really appreciating fifty.

When I got to Stockholm I was badly underweight, foul-smelling, exhausted, carrying everything I had on my back, having just spent two weeks on a ship, and two more crossing Asia the hard way, and a mere three hours sleeping off a thunderous hangover.

Now I found myself in a fairty-tale paradise, an efficiently designed urban archipelago of dazzling architecture, full of luminous ladies and stylish gentlemen, each tall, blond, and looking as though they bicycled fifty kilometers each morning, ate nothing but Kashi, built their own end tables, and were minutes removed from bouts of loving yet experimental sexual intercourse with their sensible partners with whom they have sophisticated arrangements that go beyond marriage.

I can't take a single bit of the credit for the funness of my weekend. Left to my own devices for a weekend in Stockholm, I probably would've ended up in the basement of the National Library pulling crust from my hair and reading the complete works of August Strindberg.

The credit is entirely due to my hosts, Filip and Fredrik.

STEVE: The Story of Filip and Fredrik

If you can read Swedish, you can learn about Filip and Fredrik's absurd adolescence in their memoir *Två nötcreme och en Moviebox* ("Two Nutcreams and a Moviebox"). This book sold something like eight hundred thousand copies, which by my back-of-the-envelope calculation means everybody in Sweden bought five.

Filip and Fredrik met while working together as reporters on a Stockholm tabloid. This was mostly an excuse for them to take expensive jaunts to Los Angeles, sit around the pool of the Standard Hotel, and pretend to interview celebrities. They somehow got cast as TV presenters during the Sydney Olympics. This program was a crazy, *Chevy Chase Show*–level disaster. Then they got another chance and began an unbroken run of Swedish television hits that feature them traveling around the world doing whatever they want. Like, they'll fly to the most idyllic lagoon in the Cook Islands, then attempt to get so drunk that they can't remember it. It is difficult to explain how much the people of Sweden love this schtick.

Over there these guys are as big as Jon Stewart, Conan O'Brien, and the YouTube nunchucks guy put together.

I'd met Filip once before in LA, when our mutual friend Brian introduced us and explained that Filip was famous in Sweden. At that moment hearing a guy was "famous in Sweden" was like hearing he was really good at contract bridge or had six toes on one foot: interesting but meaningless trivia.

Now I was actually in Sweden, where my hosts' pictures were on the front pages of several tabloids.

They had me meet them in the lobby of a hotel. "We're working on our next project," said Fredrik, who speaks English like a waggish Oxford wit. "Sweden's first animated TV show."

At the moment their "working" appeared to consist of drinking Heinekens while showing me pictures of their most recent trip, to the remote mountains of Albania.

"We were testing the idea that a person can have fun anywhere. You can!"

When I asked why they were on the front pages of the tabloids, Filip translated an editorial, which, as I understood it, examined the question of whether these guys were too awesome to be solid Swedish citizens.

"But what do you think, Fredrik," said Filip, who speaks English like the smartest dude at the most degenerate frat at the University of Wisconsin. "Isn't it time we started to party?"

Suddenly the race was put on hold as I got swept into an episode of Swedish *Entourage.*

In the summer, all Swedes party extra-hard to store up fun times for the winter. Filip and his terrific girlfriend, Jennie, go above and beyond. Everywhere we went in Stockholm, we got VIP treatment as local paparazzi snapped our pictures, wondering if I was some weird-looking indie movie star they'd never heard of. I kept being introduced to people, and then it'd be whispered to me that "He directs famous music videos" or "This woman is Sweden's best new model."

Swedish celebrities, by the way, are much smarter and more interesting than American celebrities. American celebrities do nothing but crash cars and proclaim which things are "hot." Compared to them, Swedish celebrities are all poet-scholars who could hold their own at the Algonquin Round Table. A legendary Malmö soccer star or slick-haired Stockholm DJ would give me a beer and then ask me to explain obscure points about the New Hampshire primaries, or get my take on the works of Donald Barthelme.

Then we'd do a shot.

Free-flowing aquavit and expensive champagne mean I can't recall much of what happened that night. A man in a suit told me his "fresh, young, and crispy" theory of women, but I cannot now tell you what "crispy" meant, and find it troubling to consider. I was introduced to a Swedish mogul about whom it was suggested: "This man gives off the air of having exceptionally well-groomed pubic hair, no?" Twelve impossibly charming people appeared from nowhere and swept me into an incredible dinner at a swank restaurant. A model clung to my arm, and my "joke" was that I refused to talk to her, which seems epically stupid in retrospect but which had a logic at the time. I invented some dance moves.

Well into the morning, at a club called maybe Elegance or Sophistique, a bouncer tried to kick Filip out for being too drunk, which he was, but then somebody declared that "for Filip Hammar, there *is* no too drunk!" Somebody, possibly me, poured a bucket of ice over his own head, then I forget what happened, and then I woke up in an überhip hotel owned by Benny Andersson, the genius of ABBA, and there was a pile of ice cream melted into the rug.

All through the night I remember thinking, "I need to sell all my possessions, move to Sweden, become famous, and live the rest of my life like this."

In the morning, however, Puritan Guilt Voice showed up in my brain. "Hey," he said, "you're in a race, jerk. You're not here to have crazy party times."

He was right, of course. "This very minute," he said, "Vali is dashing across Asia, gaining on you!"

"Okay, okay," I replied.

"Good. Now," said Puritan Guilt Voice, "you're here in Sweden for one reason—to go on a blind date—FOR COMEDY PURPOSES ONLY—and that's *it*. So let's get that accomplished and win this race. Now brush your teeth, they're disgusting."

STEVE: 'Holm Is Where the Heart Is

A blind date in Sweden. That's what I'd come up with, when I'd looked at a map of the world and tried to figure out how to win the Awesomeness Contest without costing myself too much time in the race.

Filip and Fredrik understood perfectly. When I'd called them from Russia, Fredrik reported that he'd arranged for me to go out with one Carolina Gynning.

"She was just elected Sexiest Woman in Sweden," he explained, as my eyes cartoonishly exploded out of my head. "She hosts a show on the same network as us. We're trying to convince her that dating you is like Marilyn Monroe marrying Arthur Miller."

Exactly correct. There was no way Vali would top me, disgusting, train-weary, stinking of Mongolian horses and Chinese vomit, splitting a milkshake with the girl who's face was smushed under the mattress of every teenage boy from Ystad to Lapland.

Unfortunately—or so I thought—Carolina Gynning didn't buy this Arthur Miller argument. At the last second a substitute date was found.

If you're thinking about writing a romantic comedy about my blind date in Sweden—and you should—then the tagline to your movie should be this: "There was one thing he didn't plan on: falling in love."

Try to get Zac Ephron to play me.

Her name was Ingrid Svendegaard.* The perfect Swedish name.†

She was Jennie's high school classmate, now a college student studying the art of textiles, which means she knew how to dress really cool. She was blond and bubbly and her laugh was like the song of a little bird.

The success of our date owes a lot to her limited English skills. She adorably confused the words *fun* and *funny*, which alarmed me at first when she kept saying, "We are having a funny time, no?"

Also she had incredibly low expectations. "When they told me I was going on a date with an American man," said Ingrid, "I thought you would be more like the fat man? From *Seinfeld*? Newman?"

I did not look like Newman—weeks of travel had withered my trunk and limbs down to sinewy cords, which sounds repulsive, but this is a look Swedish guys cultivate.

Because I'm a gentleman, I'm going to cut out much of what happened on our date. I'll fill in the gaps with Interesting Trivia About Sweden's Rich History.

We went to a magnificent restaurant and were seated by the harbor. We got to talking about which of us was better at drawing, and decided to settle it by having a contest where we took turns drawing various animals. Ingrid's drawing of a lobster would be enough to win over any sane man. At least any sane man who loves lobster drawings as much as I do, which is above average.

Then we began an earnest conversation about educational systems.

*Not her real name. Also the name I later give for her sister is changed, too.

†Her real name was only slightly less perfect.

INTERESTING TRIVIA ABOUT SWEDEN'S RICH HISTORY, #1

Sweden's King Gustav III had a difficult reign marked by disputes between the comically named Hat Party and Cap Party. In 1792, Gustav was assassinated while attending a masked ball!

We now resume the date in progress—we're still at the restaurant, but we've finished eating.

"OH STOP IT, YOU ARE BEING FUN."

"I'M NOT. I'M FOR SERIOUS, YOU LOOK LIKE KIM CATTRELL, YOU DO, BUT, LIKE, YOUNGER. LESS, YOU KNOW, WITH—THE FACE. HEY, YOU KNOW WHERE WE SHOULD GO?"

(There was no need for us to be shouting in a nice restaurant, but we were.)

"WHERE?"

"KIRUNA! WE SHOULD GO TO KIRUNA!"

"YES! I HAVE NEVER BEEN THERE!"

(Kiruna is a town in the extreme north of Sweden, above the Arctic Circle.)

"WE SHOULD GO TO KIRUNA AND RIDE REINDEER."

(I had heard that at that time of year, that far north, the sun was out twenty-four hours a day, and that even limited exposure to this makes people go crazy. I kinda wanted to try it.)

"YES! OF COURSE THAT IS WHAT WE SHOULD DO! WE WILL GO TO KIRUNA!"

"WE'RE DEFINITELY GOING TO KIRUNA!"

(It takes two days to get to Kiruna.)

"YES! WE WILL GO TO KIRUNA! TOMORROW!"

"TOMORROW!"

"YES! THE MORNING TRAIN!"

"I'LL WRITE IT DOWN SO WE DON'T FORGET!"

(I wrote a document explaining that Ingrid and I would go to Kiruna. We both signed it.)

"WE ARE HAVING SO MUCH FUNNY!"

INTERESTING TRIVIA ABOUT SWEDEN'S RICH HISTORY, #2

In 1628, Sweden was at the height of its power under the reign of King Gustavus Adolfus, who decided to build the world's finest warship, the *Vasa*. He spared no expense, hiring Europe's finest shipwrights. On its triumphant maiden voyage, as crowds of dignitaries proudly looked on, the *Vasa* emerged, proceeded about one mile, tipped over, and sank.

In the 1950s and '60s, engineers raised the well-preserved vessel from the floor of Stockholm harbor, and you can now view the *Vasa* in a specially designed, climate-controlled museum!

We now resume the date—it's sometime around three a.m., the northern sun is already rising. We're in a park outside my hotel on the island of Södermalm, having been kicked out of a taxi.

"YES! OF COURSE I WILL MOVE TO AMERICA WITH YOU!"

(Ingrid had expressed a great love for the United States, which, in her vision, consisted mostly of sassy black waitresses who would pinch her cheeks and give her pie.)

"DONE! YOU'RE MOVING TO AMERICA!"

"I AM MOVING TO AMERICA!"

"IT'S GREAT! YOU'RE GONNA LOVE IT! THERE'S BUFFALO WINGS, AND YOU WON'T BELIEVE HOW MUCH GOOD STUFF IS ON TV! NOW, I LIVE DOWN THE STREET FROM VALI. HE'S THIS JERK I'M RACING AROUND THE WORLD . . ."

A pause here as a practical consideration dawned on me.

"WAIT . . . I don't know if I have enough room in my apartment for your stuff."

Ingrid considered.

"We could put my things on the floor."

It was hard to believe how perfect this woman was.

"YES! THE FLOOR!"

"YES!"

"PERFECT! OKAY! I BETTER CALL MY PARENTS AND TELL THEM YOU'RE COMING. WAIT, NO, WHAT AM I THINKING?! WE'LL JUST SHOW UP! [This part sung to the tune of ABBA's "One Man, One Woman":] *WE'RE MOVING TO AMERICA . . .*"

"Steve?"

"Yes?"

"I do not know where is my shoes."

INTERESTING TRIVIA ABOUT SWEDEN'S RICH HISTORY, #3

In 1810, Sweden needed a new king, and there wasn't any clear candidate. But some Swedish soldiers remembered that one of Napoleon's marshals, a Frenchman named Bernadotte, had seemed like a solid guy. So Bernadotte, who did not speak Swedish, was offered the throne. He accepted and ruled Sweden for thirty-four years. His descendants are the current royal family of Sweden, and from what I hear they're a bunch of fun-loving, fast-driving, sailboat-racing maniacs.

We now conclude the date—it's 11:00 a.m. the following morning.

Ingrid didn't move to America with me. We didn't even make it to Kiruna.

We made it back to Filip's apartment, where she was staying. We ate cucumber and cheese sandwiches. An unwelcome third party was my Puritan Guilt Voice, who reminded me I was in a race. He told me that Ingrid may well be a seductress in Vali's employ. He pointed out if I went to Kiruna, it would cost me a week while Vali was trekking across Asia.

Vali might've reached the Pacific by now. I couldn't stop. It wouldn't be good sportsmanship. He and I had agreed to a challenge. I'd be cheating him, ruining our whole idea, if I let my heart get in the way of it, and stopped moving west.

I needed to dash to Antwerp, and see if I could get on a ship.

Ingrid, for her part, realized that she was supposed to get back to school and take a test on dyes, or something.

So we found her some shoes and then said good-bye. That was the rational thing to do.

What did it matter if I was miserable I'd never see her again? There was the race to consider. Besides, we'd always have almost-Kiruna.

STEVE: The Worst Slum in Sweden

I was worried that I'd gotten a skewed view of Stockholm, because at the moment I considered it a terrestrial paradise filled with only the most beautiful and charming people and things.

So I did one more thing before I left. I asked Filip to direct me to the worst slum in the city.

He sent me to Rinkyby, a long subway ride away. Swedes will tell you that Rinkyby is a morass of crime and poverty and dismal public housing.

Do not believe them. The projects of Rinkyby look like the campus of an expensive college in Vermont. They are clean, well lit, and crisscrossed with tree-lined bike paths. Most of the people there seemed to be Kurdish and Ethiopian immigrants, and that put an end to the one knock I could think of on Sweden, that it's too homogenous. Kids and families were sitting outside, playing soccer, chatting, reading poetry, and contemplating tasteful works of public art. A little girl on a bike—I swear this happened—challenged me to a race, and smiled when she beat me. Within minutes of arriving, some friendly strangers directed me to a delicious Turkish restaurant where I had a heaping bowl of spicy chicken stew.

You do need to be careful in Rinkyby. If you wander too far, as I did, you might end up lost in a beautiful birch grove before emerging into the shade of an old church.

It's hard to imagine Sweden was once a land of frenzied Vikings. These days Swedes seem embarrassed that their ancestors were always raping and chopping heads off instead of, say, going on hikes. Modern Sweden insists on being broad-minded to the point of absurdity. Both men and women get roughly six years of maternity leave. Swedish prisoners are allowed to watch porn in their cells, and they used to be allowed to participate in experimental theater projects until a bunch of incarcerated bank robbers, who'd been let out to appear in a play, decided to use that opportunity to escape.

Swedes will argue with you if you tell them their country is perfect. They will raise complicated points about the stifling nature of their society. They will refer to their national concept of *Jahnteslagen*—which basically means everybody treating each other decently—as though it's a national flaw.

Do not believe them. They're crazy. Or else they're being modest. Because they're perfect. Because they're Swedish.

STEVE: Bad Times on the High Atlantic!, or, The Incredible, Heroic Ocean Journey I Made, Just Ahead of Vali, to Seal My Race Victory!

The *M. V. Independence* left Liverpool on May 25 and took twelve days to cross the Atlantic through heavy seas before arriving in Philadelphia on June 5.

But I can't really tell you any more about it, because I wasn't on it.

I can, however, tell you about the town of Borås, Sweden. It's on the western side of the country, about a four-and-a-half-hour drive from Stockholm, and it's home to the Textilhögskola, the Swedish School of Textiles. There is a courthouse, a small zoo, and a picturesque old water tower, and the whole place appears to be surrounded by pine forests.

There's no reason to go there. Unless you're about to leave Stockholm, and Ingrid Svendegaard says there's an extra seat in her friend's car, and if you're up for the road trip, she'd be happy to put you up in her apartment and spend the next day showing you the sights of her hometown.

"Of course," said Ingrid, "in the car you will have to be squeeze between me and my sister. Ilsa. She is nineteen."

I thought about the race for one minute.

I'm ashamed of that minute. When it was over I said "screw it" and got in the car.

If Vali beat me to the Victory Scotch because I went to Borås, fine. I could explain this one to my grandchildren with pride.

So I rode in the back with Ingrid and Ilsa as their friends Leonard and Erik took turns driving the Volvo and we listened to the Fugees. On the shores of Lake Vättern we ate meatballs and watched the sun go down over the water, and Leonard made a valiant effort to play some Fugees songs on his nose flute.

The next day Ingrid and I ate lunch, and went to the zoo, and had coffee with her friends, and did nothing else very exciting. It was the best day ever.

I knew enough not to ruin it by sticking around. Before long, her English or my Swedish would sharpen up, and we might realize we weren't actually soul mates.

So that night I kissed Ingrid good-bye as I raced for the last train out of town.

We live in an age where you easily obtain chemicals that will flood your brain with pure serotonin, thus overloading your pleasure receptors, and while this is happening you can sit in an ergonomically designed massage chair, eating twelve kinds of ice cream at one time, rubbing yourself with grapefruit-kiwi body lotion, listening to Sam Cooke through Bose headphones while going on the Internet and examining any sort of video that might interest you from an infinity of options.

Whatever. I've done at least half of those things. And kissing a girl as you run for the evening train is better than that.

I was used to the trains of Russia and China, where the toilets are mere holes onto the tracks. So after I used the futuristic hygiene chamber I found now, I felt obliged to comment on it to the bespectacled woman working on her laptop across from me.

"Hey! Pretty snazzy bathrooms on this train! It's not just a hole!" I said.

She stared at me, perplexed. "But—of course," she said. "You're in Sweden."

VALI: Trying to See the Most Famous Belly Dancer in Cairo

I called ahead and booked a table at the Haroun al-Rashid nightclub at the Semiramis InterContinental Hotel. The voice on the other end of the phone confirmed what I was hoping: Dina would be performing that night.

These days, the best belly dancers in Cairo perform exclusively at the city's fanciest hotels. The dancers are apparently pretty renowned, but the hotels still attach "Famous" to their names when describing them: the Famous Dina, the Famous Soraya. So they're not so famous you'd know them without being reminded that they're famous.

I had never really thought much of belly dancing before. But maybe I had never seen good belly dancing. Maybe it was like how I thought I hated meat loaf because the only meat loaf I had ever tasted was from the school cafeteria. Then, one night, I had homemade meat loaf at a friend's house and discovered that the stuff could be incredibly delicious. Maybe belly dancing is the meat loaf of dancing—below a certain level it's crap but when good it's amazing.

The al-Rashid was a nightclub in the Rat Pack sense of the word. There weren't girls dancing in cages, fifteen kinds of superpremium vodka behind the bar, or a blacklight-lit dance floor. There wasn't even a visible bar. It was more of a white tablecloth joint where well-dressed tourists and wealthy locals smoked cigarettes and watched the onstage entertainment.

Since I was alone, I was relegated to the side of the viewing area. Large groups and loud men with more money than me generally got the best seats. To get a worse seat than I did one would probably have to have several open and bubbling wounds.

But for some reason the most important guest that night, a large Arab man dressed in slacks and a short-sleeve button-down shirt, chose to sit at the table next to mine. I had no idea who he was or what he did, but within ten minutes of sitting down every employee of the nightclub came by to shake his hand. Then every item on the menu was brought to his table. He ate what he wanted and sent what he didn't want back to the kitchen. It seemed like more of a hassle than simply ordering off a menu, but the nightclub was determined to treat this guy differently from everyone else.

Two cute Japanese girls on vacation sat nearby. I shifted the position of my chair to make sure they could see me.

VALI: What I Was Aiming For

I took a long drag off my cigarette before resting it on the edge of the ashtray. Then I swirled the cheapest scotch on the nightclub's menu around in my tumbler before taking a small contemplative sip. *Ahh life,* I thought.

"I notice you were sitting alone, writing in a notebook." I looked up to find the cuter of the Japanese girls. She licked her lips and continued: "Do you have some sort of book deal?"

VALI: What Ended Up Happening

The Japanese girls giggled like Japanese girls in movies do as the Important Arab Guy, who by then had started drinking the most expensive scotch on the nightclub menu, charmingly teased them, then invited them to sit at his table.

I continued drinking alone.

Finally, around one a.m., the show started.

It wasn't Dina. It was the opening act, a cheesy Egyptian version of Ricky Martin. His hair was slicked back and he wore a form-fitting white T-shirt along with some sort of Franken-jeans—a pair of blue jeans that looked like they were sewn together from a bunch of ripped up, murdered blue jeans. If you're wondering whether the Egyptian Ricky Martin liked to come offstage and dance on people's tables, the answer is yes. If you're wondering if the Egyptian Ricky Martin liked to snap his fingers while charismatically singing and thrusting his pelvis around the room, the answer is yes. If you're wondering if the Egyptian Ricky Martin's enthusiasm was matched by approximately twenty-five male backup dancers with tambourines, the answer is yes.

And not all tambourine-playing Egyptian male backup dancers are created equal. Two stood out from the pack. One was medium height and lithe-bodied and the other was medium height and fat. Every once in a while, during the chaos that comes with unchoreographed dancing, they would end up next to each other and for a split second it would look like the number 10 was dancing.

The function of the backup dancers was to make the entire nightclub experience as interactive as possible. They pulled people out of their seats and into the aisles. At one point the skinny member of the energetic duo, the number 1, brought his skeletal face six inches from mine and started shaking it back in forth rapidly, much faster than the beat of the music, as if he had been suddenly possessed by a poltergeist. This was supposed to make me dance. It did not.

At first this was entertaining. After an hour, it grew tiresome. For me, at least. The Japanese girls were dancing in the aisles and Important Arab Guy snapped his fingers with his hands in the air.

Finally, shortly after two a.m., the opening act ended. Then the lights came on and people slowly started getting up. What was going on?

"What happened to Dina?" I asked my waiter.

"Since everyone was having fun and the opening act went

long, the Famous Dina will not be dancing tonight. I hope you enjoyed the show."

No, I did not enjoy the show! It was terrible! They canceled the main act because the Egyptian Ricky Martin and his twenty thieves played too long? I wanted to see the best belly dancer in Cairo!

"Dina will be dancing again tomorrow," explained my waiter.

Again? Don't act like she danced today. *If* she dances at all tomorrow, she won't be dancing *again*. She'll just be dancing.

Why was I the only person angry about this? Why wasn't everyone lighting their chairs on fire and throwing them at the stage?

Before leaving I vowed never to patronize an InterContinental Hotel for the rest of my life.

VALI: Thoughts on Foreign Cabbies

Tired and angry I stormed out of the hotel and flagged down a cab in the street. After nearly five weeks of traveling, I had learned the two most important skills shared by cabdrivers around the world. The first is their ability to summon up a face of pure bewilderment whenever necessary. I usually saw this face just after offering the proper price for a journey. The driver's eyes would widen with amazement and his brow would furrow with sorrow—amazement that my feeble brain would have trusted whatever source provided me with the wildly low estimate and sorrow that I had been lied to regarding fair taxi pricing. The second most important skill is their ability to confidently state that they are not lost while making their fourth U-turn in the middle of traffic.

In Cairo, proper taxi etiquette is to give the driver your destination then pay a fair price when you are dropped off. Pricing is rarely discussed during the course of the ride. If the driver brings up pricing, tourists are advised to firmly name a fair price.

After we had driven a mile toward my hotel, the taxi driver eyed me in the rearview mirror and asked, "How much?"

"Twenty pounds," I told him. The real price, including tip, was fifteen, but I was so fed up by the Dina fiasco I was willing to pay extra to avoid haggling.

"Thirty pounds," the driver countered.

"I know the price is fifteen pounds."

"Okay. Fifteen pounds for taxi and fifteen pounds for tip."

You win, I wanted to scream. You win, I hate Cairo. Not even the beauty of the pyramids and the serenity of the mosques make dealing with the Egyptian hustler worth it.

"Twenty pounds total," I insisted.

"Twenty pounds for taxi and ten pounds for tip."

"Pull over the taxi!" I yelled. I had no idea where we were. Thankfully the taxi driver ignored me and kept hustling.

"Twenty pounds for taxi and ten pounds for tip," he repeated.

I was beaten. What could I do? I was already in the cab and it was after two a.m. I was powerless. I agreed to the price, then stewed for the rest of the ride.

It wasn't the money. Another ten Egyptian pounds was less than two dollars. It was the constant assault on my dignity, the manhandling, that infuriated me.

By the time we reached my hotel I had worked myself into a fury. I handed the taxi driver fifteen pounds total and stormed out of the car.

He started yelling at me. What was his goal, I wondered? Did he expect hotel employees to think that the *tourist* was cheating the *taxi driver*? Good luck, pal. I calmly walked into my hotel and up to my room. I wasn't proud, but I felt strangely happy. Every once in a while it feels nice to say, *No, screw you.*

VALI: The Pyramids, Part II: Avenging Baksheesh

I awoke the next morning feeling terrible. I had let a bad day affect my attitude. Yes, I was getting hustled. Yes, it was annoying. But I hadn't even tried to understand what was going on.

When I thought about it, the aggression of the hustlers started to make sense. They were relatively poor and I, with my dollars, was relatively rich. Plus the unemployment rate in Egypt was 11 percent, more than double that of the United States. Which meant there were many more street hustlers competing for every tourist dollar.

It should be noted that when I strayed away from the tourist areas, when I just allowed myself to get lost in Cairo, nobody tried to rip me off. The Egyptian man running the convenience stand charged me the normal price for a bottle of Coca-Cola. The cabdriver I found near the cemetery, where Cairo's poorest live among the graves, gave me more change back than I asked for.

It was the Egyptians who sought out the tourist spots, the ones who interacted with the most foreigners, who offended me so much. But there's an old saying that goes, Click click click click clack click. Eventually man developed language and that saying became, "Don't judge another man until you've walked a mile in his shoes." You would think judges would find this advice especially useful. But I've never even heard of one of those lazy bums requesting a defendant's shoes.

If I was going to understand the Cairo hustler, I decided, I needed to become one. So I went out and bought myself some Egyptian clothes, combed my hair like the men I saw in the streets, purchased half a dozen Sphinx figurines, and headed back to the pyramids.

I wanted to feel the feelings of the hustler. I expected to first feel enthusiastic, then slowly grow resentful.

Why are you ignoring me, I would think. *I am simply*

trying to earn money so I can get married and support a family. I'm sorry my father wasn't a rich businessman who could give me a job after I drank my way through college. I need to work to live and with 11 percent unemployment I don't have a ton of options. So please, nice foreigners, take a look at my Sphinx figurines. They make great gifts and souvenirs! Why are you still walking? No. No. Don't look at that guy's Sphinx figurines. Are you serious? I can't believe that worked. He was being annoying for chrissakes! Wait, here comes another one. Hello, my friend!

It turns out the same hustlers work the pyramids every day. They know one another, they know the cops, and the cops know them. So when I showed up with my white towel, six Sphinx figurines, and LOW PRICE GUARANTEE: WE WILL NOT BE UNDERSOLD sign (written on papyrus), I attracted some unkind attention from the other hustlers. They took a momentary break in harassing tourists to stare at me. The cops did the same. But nobody made a move.

Once set up, I sat back and waited. I was sure my professionalism and people skills would earn at least a few sales. The first group of tourists passed by without even looking at me. Maybe I needed to be a smidgen more aggressive. A second group of tourists, all Japanese, approached. "Hello, my friend!" I greeted them. They didn't break stride.

This is when I expected the resentment to begin. Instead, I was elated. Yes! Ignore the annoying Egyptian hustler. A victory for the tourists!

A white couple approached. "Souvenir, madame?" I asked. Her earflap-hat-wearing husband stepped between the two of us and they kept walking.

Another victory for the tourists!

By this point, the other hustlers must have figured out what was going on. A few of them, including one on camelback, had gathered to watch me. Once my ineptitude became clear, they found my performance incredibly amusing.

A busload of tourists passed by, none even stopping to inspect my wares. My sales ability was too pitiful for the

Egyptian hustlers to bear. The camel driver yelled out, "Buy from him, he is Egyptian!"

But it was no use. I didn't have the ability to really get in people's faces and smooth talk them into paying for something they didn't want. I didn't have the hunger to sell.

I wrapped up my figurines and made my way down to the café at the foot of the Sphinx. I had sold zero souvenirs. On my way, I passed a young European backpacker buying a book of postcards from a smiling hustler. "Danke Schön," he thanked her.

VALI: It's Complicated

From the café I could see the Sphinx in the foreground, the pyramids in the background, and the rusty desert sand everywhere else. I sipped on a mango juice and thought about leaving Cairo. It felt weird. Cairo was the most frustrating city I'd ever visited in my entire life. But I also didn't want to leave. It was like being hazed before joining a fraternity. The work I had to do to get past the unpleasantness made the benefits—the culture, the pyramids, the Nile—seem much more wonderful.

After finishing my juice, I noticed a group of local kids behind me. They crowded around a table of bussed dishes. Their tiny six-year-old hands were reaching up and grabbing unfinished food off the plates and shoving it into their mouths. Every few minutes a waiter would shoo them away. Thirty seconds later they would return for scraps of shrimp, saffron rice, cold fruit juices, spiced lamb kebabs, fresh hummus, and whatever else diners had left on their plates uneaten.

I hadn't noticed the children at first because the neediness they represented was commonplace in Egypt. I had steeled myself for traveling through the third world. I had trained myself not to see.

Chances are these kids will not grow up to be doctors or lawyers or captains of industry. They might learn a trade or they might grow up to become hustlers like the ones operating up the hill, under the hot sun, next to the trophies of a powerful civilization now gone and visited by tourists from the new powerful civilizations.

I'd like to think next time I hear "Hello, my friend" and someone tries to charge me five dollars for a Coca-Cola, instead of getting angry I'll think of these kids and the circumstances that produced the offending hustler. But, honestly, in the heat of the moment, I'll probably forget about all the advantages I've been handed in life and start cursing.

STEVE: How Things Stood in Malmö

Improbably, the bar in the train station in Malmö, Sweden, is Boston Red Sox–themed. It was here that I planned my next stage.

The best move for me now in the race was to forget about freighters and make my way to England to catch the *Queen Mary 2*, the fastest transatlantic ship in the world, running from Southampton to New York in six days, earning me back some time.

But the *QM2* wasn't sailing until June 4. Between me and it was Europe—a magnificent salad bar of a continent—and a week and a half of empty days.

I could've sat around for those days, sleeping and nursing my blisters, or at least making a topographical map of their various ranges and valleys. That would've been wrong. When this race was finished, I'd have to account for those days to Vali. He was my worthy opponent, and I believed I owed it to him as one honorable athlete owes it to another to compete vigorously, strenuously, and fairly. And I'd have to account for those days to myself. I was twenty-seven and I had ten days to make my way westward doing whatever I wanted, a stupidly good chance for comical adventures. If I blew it now then I'd deserve every fitful sleepless night in a run-down nursing home fifty years down the road. And I'd have to account for those days to you, Reader, who probably doesn't want to hear about me sitting around in Sweden rubbing ointment on my feet.

So consider these pages an accounting for a week and a half in Europe. Let's see how I did!

STEVE: The European Awesomeness Tour: An Accounting

I slept through Denmark on the train. Not a great start.

I woke up in Berlin, and spent just enough time there to try to find Hitler's bunker. The Germans I asked responded with a range of awkward politeness and detailed instructions. As I understand it, it's now a children's playground. Maybe the world improves. Then it was on to Munich.

In Munich hangs *The Four Apostles*, by Albrecht Dürer, and it's the single best painting in Europe—at least according to Professor Martin Kemp of Oxford University. He's the only one of about fifty art historians who responded to my e-mail query about what one painting I should see if I were racing across the continent in a hurry, although after my attempt at a free Chinese history lesson it's possible my e-mails are blocked at most universities.

Professor Kemp has written about *The Four Apostles* and why it's an astounding human achievement. To his writings I can add nothing, except to say that I stared at it, unbored, for one solid hour, while thinking, *A guy took two hunks of wood and put this painting on it.* Remember that the hunks of wood had NO painting on them until Dürer showed up.

Then my hour was up and I rented a car—ideally it would've been a Mercedes, but for some reason (the amount of money I was willing to pay) they gave me a Ford Fusion. Fine, that's funnier anyway.

I drove south across Austria. I drove over—or rather through and around—the Alps. I kept seeing places and deciding, "There! That is it. That is the perfect valley. There

Nature has created a more perfect valley than my mind could imagine." Ditto "mountain," "lake," "stream," and "cottage," and "cow." I passed gloomy crumbling castles where they once tortured infant duchesses.

I crossed into Italy, and in a town cut into the mountains called Bozen I stopped to wait out a thunderstorm. I had coffee beside an elderly Italian man in a suit whose hand shook as he fussed over the papers and dribbled espresso from his mouth, while the indifferent barkeep rubbed his own filthy and unshaven face. I stared out into the rain as gloriously proportioned women in tightly fitted business suits jockeyed past one another on Vespas.

Through the Dolomite Mountains my drive got especially exquisite, because storm clouds smeared the sky. It was catch as catch can radio-wise up there, but just as lightning was describing itself across a valley, Eric Clapton's "Layla" came through. "Not bad, radio," I said. I talked to my radio a lot during this drive. Also sometimes I pretended I was a heroic pilot escaping from a Nazi POW camp in a stolen 1944 Ford Fusion.

I had a guidebook to Italy, but on principle I decided that using a guidebook in Italy was cheating. Better just to fumble along and see what happens. That night I stopped when I saw a sign for Verona, because I remembered hearing that name—didn't two guys come from there, or something?

It turns out Verona is where Shakespeare set *Romeo and Juliet*. This is kind of an odd claim to fame, because Shakespeare never visited there. But it turns out Shakespeare was pretty good at imagining stuff, because the streets of Verona are ancient and narrow and arched over by balconies, and you could totally see yourself—*ROMEO AND JULIET* SPOILER ALERT—drinking poison over the corpse of your lover in this very city. Over Campari sodas I asked three different bartenders for the best trattoria in town. I knew which one was correct because inside were swaths of Italians cramming bread into their gaping maws.

After my meal (I ordered using a prepared note written in Italian that said "Bring me the best thing you have, please. I am a worldly gourmand"), I was exhausted again. The main point of Italian cooking is to exhaust the eater.

The next morning, as I drove out of Verona, I put on a CD called *Drive-Time Italian.* A good 30 percent of this CD is devoted to stressing very emphatically that you should *not* attempt to write out the workbook exercises while driving. This must've been a problem, and possibly a very funny lawsuit. The only Italian I learned was "I have a car" and "There is a car," phrases that can take you only so far in conversation.

By the way, if you want to forget about a girl in Sweden, go to Italy. In Ravenna, in the time it took me to get gas, espresso, and a salami sandwich, I fell in love with three different girls and fell into at least semiuncomfortable man-crush territory with one guy. He's the only one I talked to. He was dressed all in black, wearing the coolest sunglasses I'd ever seen, and I asked him if I could take his picture so that later, back in America, I could copy his entire style. He gave me the only response such a man would possibly give, which was that I could do whatever the hell I wanted provided it didn't interfere with his smoking a cigarette.

One thing that you don't have to worry about on the Autostrada in Italy is getting stuck behind some old granny who's driving too slowly. In Italy that granny guns past you in a souped-up Maserati at 125 kph while suggesting with her hands what you do with your butt.

Just to prove to myself that you can't go wrong in Italy, I got off the highway and drove narrow roads up into the hills. Sure enough, before long I found myself staying at a farmhouse in a tiny village by an immaculate lake, being fed mountains of pasta and lamb cooked over an open fire and all the red wine I could drink, which was a lot.

I drove down the Adriatic coast, past Rimini, which seems to be the Jersey shore of Italy. That was surprising, because I'd thought the Jersey shore of Italy was the Jersey shore. But Rimini offers all the trashy condos, minigolf, terrible pizza, and hairy dudes stuffed in mesh T-shirts that we've come to love over here.

Then I left Italy for about twenty minutes. I went to a

lot of countries on this trip, but San Marino is the only country I'm willing to call "silly." I'm qualified to say this because I saw with my own eyes at least 45 percent of the entire nation.

The republic of San Marino consists of a big mountain on Italy's eastern coast. If you are wondering why or how San Marino became its own country, don't ask anyone in San Marino. "Why?!" said the hotel bartender I asked. He said this as though I'd just asked why birds poop or why people like *The Price Is Right.* "Why its own country? Because it is, from old times!" With that he scoffed and walked away.

Maybe he was right. The whole idea of "Italy" is strange enough: a cobbled-together bunch of fiefdoms that's had something like forty governments since World War II. Why is anything anything, really? On the way to San Marino I'd passed a cemetery for Ghurkas—Nepalese soldiers who'd died in Italy on behalf of the British who were fighting the Germans in a war that started because Germany invaded Poland. If you start thinking about why *that* is, there's no end to it. Better just to drink your Peroni and stare out the window at the roof down the hillside where a woman is sunbathing topless.

The important thing about this detour is that San Marino *is* its own country, and "an active player in the international community," as the U.S. State Department Web site puts it. I'd stopped there because Vali and I had a side wager: $500 on who would visit the most countries. San Marino counts.*

Driving south, the Adriatic Sea was out my window. Across it lay Bosnia, Croatia, and Albania. Filip had suggested I visit these places. He'd also suggested I visit Greenland, Svalbard, Nigeria, Kazakhstan, North Korea, Tibet, "the *real* Finland," and Papua New Guinea. Great ideas, all, but instead I decided to see some relatives.

*I'd end up winning, 15–14.

STEVE: The European Excellence Tour: Volpe Family Reunion

Louis Volpe is a retired granite quarryman/high school history teacher/football coach. There's nothing remarkable about him, except that he's kindly and hilarious, everyone loves him, he sings imaginary Italian operas, claims to speak Finnish, and grows deformed zucchini. Also he's my grandfather. And *his* father, my great-grandfather, was born in a village in Italy called Introdacqua. This village is in Abruzzo, a rural mountainous country that's sort of the Ozarks of Italy, but with homemade red wine instead of moonshine.

I'd never met any of my Italian relatives—anyone still in Italy is pretty far out there on the family tree. But I had a note with me in English and Italian, which said this: *Hello, my name is Steve Hely. Luigi Volpe was my mother's father's father. He was born in this village. I have come here from the United States to buy a drink for anyone who is related to me.*

After taking several wrong turns, roads that ended by bumping into rockslides or fading into brambles, I found Introdacqua on a Saturday morning. The whole place wasn't much bigger than your average American movie theater. It was a spiderweb of tight-squeezed streets and cracked stone steps that looked like they'd been there for a thousand years. Italy is paradise for historic staircase hobbyists.

It is not hard in any town in Italy to find a bar with several old men hanging around the way American old men hang around at the hardware store. I walked in, and presented the bartender with my note. He read it, and laughed, and then summoned the Council of Hanging Around Old Men with Nothing to Do.

They were very grateful for the excitement I provided and made the most of it. There followed about half an hour of emphatic chattering in brusk hill-Italian, which sounded like this: "*Stada de vadi esca Volpe?! Esto filanchato birigagiatta besteni! Eh Volpe!*" [WILD WAVING OF HANDS.]

Sometimes one of the old men would ask me, in Italian, to clarify a point, to which I would respond *"Cè una machina."* ("There is a car.") Sometimes they'd examine my nose or chin, in case there might be some clues there. Genealogical tables were scrawled on the margins of sports pages.

Finally they decided to find the one guy in town who could speak English, a plumber. He arrived and received a twenty-minute debriefing, which he translated to me as "They-eh, don't know anything." The problem being that just about everybody in Introdacqua is named "Volpe."

Another fifteen minutes of yammering and hand waving and scrawled genealogy and face examining. Then somehow the line of descent was figured out. The plumber and I got in my car and we drove up into the hills. He led me a few miles out of town to an overgrown farm, and urged me on as I forced the Fusion down a muddy path.

At the end of it was a broken-down tractor that looked as though it had been made fifty years ago from leftover pieces of a sewing machine. A toothless man with huge meaty hands and a scrawny assistant were viciously battering this unfortunate tractor with feet and tools.

The plumber and I got out of the car. There followed a ten-minute discussion in Italian, which sounded to me like the bitterest argument I'd ever heard, and I assumed it would end in murder, but it ended instead when the plumber pointed at the toothless man and said, "This man is your grandfather's second cousin." My relative embraced me with his giant mitts. "You gonna eat with him," said the plumber.

So it was that I ended up having lunch with my grandfather's second cousin Pepino. Also Pepino's wife, and their Romanian hired woman who was in charge of Pepino's mother-in-law, who was at least a hundred and seventy years old and not well, and existed as a pair of white eyes emerging from a pile of blankets on a chair. Conversation was vigorous, but I understood not a word except sometimes Pepino would point at me and say "Volpe?" and I would say "Volpe!" and he would pound the table with joy.

I was then force-fed mounds of pasta and stewed beef,

and barely powered through without collapsing. Just when I was finished, Pepino's wife presented me with a lump of homemade sheep ricotta the size of a fat baby's head.

"Mange!"

Heroically I forced my trembling arm to cut off a sliver and shove it in my mouth as I said, "Oh my yes it's very good thank you."

This was not adequate. Pepino's wife leaned over me and pointed at the cheese. "MANGE *TUTTI*!"

"All! Eat all!" translated the Romanian hired lady.

"All! Tutti!" said Pepino's wife.

"Volpe!" shouted Pepino.

"Volpe!" I said, as I attacked the cheese softball and he pounded the table in glee and poured us all more wine.

Eating this lunch was the most exhausting physical challenge of my life, and I was incredibly relieved when I'd survived it, until I realized that Pepino was putting his boots on, and leading me to my car, and it dawned on me that he was taking me to more relatives, and that these relatives were also going to make me eat.

Second Lunch was at another farm up the road, and it was already crowded when Pepino and I arrived. He pounded the floor with his cane, and the table of twenty or so looked up as he pointed at me and said something like *"Chetrada mistondo britiaga illa che'ta VOLPE!"*

And at the magic syllables I was somehow lofted across the table and into the arms of an elderly matroness who squealed with delight and smushed my face into her ample bosom, held it there until I was purple with near-smothering, then lifted me by the hair and forced my face into a platter of the finest meats and cheeses in all Abruzzo.

At Second Lunch there were a number of Volpes who could speak English, and they started figuring out the family tree. For a minute they got stuck. It appeared that maybe I'd stumbled into the wrong line of Volpes. Confusion grew. All bosom smotherings were put on indefinite hold until my lineage could be confirmed. I began to get worried I'd be put in Italian jail for accepting cheese under false pretenses.

One of the Second Lunchers said that in 1960 he'd visited Quincy, Massachusetts.

"You had a great-aunt, Philomena, who was always trying to make me do the dishes! She had big arms and she was a tough lady!"

"Yup," I said, because this was a precise description of Auntie Phil. Table pounds, wine pouring, bosom smothering, and forced consumption of cheese followed for several hours.

Finally, at the end of the lunch, somebody asked me how I'd gotten here. "Did you come just to see us?"

"No, not really."

"So, you flew to Italy to have a vacation?"

"Well, not quite, I was kinda in the neighborhood . . ."

"You're on business?"

"Well . . . sort of."

"You come just to Italy, or other countries?"

"Well . . . a bunch of countries."

"Where did you fly in?"

"Um, nowhere, actually."

(Confusion, wine pouring.)

"How did you get here?"

In my cheese-fever I thought about this, tracing my path back through Sweden and Russia, Siberia and Mongolia, across China and the Pacific, back to Los Angeles. Then I went further back in time, back to Boston, through my mother, and my grandfather, and toothless Pepino, who was somehow part of it, part of the thread, anyway, that came back here to Introdacqua, one of infinitely forking threads that stretched back to Ireland and France and wherever else—probably with a stop in Genghis Khan's loins.

"Well . . . it's a long story."

STEVE: Rome Is Where the Art Is

I had time to tell my whole story the next day. I was going to Rome, and so was my mom's third cousin and his soon-to-be second wife, so I was pressed into service driving them to the airport.

I didn't end up telling my story, because my mom's third cousin spent the four-hour drive delivering a monologue/one-act performance piece about his own life, which also included a digression on the art of mushroom hunting, a thorough analysis of the real estate business in Ohio, anecdotes about elderly relatives of mine, some scandalous suggestions about what I'd been doing the night before with some Irish women whom I'd encountered,* and several sung arias, unprompted singing of Italian opera apparently being a genetic trait in the Volpe clan.

I drove on, with my mom's third cousin constantly offering me a mortadella sandwich, which I kept refusing, because I was determined to say no to at least one piece of food in Italy.

Finally, we reached Rome.

STEVE: A Stern Warning

Back at the tourist office in the Munich train station, I overheard a woman speaking in what I correctly guessed was Boston-accented German. She told me she was from Revere, I told her I was from Needham, we talked for a while about Kelly's Roast Beef, and then I asked for advice.

"I'm about to rent a car."

"Oh, driving in Germany's no problem—people drive fast, but they're safe."

"Well, I'm also going to Italy."

She sucked air across her teeth. "Italy's a different story." She looked me over. "Well, you've driven in Boston, right?"

"Yup."

"You've driven on Storrow?"

"Yup."

* Improbably, the most happening spot in Sulmona, Italy, is an Irish pub called Gallagher's. This allowed me to drink Guinness in Italy, which, genetically, is exactly what I'm built for.

"In rush hour?"

"Oh yes."

"That's as bad as anyplace, I guess. If you can handle Storrow, you can handle Italy. Just be very, very careful. Where are you headed?"

"Up into the hills," I said. "And then to Rome."

At this she grabbed both my arms. "No," she said. "*NO.*" She gripped my arms so hard I still have bruises. Little flames appeared in her eyes.

"Whatever you do, *Whatever* happens—do *not* drive in Rome. Drive in Sicily, drive in Florence, hell, drive in *Naples*—but do not—DO NOT—drive in Rome."

It was too late now.

There are no traffic laws in Rome. There's a vague agreement that right-of-way goes to the coolest car, but you're welcome to challenge this. Most drivers are having running conversations with two or three other drivers, exchanging wine and deli meats across lanes. Vespas zip around, sliding off the road to take shortcuts through buildings. Several scooters rode over the Fusion, and I'm pretty sure at least one guy managed to slide under me at one point. The "roads" are any space between fountains, statues, and buildings into which you can wedge your car. The only thing that ever stops traffic is a beautiful woman passing by, at which point people start honking and applauding and crashing into one another in celebration. Full eleven man teams play soccer midtraffic.

Add to all this that my mom's third cousin insisted I get a tour of the city, so as I tried to needle the Fusion around without killing anybody or destroying any second-century monuments, he would holler out directions, except that he had no idea where anything was, so he was going on gut and whatever he could find out from yelling out the window. Also half the streets were closed on account of a parade.

Those who've been in traumatic situations, like combat or a plane crash, often speak of how their brain and senses shut down and they enter a kind of hypnotic trance state. This is what happened to me in Rome. Suddenly I entered a mystic state, beyond consciousness—what Zen monks call "perfect emptiness." I felt that the Fusion and I became one being, seamless, and without fear we moved as one past fruit stands, under laundry lines, around screaming nuns.

When I came to, I was neatly parallel parked, on a quiet, tree-lined street overlooking the Colosseum, and I believe the feeling I had was exactly what victorious gladiators felt. My mom's third cousin and his soon-to-be second wife looked at me with the awe and dread and fascination one feels when in the presence of the supernatural. My shirt was soaked with sweat and my face had a beatific smile.

"I think I'll have that sandwich now," I said.

STEVE: The Wonders of Western Civilization, Summarized

I stood in line for the Sistine Chapel, wedged between some Australian teachers and the most bratty, obnoxious family of Americans I've ever encountered, at home or abroad: a three-sister, two-parent team of fat shrieking harpies who spent four hours demanding ice cream from one another and making a list of what things in Rome smelled the worst (these folks weren't a bucket of rose petals themselves). Meanwhile the sun got hotter and hotter, and my crotch itched, but it seemed rude to scratch it in the Holy See, so that was an ongoing issue. This was four hours of joyless misery, and just when I'd concluded, ultimately, that the Sistine Chapel could not be worth it—I could see the damn thing on the Internet—they let me in. Somehow I ended up taking a wrong turn into a utility hallway or something, so that I came out a side door on the altar, extended-finger distance from Michelangelo's painted fresco.

"Oh, right," I thought, "it's worth it."

VALI: A Thought That Made Me Smile

It had been six days since Steve and I had met in Moscow. The train journey from Moscow to London, where I assumed Steve would board the vessel for his transatlantic voyage, takes less than three days. I figured Steve would spend a little additional time recuperating and taking in the sights of Europe. But I didn't expect him to lollygag long.

As I flew from Cairo to Amman, I imagined Steve at a port in London, contemplating suicide to get him out of another mind-blowingly boring travel stint. The salty smell of the ocean air, a reminder of his recently completed trans-Pacific journey, must have made him nauseous. He was probably crying as he took notes, assessing the seaworthiness of his ship, as if that was a thing anybody cared about in 2007.

VALI: Discovering Pleasant Differences Between Jordan and Egypt

I landed in Amman without enough money to purchase my Jordanian visa. No problem, I thought. I'll just withdraw some money from an ATM. It turned out it was a problem because all of the ATM machines were located beyond passport control. In other words, I needed a visa to withdraw the money I needed to buy a visa. These are the sorts of problems Marco Polo never had to deal with. His assistants probably obtained all his necessary visas in advance.

Thankfully the immigration officials eventually allowed an armed police officer to escort me to the ATM machine. Even though I wasn't handcuffed, I walked with my hands clasped behind my back as if I was. I wanted everyone who saw me and my armed escort to think I was some sort of awesome internationally wanted man—the sort of guy who did away with his enemies by forcing them to gorge themselves to death on fine caviar. Ideally, I would have been wearing aviator sunglasses, but my pair was in my checked luggage wrapped in a pair of sweaty underpants.

After withdrawing some cash I offered my armed escort five Jordanian dinars as a thank-you/post-action bribe. He angrily refused.

Honest and trustworthy cops! After Belarus and Russia and Egypt, I didn't think I would ever see the species again.

I wanted to hug him. Feelings like that are probably why I'll never be an awesome internationally wanted man.

VALI: What I Feared Was a Trap Turns Out to Be Guidance

After leaving the airport I went straight to the hotel with the hippest bar in Amman, the Howard Johnson.

Every Howard Johnson motel (or HoJo as the company refers to itself) I've ever seen in the United States was a no-frills basic orange-roofed place to sleep.

The Howard Johnson Amman was nothing like that. It was a massive space with multiple restaurants and two bars, the larger of which was the Courtyard Lounge. The social center of the lounge was a soccer pitch–sized expanse of turf dotted with beanbags and low tables. A half-hour-long Arab fashion TV show ran in a loop on a large projector screen toward the front of the Astroturf. A small group of college students, both male and female, some in traditional Muslim dress, others in jeans and polo shirts, smoked sheesha and drank tea while chatting and watching Middle Eastern models strut down a catwalk.

Then things got weird.

"Did you see the last episode of *American Dad*?" I heard one of the Arab students ask another. *American Dad* is an animated FOX television show about an overzealous CIA agent engaged in the war on terror. It is also the television show Steve writes for.

Was this some sort of trap? Did Steve somehow know

where I was and arrange for me to be messed with? No. That was impossible. I didn't even know I was coming to Amman until just a few days ago. But wait. Could Steve be following me? No. He couldn't have gotten from Moscow to Egypt and then to Amman overland so quickly. And I knew Steve would never take airplanes. But wait. Could Steve be paying someone to follow me? Like so, paranoid thoughts crowded my mind.

I scanned the room looking for anybody I recognized. Nobody. I called the waiter over and asked him who the kids were. He had no idea.

After a moment, I relaxed. In Moscow Steve couldn't even figure out how to leave a note for me at a hotel bar. There was no way he was having someone shadow me in Jordan.

I walked up to the college students and asked them if they were just talking about *American Dad*. They were. They loved the show, they told me. I told them I was racing my friend, a writer for *American Dad*, around the world. Then they invited me to sit down and bought me a beer. In a final burst of paranoia I looked the nearest member of the group in the eye and asked, "Did Hely send you?" A look of genuine confusion passed across his face. So I sat down.

The kids, it turned out, were all international relations students at the Georgetown University Qatar campus. Georgetown University, it turns out, has a campus in Qatar. Qatar, it turns out, is the name of a country.

The fourteen students were in Amman learning about the lives of Iraqi refugees living in Jordan. They informed me that Iraqi refugees in Jordan were generally well off. The doctors, lawyers, and engineers, the people with means, fled to Jordan, one of the most stable countries in the Middle East, after the American invasion. I also taught the students a few things, like where the bathroom was located and how much they should pay for my drink.

As it does in all conversations I have with strangers, the topic eventually moved toward the Arab-Israeli conflict. I wanted to run my proposed solution to the problem by the students.

"What if Palestinians blew themselves up in crowds of Israelis?" I asked.

According to the students, I wasn't the first to come up with this peacekeeping plan. And apparently it was one of those plans that does not work as well in practice as it did in theory. Too little real-world experience—that's the problem with us ivory tower academics. Thankfully, I had a backup plan.

"What if the Israelis treated every Palestinian like a potential terrorist?"

Again I was told that what seemed like a great idea on paper did not work out in the real world. Coming up with peace plans was hard. So I changed the subject.

"Have any of you guys been to Israel or any of the occupied territories?" I asked.

None had. Not even the ones with relatives there.

"Do you think I could get in?"

I was told that with an American passport I should have no problem crossing the border. I had already made plans to visit Petra, an ancient city in south Jordan carved out of rose-colored limestone cliffs. But I was less than twenty miles from the West Bank, a place I had read and heard about all my life, yet was still an abstraction to me. I had no choice. I needed to take a day trip into Palestine.

The students told me not to take my camera or any notes because the Israeli army would confiscate anything of record. The students all had strong and unanimous opinions on Israel's treatment of Palestinians. One student, while telling a story about the Israeli army accidentally killing an eight-year-old Palestinian boy, started crying. A few minutes later a smile emerged on his face.

"It's midnight," he whispered to one of his friends. Then the nineteen-year-old leaned into me. "We bought a bunch of grim reaper masks at a store today," he explained. "We're going to go put them on and scare the shit out of my sleeping roommate now."

"I'm an idiot," I muttered to myself. I thought that frequently, but never believed it. This time, I was pretty sure I was right.

I was standing in the "foreign passports" line to enter Israel at the Jordan-Israel border station. My luggage consisted of one blank notebook, one pen, and my passport. No change of clothes. No toiletries. No Israel guidebook. No ideas on how I was going to spend the next twenty-four hours. My journey had turned into a celebration of unpreparedness. Only this wasn't one of those fun celebrations. It was one of those celebrations where people wonder if they will be beaten up after falling asleep alone in the desert.

My next twenty-four hours were uncertain because the King Hussein Bridge back into Jordan had closed, causing my initial and unresearched plan to become an initial, unresearched, and idiotic plan.

The initial plan was to enter the Palestinian Occupied Territory of the West Bank (or "Israel" as it is known to Israelis) by bus, grab a cup of coffee, talk to some locals, then cross back into Jordan in time for dinner. Right now, dear Reader, you're probably thinking, "That sounds like a great plan!" That's what I thought, too. We think very similarly. (That's why I like you.) However, it was not a great plan because the bridge closed before I even got off the bus at the Israeli side of the border around two p.m. Apparently the hours of bridge operation are kept secret from people who don't bother to ask questions or read signs.

None of my fellow travelers seemed concerned by the bridge closure. Of the hundred or so travelers crossing with me, probably ten were non-Palestinians. And from what I could gather, I was the only non-Palestinian planning on staying in the West Bank. Everyone else was heading straight to Jerusalem. And of everyone there I'm pretty sure I was the only one who possessed a card identifying me as a Federal

Burka Inspector. I couldn't wait to pull that thing out at a Middle Eastern bar.

As I stood in line, the Israeli border guards acted friendly enough, but I wasn't buying it. I knew each and every one of them could kill me with a bouquet of daffodils if they so desired. They could also kill me with a gun, but that isn't nearly as impressive since almost anyone could do that.

The strange it's-a-state-but-not-really nature of the West Bank hung over the immigration hall. Nobody I saw, fellow traveler and border guard alike, looked comfortably at home.

I was still counting the number of armed Israeli border guards in my ken when my Blackberry buzzed with an e-mail from Steve.

> Date: May 20, 2007
> From: Steve Hely
> Subject: I win for all time
> Last night I went on one of the best dates of my life with an incredibly pretty and charming girl.

It took me a moment to decide how to feel. I wanted to be happy for the success of my friend. Then I looked up at all of the guns and thought about how I had been in the Middle East for over a week and how I hadn't spoken to a girl who was not a hotel employee in all that time because I was afraid of putting girls in uncomfortable positions and/or violating social mores. Suddenly, I stopped wanting to be happy for the success of my friend and started wanting to collapse to the ground and cry.

Steve was smooching girls in western Europe while I was stuck in a place that has not known peace since the beginning of time. I made a mental note to take a course on good decision making when I returned to the United States. Then my mood brightened and I made a second mental note. This note was to look into *teaching* a course on poor decision making when I returned to the United States. No reason I shouldn't profit a little bit from this.

Wanting to get my mind off how much more fun Steve was having than me in that moment, I struck up a conversa-

tion with two Aussies standing behind me in the passport line.
They turned out to be a father and daughter taking a several-month-long trip through the Middle East. The father was a serial backpacker; he had been traveling for three years straight. His daughter, a nanny, was taking a few months off to join him. They mentioned that they had recently been in Iran.

My own associations with modern-day Iran are less than positive. Iran's president, Mahmoud Ahmadinejad, is a handsome specimen who appears at official events tieless, top button open, and with a rakish two-week-old beard. But from that stylish container, Ahmadinejad spews out nonsensical holocaust-denying rhetoric and explicit threats against Israel. The associations get worse from there. "Iran" is only one letter different from "Iraq," a textbook clusterfuck. (At least it would be if textbooks loosened up and threw in a couple swear words here and there.) And most damningly, "Iran" is only one letter different from "bran," a substance that makes breakfast cereals taste gross.

"How was Iran?" I asked the Aussies.

"Wonderful. Stayed much longer than planned. Everyone we met did."

When they asked what I was going to do in the West Bank, I explained my lack of concrete plans. In response, they expressed concern regarding my ability to get into Israel. These two basically had swastikas stamped into their passports and they were worried about me? Before I had a chance to become concerned, it was my turn at the passport control window.

"Where are you planning to stay in Israel?" asked the immigration agent, a cute Israeli girl who could not have been much older than me.

"I don't know," I responded through a plastered-on smile.

"You don't know?"

"I had planned on returning to Jordan tonight, but now the bridge has closed." She flipped through my passport for a few seconds before I continued. "Could you please give me my stamp on a separate piece of paper?"

"Why?"

"I might go to other countries in the region and I'm

worried they might deny me entry if they see an Israeli passport stamp." I had heard horror stories about this. Although the official government position was that out-of-passport stamping was not allowed, fellow travelers told me that the Israeli border guards are typically accommodating.*

"Why might you go to Middle Eastern countries that do not allow entry to travelers with an Israeli stamp?" asked the cute Israeli immigration agent as she considered whether or not she was going to give me a stamp at all, let alone give me one on a separate piece of paper.

"I'm racing my friend around the world for a book we're writing." At this point, I expected the cute guard to lean over and kiss me while I, without even turning to look, raised two middle fingers at the Aussies who, just moments ago, seemed certain that I would be arrested by the Israeli police. Instead the agent leaned over her table to look for the sort of luggage a person traveling around the world might carry—probably something more than zero bags.

"All my stuff is at the Howard Johnson in Amman," I explained.

"What were you planning to do in Israel?"

"Have some coffee and walk around for a few hours?"

"Where?"

"I don't know. Somewhere in the West Bank. I was going to ask a cabdriver for a recommendation."

"Now what are you going to do?"

"I don't know. Do you have any suggestions?" She did not. However, she did sigh and give me an entry stamp on a separate piece of paper.

I will never know exactly why she gave me my stamp, but

*Always on the lookout for Zionist conspiracies, other Middle Eastern countries have wised up to the stamping scam. In response they sometimes deny entry to those with suspiciously unaccounted for time in their passports. For example, if a traveler's passport bears a Syrian land exit stamp for September 1, a Jordanian land entry stamp for September 5, and no stamps in his passport for any of the days between, a clever Middle Eastern immigration official can do the math, assume the traveler spent the missing time in Israel, and deny him entry. Some travelers get around this problem by simply having two passports and allowing Israeli stamps in only one of them.

I think it's because she felt that I was too stupid to be any real threat to Israel. A terrorist would have had some fake answers to her questions. I, on the other hand, was using notebook paper to blow my nose.

The same naïveté that made me an easy mark to the Cairo hustlers made me appear harmless to the Israeli border agent. I wish this wasn't the case. I want to appear dangerous. Upon sight of me, I want a woman's heart to race and a man's testicles to shrink back up into his torso. But not too far up into his torso because this Dangerous Vali wouldn't mind kicking those very testicles should the man in question slight Dangerous Vali in the smallest way.

In the end, my border-crossing experience was fairly hiccup-free. The only tense moment came when a customs official thought my name was "Ali" and that I was an Arab American. Once she realized I was an Indian American, she took some teasing from the colleagues she had called over to inspect me, then sent me on my way.

After immigration, I went to a moneychanger to buy some Israeli shekels. The moneychanger was not Jewish. I only mention this because every other person working at the Israeli border point was Jewish. The Jews were really going the extra mile to fight stereotypes on their home turf. I was going to suggest putting a "See! Jews aren't obsessed with money!" banner above the moneychanger, but then I realized that a vandal could easily scribble "Yes. But they are very crafty" underneath that message. That would undermine the entire operation.

Before sending me off, the moneychanger told me that Jericho was the closest city to the border—just a few minutes by cab or bus. I had heard the name, so I decided to check it out. Later, I realized that I had heard the name only because of ads for the ABC television show *Jericho*, a drama about a nuclear apocalypse in Kansas or something. And for that reason—which is to say: no reason at all—I hopped into a cab and set off to the city.

VALI: I'm So Happy I Have an American Passport

For the first time in a long time, I was not in a metropolis. Since the start of my journey I had either been in a large city—Los Angeles, Mexico City, Nashville, Rio, London, Paris, Berlin, Moscow, Cairo—or traveling toward a large city. Now I found myself in a part of the world I knew existed but never really thought about: the rural Middle East.

The scenery was dramatic. Sand ran in all directions until it met the horizon, the bottom of which was wavy with heat. I wouldn't have been surprised to hear a BEEP-BEEP and then see Wile E. Coyote whiz by on Acme rocket skates.

The cab driving me to Jericho stopped at an Israeli military checkpoint. The Palestinian Authority controls and polices only a few cities in the West Bank. The rest of the region is policed by the Israeli military. They protect Israeli settlements and keep a watchful eye out for terrorist activity.

A young guard approached the cab window. A gun, which is required by Israeli military rule to be loaded and ready at all times while in the occupied territories, hung by his side.

"Where are you from?" the guard sternly asked me.

"The United States."

"Passport."

I handed him my documents.

"You're from Los Angeles?" His face broke into a grin. "Kobe Bryant scored sixty-five points last week!"

The guard handed the passport back to me and waved the taxi through.

The interaction couldn't have been easier, but it still made me a little bit uncomfortable. I knew it would have been far more uncomfortable had I been Palestinian. Then, to the guard, I would be a potential security threat. And to me, the guard would have been an unwelcome suspicious force while I was simply trying to go home.

I started to understand where the tension came from.

VALI: I Was Kidding Before About Wanting to Burn You Down

There is one and only one hotel in Jericho: the InterContinental Hotel. A stronger, more principled man might have snubbed the multinational chain he so recently declared war on. That man would have gone into town and asked a shopkeeper for permission to sleep at his house in exchange for a few shekels and a promise not to lay a finger on his daughter. I, on the other hand, marched into the hotel, raved about the evening I spent trying to see Dina at the Inter-Continental Cairo, and rented a room for the night. Inter-Continental: 2, Vali: 0. I was absorbing some stinging early defeats in this war.

The InterContinental Jericho was a surprisingly beautiful resort, especially given the stark surroundings. Arab families on holiday swam and sunbathed at the outdoor pool. Multiple restaurants catered to guests' varied culinary whims. I never saw them but apparently there were tennis courts and a squash court located somewhere in the facility. A gift shop sold umbrellas.

Why was this hotel here? What was this significance of this place?

Jericho, it turns out, is the oldest continually inhabited city in the world. People have been living there since 9000 BC. It was a simpler time back then, when people used their imagination to entertain themselves instead of listening to rap "music" or advancing "science."

Today, Jericho doesn't have much to show for eleven thousand years of history. The Old Testament records the destruction of the city somewhere around the thirteenth century BC, give or take a few hundred years. Joshua, the story goes, brought down the city's walls by having his men march around while blaring trumpets. I'm not sure the city ever recovered from that deafening assault. Today, there isn't even a souvenir shop. What am I supposed to put on my collectible spoon rack to symbolize Jericho? A clump of dirt?

I walked through the meat of modern Jericho in about twenty minutes. It was swelteringly hot, so most of Jericho's approximately 25,000 residents stayed safely indoors. The few people I met were friendly and talkative. I got the sense that they didn't see very many solo Indian travelers in Palestine. I found explaining that I was an American of Indian descent to be pretty difficult, so I started just telling people I was Indian. This seemed to make them happy. "We are of the same blood," they said. I have no idea what that means.

I was struck by how strangely normal life seemed in the West Bank. Given all the news reports about violence in the region, I used to wonder how anyone who wasn't either too poor to leave or a crazily principled zealot—either Palestinian or Israeli—would ever want to live in an occupied territory. But Jericho made me understand.

The city was quaint and pleasant. A few small stores along the main street sold household goods. Men drank tea, ate food, and watched soccer games in cafés. And street carts sold deliciously fresh in-season fruit—dates or bananas or oranges.

After walking around Jericho I tried to go to the nearby Monastery of the Temptation. On a nearby cliff overlooking Jericho, the location is believed to be the spot where the first Temptation of Christ occurred. The apostle Matthew wrote that the devil tempted Jesus, who had been fasting on the mountain near Jericho for forty days and forty nights, by asking, "If you are the Son of God, why don't you turn these stones to bread and end your hunger?"

"Man shall not live by bread alone, but also by the word of God," replied Jesus. Strangely, Jesus made no reference to water or vitamins, which even I know are super important for life.

Unfortunately the monks at the monastery had all left for the day, so the cable car operator who controls access to the mountain wouldn't let me up. No big deal, I thought. I've already been to lots of places where someone *didn't* turn stone into bread.

VALI: Wherein I Stumble into the Most Memorable Night of My Trip

"We'll pick you up in a few hours. Be really hungry."

"Perfect," I said, and hung up the phone.

After returning to the hotel I remembered a friend of mine, Foos, had worked in Israel after college. Having nothing else to do in Palestine until the King Hussein Bridge opened the next morning, I e-mailed him saying I was in Jericho and asked if he knew anyone in the city I could meet up with. Within five minutes Foos e-mailed me back. Not only did he know people in Jericho, he was in Jerusalem and could come introduce me.

Before we cemented our plans over the phone, I hadn't seen or spoken to Foos in years. His actual name was Brian Sigafoos, but we all called him Foos because it was the funniest-sounding segment of his name. We became friends in college, where he was a hardworking psychology student and the starting center on the Harvard basketball team. After college, Foos played pro ball in Europe for a few years, then came to Israel to work for an organization called Peace Players International. With PPI, Foos coaches a basketball team made up of both Israeli and Palestinian kids. For most of the Israeli children in the program, basketball practice and games are the only times they interact with Palestinian children and vice versa. The idea is that working together on the same team will help the kids forge friendships across ethnic lines and forget some negative stereotypes they have grown up hearing. And it works. Peace Players International isn't going to solve the Arab-Israeli problem on its own, but it has increased understanding in the hundreds of kids who have participated in the program. I like to think that Brian's positive contributions to the world offset my negative contributions.

At 9:30, Foos and another one of the PPI coaches, Matt, picked me up. They had both just come from a slam dunk contest and were still dressed in their jerseys and basketball shorts. I had forgotten how much taller than everything Foos was. He even made Matt, who was in the mid-sixes, look short. Next to them, five feet and ten inches of Vali looked pathetic. I felt like these guys should have been carrying me around in a wicker basket.

"Are you hungry?" Foos asked again as we drove.

"Not as hungry as two freakish giants coming from a slam dunk contest."

"Well, you better get hungry. We're going to Allah's house for dinner." I thought this meant Foos was going to murder me so my soul could reach Heaven by dinnertime. But this particular "Allah" was the Jericho basketball coach.

On the other side of the road, a solid rectangular prism of Arab soldiers jogged toward us, in perfect step with each other.

"Mahmoud Abbas's personal bodyguards," explained Matt. "They train down the street from the hotel."

Before getting to Allah's house, we stopped to pick up Ferris, another coach, also dressed in a jersey and basketball shorts. At first I thought Ferris was African American. He spoke just like Foos, Matt, and I spoke and talked about the same movies and sports teams we talked about. Then, a few minutes after getting in the car, he asked Foos for the English translation for an Arabic word.

Ferris was a type of person I never knew existed: a black Palestinian. He deliberately affects an American accent when speaking English because he likes to go out to bars in Tel Aviv with Foos and Matt. Ferris, a nonpracticing Muslim, loves the ladies. And the ladies of Tel Aviv love black American basketball players with hip-hop style. By the time the ladies realize Ferris is Palestinian, he has already charmed his way into their bedrooms. And having spent plenty of time in Israeli bedrooms, Ferris can now also speak Hebrew. The guy oozed charisma. He was the first of many surprises I received in Palestine.

VALI: I'm Not Scared Only Because Nobody Else Seems Scared

The spread at Allah's house was delicious. He was newly married and his wife went all out. We had a tomato and cucumber salad, sliced pickles, creamy fresh hummus sprinkled with paprika, a corn slaw, and seasoned chicken roasted until the skin was brown and crispy. All served under the stars on their patio in Palestine. It was one of those moments where I looked around and thought, *My life is so stupidly good.*

I felt bad for Steve, who, while pulling off his pointless and nostalgic stunt, would never experience anything this perspective-expanding. He wouldn't have been able to appreciate it, anyway. It was too relevant to what is happening in the world today.

Allah's wife and mother, who lived with them, greeted us when we arrived but did not join us for dinner. I didn't get the sense that this was cultural. It had more to do with it being 10:00 p.m. on a Sunday. They had already eaten and wanted to relax while Allah caught up with his friends.

The conversation at dinner was surprisingly open. Allah talked about how he and his wife were having difficulty conceiving. Ferris leaned over to me and explained: "Allah can't make a baby because he is no good at sex. If you asked him to draw a picture of a pussy, he would draw something with seven holes in it."

Laughing at his own joke, Ferris got up from the table to answer his cell phone.

The food was fantastic, but I was given the same amount as the seven-foot giant who had just played basketball all afternoon. Worried I might offend my host, I slowly and methodically forced myself to finish everything. When dessert was brought out, a giant plate of fresh fruit, I almost cried.

Ferris returned and whispered something to Foos in Arabic.

"The Israeli army has entered Jericho," Foos translated. "They have intelligence that a suicide bomber is hiding out here and they're trying to find him."

We heard a crack, then saw a light slowly descend into the desert. It was a flare attached to a parachute. The army was using it to light the surrounding area so they could search for the bomber.

A few eyebrows were raised, but nobody stopped eating his dessert.

"The intelligence must be very recent," said Foos. "If they had known it at nine-thirty, the soldiers at the military checkpoint wouldn't have let us into town."

Ferris laughed and slapped me on the back. "Welcome to Palestine."

After dinner we drove to another coach, Rami's, house. He was a Christian Palestinian so he could serve us beers. I was stuffed and hot, sweating chunks of roasted chicken out my skin, but, once again, I accepted the offering to be polite.

We drank on his patio while chatting and watching more flares slowly float to the ground. After a while, we stopped noticing them. Rami told a story about how, a few months earlier, Fatah and the Israeli army had a shoot-out in front of his house. Bullets sped across the very patio where we sat. The shoot-out continued into the night. So he, his wife, and his young daughter slept on the bathroom floor because it was the room farthest away from any exterior walls of the house.

Rami disliked Fatah as much as he disliked the Israeli army. All he wanted was for his daughter to feel safe.

"If he really means that," I told the group, "he should keep her away from Ferris."

VALI: "How Am I in the Same League as Them?"

During dinner at Allah's house, Matt told me a story that took place not long after he had started working for Peace Players International.

After a basketball practice, a Palestinian player's older brother invited Matt to a bachelor party. Matt was wary of imposing, but the brother insisted it would be fun. Besides, he wanted to show the American that Palestinian men knew how to have a good time.

So Matt went home, changed his clothes, then reported to the bar where the bachelor party was being held. The scene consisted of twenty guys dancing to Arabic music while drinking Coca-Cola. Everyone in attendance was a devout Muslim so no alcohol was consumed.

Upon spotting Matt, the guy in charge of music put on his favorite hip-hop song. Then everyone crowded around Matt and cheered for him to break-dance. They assumed he could, because he was American.

Now, this wasn't the scene the new-to-Palestine Matt was expecting. But the dude knows how to roll with the situation so he started break dancing. Everyone cheered. Then they started break dancing, too.

After break dancing through the song a couple times, Matt, now having the time of his life, stepped out to the curb with a few of the bachelor party attendees to have a Coca-Cola.

"It is funny to think about our friend getting married," one of the young Palestinians told Matt. "He is very much in love."

"Yeah, it's a weird feeling," replied Matt.

"You know who I love? I love Yasir Arafat. Do you love Yasir Arafat?"

"I think Yasir Arafat's heart was in the right place. I believe he wanted peace. So, yeah, I like Yasir Arafat."

"But do you love him?"

"Okay." Matt laughed. "I love Arafat."

"What about Saddam Hussein? Do you love Saddam Hussein?"

It should be noted here that Saddam Hussein was and is beloved by the Palestinians. They see him as an Arab leader who consistently talked about the need for a Palestine and sent actual aid to the Palestinian people. Foos and Matt recently played in a Palestinian-organized "Saddam Hussein the Martyr Memorial Tournament."

"I do not love Saddam Hussein," Matt said.

"Why?"

"Saddam tortured his own people and tried to invade another country."

"Oh. You know who else I love? Osama bin Laden. Do you love Osama bin Laden?"

"Absolutely not."

"Why?"

"He's from New York," chided one of the other bachelor-party attendees. "Of course he doesn't like Osama bin Laden."

"I see. Well, I love him. I love all these men. I love Yasir Arafat. I love Saddam Hussein. I love Osama bin Laden. And . . . you. And I love you, Matt."

Break-dancing skills can take you a long way in Palestine.

VALI: Everyone Should Experience Something Like This

Foos insisted that before leaving Palestine I had to go swimming in the Dead Sea. So after leaving Rami's house we dropped off Ferris at home (he prefers to swim with ladies) and made our way to the beach.

Around two a.m., we reached a deserted unlit public beach. When our eyes adjusted to the moonlight, we saw a landscape made up of different intensities of black. Only the closest objects, inches from our face, had any color.

We walked down a rocky path to the sand. The waves were pretty strong and crashed loudly against a rocky part of the shore, just a few feet away.

The 30 percent salinity prevents any plant or animal life from surviving in the sea, which meant that, for once, I could go for a swim without worrying about giant squid attacks. The saltiness of the water also makes human bodies especially buoyant. I floated so high in the water that swimming felt strange. The easiest and most pleasant thing to do was just float on my back.

Almost immediately, water splashed into my eyes, causing a uniquely unpleasant burning sensation. It felt sort of like fireworks being launched out of my eyeballs. Had I known about this when I was eight, I would have attacked my little sister with a saltwater-filled Super-soaker every day.

But even my burning eyes couldn't ruin one of the most pleasant sensations I've ever felt. There were no lights on the beach. All three of us floated silently, enjoying the experience, without reference points for our whereabouts. Within a few minutes, we had all floated a hundred feet from each other.

As I floated alone staring up at the stars, I thought, *Of course everybody wants this land. It's perfect.*

STEVE: Rome to Paris by Train

From Rome to Paris I traveled in a half-empty compartment practicing my French on a retired mailman from Vendée who treated me to lively pantomimes of violent episodes from the French Revolution.

STEVE: Paris for Weirdos

There's no point talking about the allure of Paris. Walk around, and you keep stumbling into stuff like a pigeon alighting gracefully on a statue of Voltaire, or an old man smoking and playing the accordion outside a café. Within about twenty minutes you're like, "All right, I get it, Paris. Quit showing off!" As you're thinking this, a girl with the face of an angel reaches out on her windowsill to water a single rose that grows in an empty wine bottle.

Roughly 18 percent of all books in the world are about the magic of being a young man in Paris. I don't intend to add to that. Instead, I gave myself a more challenging assignment: to prove in one day that Paris is also a screwed-up jumble of the disgusting and the bizarre.

The Museum of the Sewers: Here, by the banks of the Seine, and not far from the Eiffel Tower, you can descend on a spiral staircase into the earth and take a tour of the Paris sewers. Any idea that Parisians are worldly and sophisticated will be considerably dimmed as you walk alongside a river of pavement-colored filthwater and smell what those people are flushing. I lasted about ten minutes before the aroma overcame me, and I lingered just long enough to purchase a stuffed sewer rat at the gift shop before surfacing.

Rue Saint-Severin: This is now a famous tourist street, in sight of Notre-Dame, where aggressive restaurant owners are not above resorting to wrestling moves as they try to lure diners in for frog-leg specials and greasy gyros. But in the eighteenth century, the Rue Saint-Severin was known for its print shops and for its alley cats. The apprentices who worked in the print shops hated these cats and their constant feline shrieking. One night in the 1730s some of these apprentices went nuts and started massacring cats on the Rue Saint-Severin. They smashed their spines with iron bars and left "sackfuls" of cat bodies in heaps on the ground. This last quote is from Robert Darnton's terrific book *The Great Cat Massacre*, which admirably attempts to make sense of this episode in light of religious practice, contemporary folklore, and economic struggle. Whatever. The point is, if you're ever in Paris, you'll end up on the Rue Saint-Severin. Know that it once ran with cat blood.

The Catacombs: In the late 1780s and '90s, the graveyards of Paris were so shoddily handled and crammed with corpses that a public health problem emerged. "Ugh, all these decomposing limbs are sticking out of the ground!" said a French guy. "What if we just piled dead bodies into an empty underground quarry?" So that's what they did.

For a few euros you can wander through these dank passages and stand face-to-face with rows of dripping skulls, translating morbid inscriptions carved here and there in French and Latin. I translated most of them as "Death (something something) life (something) time (something) beware." Unsurprisingly, many tourists to Paris do not prioritize seeing a moist and cavernous morgue, so I was alone.

The creepiest thing about the catacombs is that the skulls and bones are anonymous: stacks of priests, printers' apprentices, soldiers, blacksmiths, prostitutes, children, barbers are all piled together in a rugby scrum of the afterlife. Among them, somewhere, are various French luminaries. There are a number of skulls that were separated from bodies during the French Revolution. You can wonder if one might be that of Madame Lamballe, whose head was paraded on a pike outside the window of her best friend, Marie Antoinette. Or if a particular arm bone might've once been part of the chemist Antoine Lavoisier, who begged revolutionaries to stay his execution so he could finish an experiment. Permission denied; he was guillotined in 1794. One of the most guillotine-happy French revolutionaries, Robespierre, ended up guillotined himself; his mortal remains are somewhere down here, too.

The catacombs extend way beyond what you can see on the tour. There are ways to enter through manholes and Metro stops, and there are rumors about secret raves that go on in these recesses. If you know about these raves, please invite me, because they sound really fun.*

The Louvre: People are pretty into the Louvre museum, but personally I find it obnoxious. The Louvre is like the rich kid you knew that had way too many Transformers, and you'd go over to his house, and be, like, "Whoa! You have Seaspray!" and he'd be, like, "That? Oh, I don't even play with that one," and you'd be infuriated. That's how I feel at the Louvre. There's so much art there that you could never see it in a day. You could never see it in a month. You couldn't see everything in the Louvre in years. So why can't they give one lousy thing—Raphael's *Portrait of Baldassare Castiglione*, say—to maybe Reno, Nevada? Nobody would even miss it, and then Reno would have *one* cool thing.

I didn't bother looking at the *Mona Lisa*, which you can't see anyway from all the crowds. I figured you can only really

*helphely@gmail.com

take in one painting a day, and the painting I picked was *The Monkey Historian* by Jean-Baptiste-Siméon Chardin. This painting is of a monkey dressed in people clothes and reading a book, and it raises more intriguing questions about human nature than any other. Questions such as, *Why are people so interested in monkeys?* and *Why* don't *monkeys read books?*

The Musée Fragonard: Paris is home to the craziest museum in Europe, a museum that makes Peter the Great's Kunstkamera look like Brookstone. The Musée Fragonard is not in most guidebooks, which is shameful, although admittedly it's kinda far from the center of Paris, housed on the grounds of the National Veterinary School. It is about evenly divided, with half of its collection being specimens of horrific animal malformations, and the other half being the works of a crazed eighteenth-century anatomist named Fragonard who figured out a way to preserve human bodies using sheep resin and wax. Thus you can casually peruse distended calf rectums and no-headed sheep, and then proceed to such Fragonard pieces as *Three Fetuses Dancing a Jig*, which is exactly that. "One can imagine the reaction of Fragonard's contemporaries to these tableaux," says the English audio guide. I assure you, Audio Guide, that I absolutely cannot.

Nearby is a mounted horseman, a preserved human stripped of skin and reduced to muscle and innards. The story goes that this body was once the daughter of a local grocer with whom Fragonard had fallen in love. This is a disturbing tribute to lost love, to say the least. The Audio Guide helpfully debunks that old myth by referring you to the body's withered penis.

STEVE: Paris Strikes Back

Just when I'd finished reviewing the Insanities of Paris, and was ready to return to the English-speaking world having forever debunked the Paris Myth, I was tricked into a day of excellence. I ate at L'Atelier Joel Robuchon, where the mashed potatoes are so good you'd swear they were made with milk squeezed from the breasts of the Virgin Mary. I teamed up with my associate Durbs, who had bought two scalped tickets to the French Open, so we sat in the cheap seats at Roland Garros stadium and watched Rafael Nadal casually demolish J. M. Del Potro. Durbs missed most of this because he was working on a scheme to sneak a bottle of champagne and two glasses into the stands inside his pants. Incredibly, this was successful, and it was nearly as impressive an achievement as Nadal's.

That was by four p.m. That night I would eat more perfect food, and end up at an underground nightclub where I was taught the cancan by three dancers from the Moulin Rouge.

Rather than continue to let Paris mock me, I got back to racing. I wanted to get to America as quickly as possible, win the race, and make Vali look like J. M. Del Potro.

STEVE: Paris to London

I for one am not tired of saying "Chunnel," and I don't expect I ever will be.

STEVE: This Is London

It used to be in London that for four pence you could sleep in a "doss house." Wedged against other lodgers of dubious hygiene and limited means, you'd sleep sitting up, with a rope stretched across your chest to keep you from falling over. At five a.m. an employee would come along, undo the rope, and out you'd tumble.

There are no more doss house bargains. London is a solid contender for most expensive city in the world. Add in the puny 2007 American dollar, and a few days in London feels like your last move in a losing game of Monopoly. Perhaps this was some kind of karmic payback for me.

London was just a way station for me—I had to wait until my ship left from nearby Southampton, cross the Atlantic, dash across the United States, and win this thing. With the end so nearly in sight, and the sailing two days away, maybe I had time to rack up Awesomeness Points—perhaps a whimsical exploration into the world of the Cornish pasty, or a day trip up to Scotland for a whisky-soaked romp through the heather.

But in London, I had the opportunity to check my bank account. It is a moment I shudder to recall.

"MERCIFUL MOTHER OF HEAVEN" I shouted, to the shock and alarm of nearby British ATM users.

Turns out that "racing around the world, making all your plans at the last minute" is really, really expensive. Like, way more expensive than what the measly accountants at Henry Holt Publishing Company had seen fit to dole out.

Then, regaining my composure, I muttered, "We're going to need to sell a fuckload of books to make this back."

All whimsical explorations and whisky-soaked romps were immediately canceled. Whatever sold books was what I'd learn about in London. I walked into the nearest bookstore to learn from the best sellers.

STEVE: ONE NIGHT IN LONDON: A LURID TALE OF SERIAL KILLERS, SEX, DETECTIVES, MURDER, CRIME, STABBING, CRIME SCENE INVESTIGATING, LAW AND ORDER, MYSTERY, AND BLOOD!

At 2:30 in the morning on August 31, 1888, a forty-two-year-old prostitute named Polly Nichols ran into a friend of hers on the street in the Whitechapel neighborhood of London. Polly was stinking drunk and explained to her friend that she didn't have the four pence for a doss house. She'd earned the money several times over that night, but each time she'd spent it on gin. It wouldn't be any problem to earn it again, said Polly, pointing to her head. "See what a jolly bonnet I have now!"

Men back then were apparently way more aroused by bonnets than they are now.

An hour later, a cartman getting ready for work discovered Polly's body. Her head was nearly severed, and her lower abdomen and legs were sliced up. A doctor called to the scene noted "a wineglass and a half" of blood pooling in the gutter.

This was the first Jack the Ripper murder.

I learned all about this from Richard Jones, who leads Jack the Ripper walking tours. Immediately after leaving the London bookstore, I figured what *this* book needed was a serial killer. But I didn't want to become one, and I couldn't trust Vali to do it, so I signed up to learn from Richard.

He began his tour for about twenty paying customers by mentioning that although there were only five Jack the Ripper murders, "they were very gruesome murders indeed," and went on to describe a torn-out uterus, a chunk of kidney mailed to the police, severed necks, and strewn innards. He couldn't help but describe all this in an almost proud tone, as though murders were merit badges and Jack the Ripper was his favorite nephew.

Aside from all the vivid descriptions of butchery, the Jack the Ripper walking tour is an amazingly informative trip through the transformation of a city. We walked down Brick Lane, where the doss houses are now Bangladeshi restaurants and shops selling Bollywood movies. Richard pointed out broad-windowed buildings dating back to the 1700s, when they housed French Huguenot silk weavers who needed sunlight to work.

As he explained this, you could almost hear people thinking, *C'mon! C'mon! Get on with the gruesome murders!* Richard's been doing this for a while, he knows his audience, he got the hint.

By parking lots, snazzy office buildings, curry shops, and London School of Economics dorms, he turned our attention to the London of the murders: tiny streets crammed with thousands of residents, corners that smelled like coffee and stale fish. The police squabble with one another and try to cover their asses. Thousands of prank letters and rantings from lunatics pour in as the tabloid press prints whatever crazy crap they can make up. People couldn't get enough of this stuff back then, too—the first Jack the Ripper tours were started before the murders had even stopped.

They're still going strong. Our tour kept passing other tours, and finally I asked Richard how many of these things there are a night. "On any given night, about thirty-nine," he said. This figure continues to blow my mind. Compare it to these numbers (based on my own Internet research):

Walking tours of London themed around Shakespeare: 1.
Walking tours of London themed around Winston Churchill: 0.
Walking tours of London themed around Dr. Samuel Johnson: C'mon.
Walking tours of London themed around Jack the Ripper: *39*.

I asked Richard how he'd gotten into the Jack the Ripper walking tour business.

"Well," he said, "I started out doing Charles Dickens walking tours." He said this as if amused by his own naïveté. "Nobody wanted Dickens."

There was something about all this that struck me as distinctly English. Every place I'd been to in the world has sordid and bloody history. But the English seem uniquely adept at finding theirs to be a source of comic amusement.

I can't say we didn't all perk up a little when Richard described the particularly vicious mutilations that were visited on one Mary Kelly, the last of the Ripper victims. Richard passed around autopsy photos, and no one declined to look. He did point out that we should all feel a bit of sympathy for these unfortunate women, but even this was just the setup to a joke, the punch line of which was, "Who ordered the dead bird pornography?"

In any case, I didn't have time to fully sort out the bizarre relationship between England, comedy, and serial killing. I was only on this island to leave it, after all. I thanked Richard for helping me spice up the book. He very kindly suggested that if it was murders I was after, I may as well head down the road and have a drink at the Blind Beggar pub. There, in 1966, the infamous gangster Ronnie Kray shot a rival in the forehead.

I took Richard's advice and enjoyed a pleasant pint and some delightful overheard conversation* before bidding England farewell and heading across the Atlantic the next day.

VALI: A Person in Search of Experience Can't Make a Bad Decision in This Town

I landed in Dubai six hours later than expected, missing the departure for the nighttime desert safari I booked.

However, my disappointment ended quickly. Before even leaving the airport I realized there was going to be more to Dubai than I could possibly see in thirty hours. Every single one of my plans could fall through and I still wouldn't have a second of downtime in this town.

The airport was a monument to modernism. Electronics were used to improve everything that could be improved. Gentlemen, remember when they first started making automatically flushing urinals? Some genius made this very normal thing, the urinal, pretty cool, you thought. Imagine auto-flush-level modernization applied to everything and you'll have the Dubai airport. Ladies, I have no idea how to explain this to you. It's like the strapless bra of airports?

I had gone from the least opulent and modern section of the Middle East, Palestine, to the most opulent and modern. They were almost unrecognizably different places, but an unmistakable Arab culture tied the two together. All male airport personnel wore traditional Emirati dress: a long white robe (*kandoura*) and a white head cloth (*ghutrah*), which was cinched to the head with a black rope (*aqal*). Then there were

*Example: "I saw 'im a week before he died. 'E was the picture a health. Imagine how surprised I was then when he got hit by a car."

some practices I had not seen anywhere else in the Middle East. For example, Emirati men greeted each other by touching noses and then pursing their lips to make a kissing sound. Seriously.

VALI: Mommy, What's an Emirate?

Dubai is one of the seven states, or Emirates, that make up the United Arab Emirates (UAE). The UAE is sort of a constitutional monarchy of constitutional monarchies. A sheikh rules each emirate. And the sheikh of the largest and most oil-rich emirate, Abu Dhabi, serves as president of the UAE while the sheikh of the center of commerce, Dubai, serves as vice president. Constitutional monarchies being hereditary systems, the direction of the entire country rests in the families of the two sheikhs.

So the term *Emirate* refers to a state in the UAE. And the term *Emirati* refers to the citizens of the UAE. This distinguishes them from the nonlocals, the foreigners. And in Dubai there are a lot of those. Only 17 percent of the population is Emirati. The balance is made up of guest workers, primarily from India, Pakistan, Bangladesh, and the Philippines. They have come to Dubai because of the economic opportunities.

Dubai lacks the oil of the other Emirates. Currently oil accounts for only 6 percent of the state's GDP and the limited supply is expected to run out within the next decade. So to ensure the financial health of his country, the last sheikh of Dubai decided to make his state a center of Arab commerce and tourism. He created special economic zones with tax benefits to attract foreign banks and businesses. Then developers brought in inventive architects to house the new businesses and their workers.

As a result Dubai today has an evolving skyline unlike any other in the world. There's the sailboat-shaped Burj Al Arab hotel, the world's only seven-star hotel. (Primarily because the real rating system only goes up to five stars.) The developers built a small grass tennis court on a tiny, freestanding, disk-shaped section of the hotel roof, such that the entire surface extends only a few feet past the baseline. A small net surrounding the disk prevents players who lunge too vigorously or back up too far from falling over the edge and plunging several hundred feet into the ocean. The disk is so small, it leaves no room for seating. And the court seems too dangerous to allow hotel guests to use. So why did the Burj Al Arab build the tennis court? From what I could gather, it was simply so they could host an unofficial match between Andre Agassi and Roger Federer and take photos from a helicopter for the hotel Web site. I can't reason out why anything happens in Dubai because I still have a part of my brain that can think, *That's too crazy*.

There's also the in-progress Burj Dubai skyscraper. It looks like a few skyscrapers pushed together with the smaller ones on the outsides and the tallest in the middle, sort of like an upside-down icicle with more edges to it. When completed it will be the tallest building in the world. Exactly how tall? The construction company won't tell because they don't want anyone else to plan a taller building.

There's also much much more. And it all looks terrific.

Before getting to Dubai, I had seen photos of the buildings and read descriptions of the plans and I thought it was all a bit much. "It looks like Vegas on steroids," I told my friends as part of a quippy lecture on the subject. On the plane I expressed my skepticism about the aesthetics of Dubai to a lovely young French girl who had lived in the city for much of her life.

"Think of it this way," she said. "Venice was once the most modern city in the world. Now it's considered an architectural treasure."

After seeing Dubai for myself, I realized she was right. There was nothing wrong with how Dubai looked. It was me who was limited in how I thought about cities. Maybe it *was* time I gave up my staunch conviction that Sayre, Pennsylvania, has the most glorious skyline in the world.

So everybody's a winner in Dubai, right? Well . . . er . . . as George Saunders put it in his wonderful essay about Dubai, "The New Mecca," it's complicated.

The Emirates of Dubai are certainly winners. The sheikh distributes some of the new wealth to his citizens in the form of free schools, free health care, and occasionally free housing. His family hasn't maintained control of Dubai since 1833 by treating the constituents like crap.

For the guest workers—the ones who actually built and continue to build Dubai—the outcome is less clear. They often live six, seven, or eight to a room and send most of their income to their families back home, whom they go years without seeing. They can never become citizens, they can never achieve the social status of an Emirati, sometimes they go months without getting paid, and they are not allowed to switch jobs. On the other hand, the guest workers chose to come to Dubai and are still coming. One Indian cabdriver I spoke with told me he was encouraged to come to Dubai by his friend who was already here. Does that imply the guest workers think being treated like crap in Dubai is better than trying to make a living at home? I think it does. But still, shouldn't a wealthy state like Dubai do everything possible to protect human dignity? That seems reasonable. Should I respect the sovereignty of any nation, even one based on Islamic sharia, especially if people are allowed to come and go as they please? Yes, I think so. So what does that mean for Dubai? I have no idea. See how quickly this gets complicated?

VALI: An Imagined Meeting

Here's how I think the meeting between the architect and the developer of my Dubai hotel must have gone.

An Architect and Developer sit across from each other in a fancy Dubai office.

ARCHITECT: I think you'll be very pleased with my completed plans for the Grand Hyatt. It is a synthesis of all the most recent advances in architech—

DEVELOPER: —I want you to put the building on its side.

ARCHITECT: Excuse me?

DEVELOPER: Take the building you have designed and lay it down on its side.

ARCHITECT: But, sir, don't you want to see the plans first?

DEVELOPER: Don't need to. And after you put the building on its side, sort of cut a slot out of it.

ARCHITECT: [Begins taking notes.] Okay . . .

DEVELOPER: What kind of restaurants did you have planned for the hotel?

ARCHITECT: We have space for five restaurants, each serving different cuisines.

DEVELOPER: Great. Put all that stuff into one restaurant. Then put in seven more restaurants, three bars, and a nightclub. And the pool—

ARCHITECT: —currently I have it surrounded with thirty-seven acres of immaculate gardens.

DEVELOPER: Add a few peaceful waterfalls. Good instincts, though.

ARCHITECT: Thank you, sir. I'll submit the revised plans to you in a week. [He gets up to exit.]

DEVELOPER: Oh, and put a rain forest in the lobby.

VALI: Out in Dubai on a Monday Night

I dropped my bags off in my room and went down to the concierge desk to ask if I could sign up for falconry lessons.

Falconry, the use of trained birds to hunt, has been practiced for centuries by Emiratis. These days the UAE spends 100 million dirhams (27 million USD) a year on falconry. I'm always searching for new ways to get food without leaving my apartment so I was pretty intrigued by the sport.

"If any instructors specialize in teaching falcons to go to Trader Joe's that would suit my needs perfectly," I said.

The concierge politely told me no without ever using the word *no*. The service at this hotel was impeccable.

"Then what bar would you recommend I go to tonight?" I asked.

"What are you in the mood for?"

"Someplace unique to Dubai."

He suggested a nearby bar that overlooked the ocean. When I got there, a Filipino man and woman were working the door. The bar had a "couples only" policy during the week, they told me. They suggested I try the hotel bar at the Sheraton.

I wasn't thrilled with the suggestion. I hadn't come to Dubai to chat up businessmen who were drinking their faces off while away from home.

As I walked away disappointed, the Filipino man ran up to me and asked, "You looking for a place with girls?"

"Are you talking about prostitutes?"

He was.

I told the Filipino I wasn't in the mood for prostitutes, politely thanked him for his commitment to service, then jumped in a cab. Surely a cabdriver would know where the party in Dubai is tonight.

"I can take you to the best massage place in Dubai," the cabdriver told me with a wink.

I must have really looked like a guy who wanted to pay for sex.

"Beautiful blond girls," he continued.

The cabdriver was also Indian and our conversation took place in a mix of Tamil, the language my parents spoke at home, and English. The associations with my family life made the prostitute talk all the more uncomfortable.

"I also know an Ethiopian place. I go there myself."

Was it the way I wore my shirt? I normally leave the top two buttons undone. But maybe here that made me look sleazy. I did up another button so as to appear more conservative.

"Vali . . ." I really regretted telling the cab driver my name. It suggested a level of friendship I was not psyched about sharing with this guy.

"Vali, tell me, how many girlfriends do you have in America?"

"Umm . . . what do you mean?"

"My friends in America tell me they have five, six, seven girlfriends."

Who was this guy friends with? Jack Nicholson?

A strange truth about Dubai: the population is 75 percent male. According to my rough calculations there are around 900,000 male guest workers in Dubai who live pretty hard lives, working long hours and rarely seeing their families. This situation has created a demand for the fairer sex.

Good data on black markets are hard to come by, but it is said that the sex biz is so lucrative in Dubai many women are *choosing* to become prostitutes. And the girls aren't there only to service the guest workers. They're also out in the nightclubs, available to tourists both Arab and non-Arab. The police and the Islamic sharia government know about all this, but turn a blind eye because getting rid of the girls might put a damper on tourism and frustrate the guest workers who are building the city. So is rampant prostitution in a country where local women must wear veils a side effect of growth? The machine of society has a lot of moving parts.

When he dropped me back off at my hotel, the Indian taxi driver gave me his card and asked me to call him if I changed my mind about the massage or if I just wanted to get a dosa with him at a great South Indian restaurant he knew about.

VALI: Circumnavigating The World

The World is one of four sets of man-made islands being built by Nakheel Properties off the coast of Dubai. The first three are huge archipelagos shaped like palm trees. The fourth is a six-kilometer-long, nine-kilometer-wide collection of three hundred islands that, from a helicopter, looks like a map of the world. The islands have been built using a process called land reclamation, which basically means taking sand from the bottom of the ocean and spraying it into island-shaped piles. The islands are being sold by invitation only to crazily rich individuals and developers for between 15 and 45 million USD. E-mailing Nakheel Properties claming your invitation has been lost in the mail does not appear to accomplish anything. Not that I care. I don't want to buy an island from an organization with such poor customer service anyway.

I rented a boat and set out toward The World archipelago, located four kilometers from the Dubai shoreline. The city's impressive skyline quickly shrunk away as we approached the massive boat that actually performs the land reclamation. It didn't look like much of anything. The vessel just sat in the water, making a little noise, completely unaware that it was six months away from finishing the job of moving 320 million cubic meters of sand. Boats can be really naive sometimes.

My plan was to circumnavigate The World in my boat, without using airplanes, thereby securing a semantic victory over Steve in our race around the world. That way if he made a big deal about my cheating when I got back to Los Angeles I could feign confusion and maybe, with the help of my lawyers, still win the bottle of scotch.

Then my skipper, a tiny Ethiopian man who actually lived on the boat, told me going around The World would take three hours. This was information I could have used before leaving the dock. Three hours was 10 percent of my total time in Dubai. I didn't want to waste that time seeing three hundred piles of sand.

So I purchased a beer from the Ethiopian's personal stock and asked him to deposit me back on shore.

VALI: Wherein I Have an Awesome Time

My guide Ravi picked me up in a Toyota Landcruiser and drove me an hour out of the city into the Dubai desert. We were heading for a spot near a particularly good dune field where the desert safari company he works for stores four-wheelers and sandboarding equipment.

Within minutes Dubai City disappeared into a point. Then there was nothing. The highway cut through a sea of red sand. Occasionally we passed a small cluster of houses, built by the sheikh for some Emiratis. Massive big rigs roared past us carrying sand and cement and rock, raw materials to support the round-the-clock building going on in Dubai City. Just before reaching our destination, we saw some wild camels walking along the road. The group included two youngsters, each small enough that I could have easily wrestled him to the ground. They appeared aware of this and avoided eye contact with me as we drove by.

Ravi wore his hair in a ponytail, sported a soul patch under his lower lip, and loved listening to Iron Maiden and Metallica. His parents moved to Dubai as guest workers before he was ten but had now moved back to Pakistan. Ravi didn't

consider Pakistan home so he stayed, started working freelance for desert safari companies, and married a Filipino woman. As Dubai developed over the past decade, the cost of living rose. After having a child, Ravi decided he could no longer support his family in Dubai and sent them to live with his wife's mother's family in the Philippines. I got the sense there was more to this story, but I didn't think it was within the bounds of our guide-foreigner relationship to delve deeper.

Once we reached the four-wheeler storage area, Ravi gave me a vehicle, a pair of yellow goggles to protect my eyes from the sand, a tiny helmet that would have simply made a head wound harder to clean should I get in an accident, and the sandboarding equipment—a snowboard with broken bindings.

Then we were off. And it was insanely fun. I had ridden four-wheelers around the mountains in Pennsylvania where I grew up but it was nothing like this. Some of the dunes carved out of the sand by the desert winds were two or three stories high with sixty-degree inclines. I drove along slight hills that suddenly crested revealing massive bowls scooped out of the desert. If I didn't ride down one side of a bowl fast enough, I wouldn't have enough momentum to get back out of it on the other side. When this happened, I had to ride up as far as I could, then, just before the wheels started digging into the sand, cut around and go back down the hill using the extra push of gravity to build enough speed to make it a little farther up the other side of the bowl. Like so, I cut back and forth, making it a few feet farther up the slope with each crossing, until finally bursting out of the bowl.

Sandboarding was remarkably less exciting because each dune I boarded down I then had to walk back up. Walking up sand in a pair of Converse hi-tops is as exhausting and time-consuming as it is not fun. Also, I fell every single time. So I went back to the four-wheeler.

I wouldn't say I ever got good at four-wheeler riding, but I definitely improved a lot. Ravi even said riding with me was fun. Then, just before we finished, I somehow ran my vehicle into the only tree in the entire desert. My official stance is that the tree moved into my path. The four-wheeler wasn't really damaged, but it was a pain in the butt for Ravi and I to pull it out of the tree. I'd say the incident had a chilling effect on our burgeoning friendship.

After dropping the equipment off and washing up, we had tea with the Emirati owners of the safari company who had stopped by. The three men wore the traditional white robe and white head cloth with black rope and nontraditional Dior sunglasses. They were pleasant but the pecking order was clear, with I, the South Asian tourist, being slightly above Ravi, the South Asian guest worker. We left before either of us finished our tea.

VALI: I'm Out

I caught a three a.m. flight out of Dubai, ending my stint in the Middle East. I haven't checked the papers since then, but I'm pretty sure I achieved my goals of dismantling the terrorist networks and bringing everlasting peace to the region.

Next challenge.

STEVE: How I Crossed the Atlantic, or, Six Days Trapped on the World's Most Luxurious Floating Nursing Home!

During World War II, the luxury liner *Queen Mary* was used as a troopship, taking as many as sixteen thousand soldiers at a time across the Atlantic. One night in 1942, an escort ship, the HMS *Curacoa*, cut in front of the *Queen Mary*'s bow. The *Curacoa* was not small—she was 451 feet long, with armor three inches thick. The *Queen Mary* sliced it in half. Three hundred and thirty-eight of the *Curacoa*'s sailors drowned, in a disaster that was kept secret until the end of the war.

That's how big the *Queen Mary* was. Big enough to slice another ship in half.

The *Queen Mary 2* is much bigger than that.

She* is as long as the Eiffel Tower is tall. Her hull weighs 50,000 tons, the weight of 330 blue whales. I'm not figuring this stuff out for myself—I'm cribbing it from the *Queen Mary 2 Book of Comparisons*. The *Queen Mary 2* is longer than three bajillion copies of the *Queen Mary 2 Book of Comparisons*.

Personally, I could care less about how big *QM2* is. It

*I'm using "she" instead of "it." I realize that's a little silly, but that's what the Cunard people insist on.

doesn't matter to me either that her passengers eat 62,425 pounds of lobster every year, although I agree that's disgusting.

What mattered to me was speed. *QM2* can cross the Atlantic in six days, about half the time it takes a container ship. That would put me in New York on June 10. For all my delays and distractions I could still race across the United States and win the race. Unless Vali had a gift for extracting favors from Chinese mariners.

Most people, of course, don't use the *QM2* for transportation. So the Cunard* business model relies on people having a kinda weird, fetishistic nostalgia for the days of grand transatlantic ocean liners.

Now, given that the most famous transatlantic ocean liner of all time sank, and that literally every person in the world has seen James Cameron–awesome effects shots of its passengers weeping as they abandon their children, smashing against bulkheads, and bobbing about with icicles hanging from their noses after freezing to death, you'd think this wouldn't be a good marketing plan.

Actually, there's a whole historical display about the *Titanic* inside the *Queen Mary 2*. You're encouraged to know that *QM2* is three times bigger than the *Titanic*. And that it's way, way safer. Practically unsinkable, in fact. Seriously.

It would be just too crazily mind-bendingly history-repeating-itself-as-farce ironic for the *QM2* to sink, so I didn't worry about it.

I assumed at least a third of the passengers on the *QM2* would be gentlemen sportsmen engaged in airplane-less races of some kind. Incorrect. It turns out the main customers who go on six-day transatlantic ocean voyages on the basis of nostalgia for a lost golden age of liners are (1) extremely old people, (2) perfect couples who are into cheesy romantic stuff, and (3) gay men.

It was six pretty awkward days.

The extremely old people are the vast majority. I would've

*The old company Cunard has been bought out by Carnival, but they still slap the "Cunard" brand on everything because Cunard has a history of classiness and tuxedos whereas Carnival has a history of Kathie Lee Gifford.

realized this if I'd looked a little more closely at the pictures in the brochure, which all depict silver-haired foxes leading their handsome wives around the dance floor. The bulk of my fellow passengers were equally old but way less mobile. I'd guess that at least half the people on the *QM2* were old enough to have heard about the *Titanic* when it happened. So they should've known better, but here they were.

The second group was a tiny but infuriating percentage. I was assigned to sit next to one of these perfect couples at dinner all five nights. The wife was a former beauty pageant winner who edits a magazine about dogs. Her husband was a former air force officer who told me about how he'd been sent to Afghanistan with three hundred thousand dollars in cash and set about hiring Afghanis to build airfields. During the whole trip I tried to poke holes in this couple's perfection. But to the best of my research they are upstanding citizens, devout but unimposing Christians, enterprising but compassionate businesspeople, and very much in love. They clearly would've rather been seated next to another perfect couple instead of a disheveled lonesome drunk who rambled on about Mongolia. But they never said a word.

Possibly out of fear of offending the extremely old people, the official Cunard literature doesn't make a big deal about the third group, gay men. On the first day, in the "Daily Programme" I saw listed "5:00 p.m.—Friends of Dorothy—The Commodore Club, Starboard Side." I guessed that this was a weird circumlocution for "gay," but I wanted to find out for sure, being a serious journalist and all. So I went to the bar at the Commodore Club at 5:00 p.m. I sat exactly amidships, just in case this "Dorothy" was some wretched harpie I wanted nothing to do with.

Sure enough a group of smartly dressed men convened to my left and started having a great time. After a few minutes, I detected some whispering, and one of them, a bald man of about seventy, came up and sat next to me at the bar.

We embarked on an idle conversation about New York City. It seemed innocent enough. But then I realized that he'd taken some kind of wager from his tablemates. His job was to find out how friendly I was toward Dorothy. This was his method: He told me a scandalous anecdote about Angela Lansbury. Then he leaned in and studied my face to watch my reaction.

Now, I'm pretty into Angela Lansbury. And the story he told me was definitely interesting. It's also been my experience that gay men make for better conversationalists than either extremely old people or perfect couples. So I explained to him what'd happened, he laughed, and I got to meet a bunch of charming gay dudes. I say this as a personal, observed observation that I observed, *not* as a stereotype: gay dudes know *way* more anecdotes about Angela Lansbury than straight people.

I asked one of the bartenders if this "Friends of Dorothy" bit ever caused any confusion. He nodded. "Oh, all the time. Every trip some old lady comes up here and says she wants to meet the famous Dorothy."

The previous eastbound trip of the *QM2* had been a private, chartered all-gay cruise. I got to know most of the bartenders on the ship, and invariably they talked about this all-gay trip the way people in Boston talk about the Blizzard of '78: as an overpowering encounter with a force of nature that was traumatic at the time but which was in retrospect both unbelievable and wondrous. Apparently by day three of the trip Dorothy's Friends set the all-time *QM2* martini-consumption record. If the Cunard folks have any marketing sense at all, they celebrated the occasion by inventing a new martini. Toward the stern of the ship there's a function room called the Queen's Room, then a small nightclub called G32. During the all-gay cruise, the Queen's Room had to be converted into an all-night dance club. G32 became a leather bar.

That would've been something to see. On this trip, however, G32 was returned to its status as an obscenely awful pit of remixed Supertramp and pudgy, sleazy German men. Here I discovered the only four single women on the voyage. They were a gaggle of condo saleswomen who spoke in some kind of squawking middle England accent/goose-cry language.

They were also absolutely committed to spending every minute of every night in G32. I was stuck with them on a ship, and I was the only single straight nonsleazy German man around, so this was probably my best-ever chance for some kind of twisted five-person sexual extravaganza. But I couldn't bring myself to descend there again, into the pit of squawking and Gloria Gaynor. I left them to the Germans and saw them only when they came up for muffins and french fries.

Meanwhile, on the upper decks I had to avoid the advances of an eighty-year-old woman from Texas who kept trying to invite me to "cocktail parties," which I think were just her in her room.

Nearly all of the other activities on the ship were skewed toward the elderly. There were health presentations every day, with titles like "How to Stay Healthy, Live Longer, and Stay Out of the Hospital" and "Answers to Every Question You Ever Had on Heart Attacks, Angioplasty, & Bypass Surgery." There were art auctions where no one bought anything despite the increasingly wild claims of the auctioneer. There was a retired producer from the BBC aboard who every day gave a lecture about a classic movie star. Invariably these talks were at least 20 percent devoted to the actor's height, an obsession of the lecturer's, with praise heaped upon "Ingrid Bergman, all five foot nine of her!" and mild scorn visited on lowly Dustin Hoffman. One night there was a passenger talent show, where several men sang songs of their own composition and two women played some kind of miniature bagpipe. I thought about entering with a song from *Barren Mountain Tears*, but decided against it.

There were also professional shows every night. At the end of "Rock @ the Opera," an MC came out to further whip up the already enthusiastic crowd.

"Ladies and gentlemen, how about these performers?" he said, as the audience clapped their arthritic hands. "Their energy! Their talent! Their *YOUTH!*" At this several members of the audience nearly had applause-induced strokes.

The two main activities aboard were (1) eating and (2)

complaining. Two strangers would sit at a table together and immediately begin parsing every tiny flaw in the service—how the french fries were soggy or the tea was weak. I found it hard to participate in this, because I thought the food was great. No one seemed very interested when I'd point out that it was a lot better than what you could get at the train station in Nizhny Novgorod.

I'd imagined that people aboard the *QM2* would be interested in hearing about my race—that wealthy dukes and so forth would introduce me to their lovely granddaughters and demand I join them for a stag hunt in the Highlands next summer. Wrong again, Hely! Most of my conversations ended up like this:

EXTREMELY OLD PERSON: So . . . how did you end up here?

ME: I'm competing in a race around the world without the use of airplanes.

EXTREMELY OLD PERSON: Oh. (LONG PAUSE) The chicken was too dry last night.

I spent most of my time on Activity (3), drinking. This was illuminating, as fellow bar patrons taught me a great deal about the carnation business, camping in Scotland, the making of Rolls-Royces, and why you shouldn't print out pornography on your work computer, not even on Saturday.

One thing you kind of forget about on the *QM2* is the actual ocean, the giant, monstrous Atlantic. I confirmed that the Atlantic looks more or less like the Pacific. But from my extra-cheap interior cabin I couldn't see the water, so it often slipped out of my mind. So much so that one day, as I sat in the Canyon Ranch Spa,* I spotted a pod of whales out the window and wondered, "What are *those* guys doing here?"

I hope I don't sound ungrateful about all this, because I appreciated that for most of its passengers this trip was their dream vacation. I was lucky to be there—the *QM2* is really magnificent. There's a grand glass-paned library, and a lovely

*Astute readers will note this is the second time during this race that I went in a steam room on a ship.

pool, and white-gloved teatime. And it's possible, alone on the staircase or out on the bow watching the spray and the fog, to transport yourself back to the days of the great transatlantic liners, when you were forced to take your time getting places and make the journey half the adventure.

But for me the *QM2* was just a leg in the race. When we saw the Statue of Liberty in New York harbor, I felt exactly as joyous as a tubercular nineteenth-century immigrant escaping centuries of persecution.

The Victory Scotch was now only a continent away. Where Vali was I did not know.

VALI: Does That Guy Ever Blink?

I rode a *moto*, a motorcycle taxi, from the airport toward my guesthouse along the Tonlé Sap River in Phnom Penh. My luggage rested between the driver's legs while I took in the Cambodian scenery from the back.

On this Wednesday night, hundreds of locals walked along the river, lounged on the curbs, and slept in the back of *tuk-tuks*—small taxis that were essentially four-person carriages attached to a motorcycle.

Many of the locals sat still, their faces vacant in drug-induced stares. The following morning I would see them and their stares in the exact same positions.

We passed bars advertising happy hours and restaurants that only sold "happy pizza"—pizza with marijuana-laced sauce. Much less prevalent were advertisements for "unhappy pizza"—pizza covered in reminders of what a useless failure you are (e.g., half-filled-out law school applications, an unassembled Bowflex, way too much pepperoni, etc.).

The moto driver stopped at a roadside gas station and handed the attendant one United States dollar. Cambodians have their own currency but everybody accepts and uses dollars at four thousand riel to the dollar. The gas station was nothing more than a card table covered by glass Coca-Cola bottles filled with gasoline. It could have doubled as a Just Add

a Rag! Molotov Cocktail Store. The attendant poured half a bottle of gasoline into the motorcycle tank and sent us on our way.

Right away I knew Cambodia was going to be different.

VALI: One Night in Phnom Penh

At the guesthouse I met up with my college acquaintance Katrina.

When I first decided to cheat and see as much interesting stuff as possible during the Ridiculous Race, I felt freed because I could go anywhere. Then I started to feel overwhelmed because I couldn't go everywhere.

Katrina, who I barely knew, found out about my conundrum and e-mailed me, making a strong case for visiting

Cambodia. Most of this involved explaining her college thesis, which was about cannibalism in Cambodia under the Khmer Rouge. Despite the personal danger involved (I am extremely delicious looking), I was sold. Katrina had so many suggestions for interesting things to do and people to see, I eventually just asked her to meet me in Cambodia so she could show me around herself. She accepted the invitation, perhaps because she had me confused with someone else.

By the time I arrived, Katrina had drawn up an itinerary for the night.

Our first stop was a nearby carnival. The rides were as cheap as they were safe, which made them all the more fun. We drove gas-powered bumper cars around a dirt circle, repeatedly crashing into a six-year-old girl riding around with her three-year-old brother on her lap. At one point I thought I broke his face, but he turned out to just be laughing really hard. His sister then high-fived me.

Afterward we went on a rickety Ferris wheel. There were no other passengers waiting, so the operator was prepared to let us ride indefinitely. When I gave him what I thought was the international signal to stop, he *increased* the speed. This made communicating with him even more difficult. After fifteen minutes I became certain I was going to die of old age on that Ferris wheel. After twenty-five minutes I started hoping I died really young. Thankfully, after thirty minutes we discovered that screaming was the ticket to getting let off.

My favorite thing about carnivals is usually the food. Nobody combines fat, sugar, and creepiness better than carnies. After some searching, I learned that the Cambodian equivalent to deep-fried Oreos is Pong tea khon, boiled chicken eggs with near fully developed embryos inside. I am a carnivore and rarely back down from a new eating experience, but something about Phnom Penh, maybe the pall of violence and violation that still hung heavy over the city, made my stomach queasy. I felt extra obligated to make moral decisions while there. So instead of chicken fetus, I ate some vegetarian noodles.

"Want to go see some intense stuff now?" Katrina asked as we finished eating.

"How intense?"

"Last time I was here there was a place where you could kill a cow with an AK47."

"I don't want to do that."

"Good. I was worried you were a sicko. Though I'm still not convinced you aren't. Let's go to Sharkey's."

There are exactly two types of people in Sharkey's: expat men and out-in-the-open prostitutes, euphemistically referred to as taxi girls. The experience was particularly shocking having just spent the past two weeks in the Middle East where I never even saw a thigh.

A European man in his mid-thirties walked into the bar after us, sat down, and ordered a whiskey. Nearby, a group of twenty-year-old Cambodian girls wearing Daisy Duke shorts and tight T-shirts played pool. After a minute, one of the girls sat down two seats over from the new entrant and ordered a drink. Seconds later she initiated a conversation and, making no big deal out of it, slid into the seat next to the man. Two minutes after that her hand was massaging his crotch. This girl had it down to a science.

"Want to go somewhere else?" Katrina asked.

A different man, one I hadn't noticed earlier, walked out of Sharkey's carrying a smiling Cambodian girl on his back.

"Let's go to a bar where locals our age hang out," I said.

The local bar was named Heart of Darkness. A sign near the door explicitly forbade bringing knives, firearms, or grenades inside. Worried that it's impossible to have fun at a bar without weapons? Don't be. The ever-resourceful wealthy Cambodians have figured a way around this problem: Bring massive bodyguards. I heard the bodyguards also serve as excellent wingmen.

Before I entered the Heart of Darkness, one of the bouncers stopped me for a search. *Finally*, I thought, *a country that takes my threat of violence seriously*. He started digging through my bag, then found something that caused his facial features to converge to a point of pure confusion at the center of his head. He pulled out the offending object. It was a good luck charm given to me the day before I left: a tiny soft plastic left foot. Convinced he was holding a severed baby's foot the bouncer started screaming in terror.

"What is that?!" he asked.

I was laughing too hard to answer so Katrina explained for me: "He is crazy."

VALI: Why Is the Median Age in Cambodia Twenty-one?

Cambodia is a scarred country.

I'm generally not one of those those-who-cannot-remember-the-past-are-condemned-to-repeat it types, but it's impossible to understand anything at all about modern Cambodia without knowing a little about the country's recent history.

First there were the French, who, while they had control of Vietnam, figured they might as well give Cambodia a go, too. This must have been one of those rare cases of imperialism causing problems because the Khmers, as the locals are known, were not psyched about the whole deal.

Their savior, sort of, came in the form of Norodom Sihanouk. Sihanouk was crowned king at age nineteen by the French, who figured he'd be a pushover. They were wrong. By thirty, Sihanouk had secured Cambodian independence. In 1954, the Geneva Conference recognized an independent Cambodia. This was good news. Smiles were smiled, dances were danced, fists were pumped.

One year later, Sihanouk abdicated the throne but continued to rule Cambodia through his newly created People's Socialist Community Party. Then his mind began to wander. He became obsessed with movies.

During the five-year period between 1965 and 1970, Sihanouk wrote, directed, and produced eight movies. He acted in some of them, too. Eventually people had gotten a little fed up with Sihanouk's method of governing through filmmaking and in 1970 Sihanouk's cousin pulled together an army and exiled him to China. This ended the recent period of Cambodian history when things were relatively normal.

Meanwhile the United States, embroiled in the Vietnam War, began a secret bombing program with the idea of eradicating communist base camps in Cambodia. This went on for four years and killed up to a quarter million Cambodians. When the bombings ended, the people were angry and the government was weak. A Maoist revolutionary group called the Khmer Rouge took advantage and, in 1975, gained control of the country. They killed a couple hundred thousand people in the process. And that was their nice period.

The leader of the Khmer Rouge, Pol Pot, was obsessed with implementing a radical agrarian form of communism. The first step was taking the urban population, the "new people," and turning them into agrarians, "old people." So the Khmer Rouge marched every city resident—including children, the elderly, and the sick—into the countryside and forced them to labor for over twelve hours a day. Those who disagreed with the radical practice were told, "To keep you is no benefit. To destroy you is no loss." One gets the sense that there wasn't a foosball table at Khmer Rouge headquarters.

The Vietnamese finally pushed the Khmer Rouge out of Phnom Penh in 1978, but the organization did not die. It continued to terrorize the nation with guerrilla warfare and terrorist attacks until the late 1990s.

Seeing the evidence of the Khmer Rouge's activities was even more upsetting than I expected. At Tuol Sleng, a high school converted into a torture facility, a sign on the playground listed the rules of the facility:

1. Don't be a fool for you are a chap who dare to thwart the revolution.
2. You must immediately answer my questions without wasting time to reflect.
3. While getting lashes or electrification you must not cry at all.
4. Do nothing, sit still, and wait for my orders. If there is no order, keep quiet. When I ask you to do something, you must do it right away without protesting.

5. If you don't follow all the above rules, you shall get many many lashes of electric wire.
6. If you disobey any point of my regulations you shall get either ten lashes or five shocks of electric discharge.

Rule 6 looks like it was added after someone lost the electric wire mentioned in rule 5.

Afterward I visited the killing fields of Choeung Ek, an extermination camp where 17,000 people were killed and buried in mass graves. Victims were often killed by bludgeoning or simply buried alive to save bullets. Today, a glass-sided tower containing 8,000 unearthed skulls memorializes the dead. My mind couldn't believe what my eyes reported. *This is surely a prop on a movie set,* I thought.

It is estimated that the Khmer Rouge killed between one million and three million people of Cambodia's population of seven to eight million. The Khmer Rouge's goal was to create a classless utopian society. Historians disagree on whether they succeeded or not.

VALI: Why Do Drugs When You Can Dance?

Thirty Cambodian kids aged six to eighteen sat around the perimeter of the linoleum-floored room on the second floor of KK's modest house. KK stood in the center of the group, facing a mirrored wall. He wore a helmet, yellow Adidas windpants with one leg pulled up, and a black tank top. A hip-hop beat played in the background. When he was ready KK dropped into a side-split, hoisted his body up with his hands, then started swinging his legs around, lifting his arms out of the way just in time for each leg to pass under. I watched from the corner of the room as KK twirled like this for a few seconds, then pulled the back half of his body into the air until he was in some sort of crooked headstand. Locked in this position, he started doing vertical push-ups. The thirty Cambodian kids clapped respectfully.

After KK ceded the floor, a six-year-old who had ridden his bike several miles to come to the house took the center of the circle. He did a few quick hip-hop steps and attempted a headstand. Then it was someone else's turn. Like this, it went on for three hours every night.

KK learned how to break dance in Long Beach, California, where he lived most of his life as a Cambodian refugee, one of 147,000 the United States admitted between 1975 and 1998. There KK joined a gang and started doing drugs, decisions, which in true after-after-school-special style, had a devastating effect on his life. Before long, he found himself in state prison.

In the United States, any foreign national who commits a crime with a minimum penalty of one year in prison can be deported. This includes refugees whose countries, like Cambodia, have been deemed safe for return by the U.S. government. When KK completed his sentence, a judge invoked this policy and sent him packing.

Even those of us who aren't right-wing talk radio show hosts can understand the spirit behind deporting noncitizen criminals, especially refugees who have responded to U.S. generosity by breaking her laws. A government must protect its own citizens before aiding noncitizens, right? I think so.

But when talking to KK, it was hard to ignore the profound sadness I felt for him. He was returned to Phnom Penh three years ago. He knew of no relatives, had no friends, and couldn't speak Khmer. His mother stayed behind in Long Beach, along with his babymama and son. KK calls home occasionally but never speaks to his son even if he's there. "I can't handle it," he said.

Many of the 160 or so American deportees in Phnom Penh have returned to the lifestyle that got them deported in the first place. But KK wanted to make a change. So he quit drugs and alcohol and, at the urging of some friends he made while volunteering with a local nongovernmental organization, he started Tiny Toons Dancers.

Anyone who wants can join. But if a kid is caught skipping school or doing drugs, he or she is kicked out of the group until the behavior changes. KK has kicked three kids out so far, including the best dancer in the group.

A few of the kids, who generally do not come from a background anyone would choose if that was how it worked, have even lived with KK for periods of time. Sometimes they steal from him (one of the kids took his laptop), but he continues to offer up his house to those in need.

Why does KK put himself through this? It's a lot of work; he still works every day at the NGO before coming home and dancing for three hours. It might be morally satisfying, but I didn't get the sense KK was very happy. Three years after coming to Cambodia, KK still knew very little Khmer, he had found no family, and the kids he loved to help often exhausted and occasionally took advantage of him.

I fucked up, he seemed to want to say.

I don't think KK really hoped to improve his life in Cambodia. His focus was on making sure his kids, the Tiny Toons, didn't make one big mistake they could never bounce back from.

VALI: The Story of Cambodia

According to legend, Cambodia came about as follows.

Once upon a time an Indian prince named Kaundinya wandered about some watery lands, which were ruled by a race of dragons, or "Nagas." Being Indian, this Kaundinya was quite a catch: smart, funny, handsome, a wise investor, etc. So it was no surprise when the daughter of the Naga king fell in love with him.

When the two decided to wed, the Naga king drank up the water covering his kingdom and presented the land to Kaundinya as a dowry. (He then missed most of the wedding because he was peeing.) The land became Cambodia. And the children of Kaundinya and the princess were the first Khmer people.

So Cambodians are half Indian and half dragon. I can't think of an awesomer genetic makeup. On the other hand, early Cambodians must have had some serious identity struggles. ("I'm caught between two cultures, neither completely Indian nor completely dragon. My grandmother on my father's side thinks I don't like spicy food just because I breathe fire all the time. But I do! The fire breathing is completely unrelated to the spiciness of the food! Who doesn't love tandoori chicken?! I'm half dragon, not a savage.") In comparison, I have it easy.

VALI: Getting to Siem Reap

"We can take a boat to Siem Reap for eighteen dol—" Katrina started.

"—Let's just fly," I interrupted.

"It won't take that much longer to drive."

"It's about the principle," I explained.

VALI: No, I'm Pretty Sure We Won't Be Needing Anything Else

Siem Reap, located just a few kilometers away from the temples of Angkor, is a world away from Phnom Penh. There are no piles of bone and skin staring out through drug-numbed faces. Prostitutes are not as prevalent. Siem Reap is growing, not struggling to stay alive, and I could feel it.

The taxi driver told us that the city had many job opportunities because, after years of being scared away by violence, tourists were returning to Cambodia. (Even in the late 1990s, the Khmer Rouge would occasionally kidnap and murder tourists.) Now over a million tourists visit the country every year, almost all of whom visit Siem Reap. (It would be a great ironic twist if the tourists started kidnapping and murdering Khmer Rouge members, but nobody I spoke to had ever heard of that happening. My attempts to be the first went nowhere.)

New infrastructure has sprung up to support all the new visitors. Last time Katrina was in town, back in 2002, she said there were two or three bars. Five years later, we passed at least ten on the way to our hotel. A roller coaster passing over Angkor Wat can't be too far off.

The One Hotel, where we stayed, came in with the recent tourism boom. It is literally a one-room hotel. It is not a bed and breakfast. It is not a guesthouse. It is a full hotel with a restaurant, a bar that serves the best pineapple-juice-and-rum cocktail I've ever tasted, and a hyperattentive twelve-person staff that makes the most doting grandmother seem like a careless wastrel.

To make sure there was no confusion, all of the room's features were explained to us in great detail by a slight Cambodian man who could have been anywhere between fifteen and fifty years old. He stood around awkwardly even after I gave him a tip. I thought maybe my tip was too low so I offered him another tip. He refused but continued to stand there.

Katrina and I stared at each other, unsure what to do. After about a minute, he shook my hand, thanked me, and left.

VALI: In Which My Jaw Is Constantly Agape in Awe

Have you ever seen anything so beautiful you wouldn't have minded seeing only that image for the rest of your life? It's a pretty short-sighted decision. You'd constantly be running into things afterward. But to see one of the temples of Angkor forever, it might be worth it.

The temples, built one at a time over a period of six hundred years by kings also revered as gods, began fairly modestly and ended with the most amazing structure I have ever seen in my life. And I've seen an igloo made out of mashed potatoes.

The first temple Katrina and I visted, Bayon, was a gargantuan dark sandstone building featuring somewhere around eleventy billion impressive bas reliefs of people beating the crap out of one another. Every square foot of the wall had so much to see: a monkey sitting cross-legged in prayer, a group of defeated soldiers drowning their sorrows with alcohol, a tiny dragon-faced demon flossing his teeth with twine (my interpretation). However, the highlights of Bayon are the

216 massive and identical smirking faces that stare out from every vertical surface. Each face is the size of an entire human. Time has eroded them enough for us to see the individual sandstone blocks that make up each one. Taken together, the faces, which at some spots in the temple looked in at me from all directions, are mesmerizing and oddly calming.

I saw an impressed eleven-year-old American kid staring at a tower with four faces.

"Pretty creepy that this is a natural rock formation," I said.

"Really?!"

"Yeah. Just the winds of the Cambodian jungle."

He ran off toward two adults: "Mom! Did you know . . ."

That was my cue to leave.

At Ta Prohm the jungle has slowly taken the land back from the temple. In one corner, the roots of a giant tree have simply enveloped the wall. It looks like someone wounded the temple and, instead of blood and tissue, thirty feet of thick root system had oozed out and dried.

Ta Keo, a first-century temple that was never finished for unknown reasons, actually looks strikingly modern. Undecorated and unsmooth, it is a massive structure of boxy sandstone blocks, each jutting out different distances. It looks like a cubist interpretation of a great Hindu/Buddhist temple.

At the top of Ta Keo a young Cambodian girl and her younger brother were selling postcards to tourists. The girl was basically conversational in the languages of the most frequent tourist groups. She could start a conversation in Japanese, Chinese, German, Spanish, and English. Her younger brother, on the other hand, was still picking up the languages. In the meantime, all he did was look up with moist eyes and repeat, "Postcards . . . postcards . . . postcards?"

"Do you want to buy postcards?" the girl asked me.

"Can you guess where I am from?" I asked back.

She looked me up and down, then thought for a moment. "The moon?"

I bought a book of postcards.

All of that was just a fraction of what there is to see at Angkor. There are several other fantastic temples, some of which are still surrounded by undetonated land mines from the Khmer Rouge days. Then there is the Terrace of the Leper King, the Terrace of Elephants, a bridge lined with Buddha heads, and more. All of it is just as impressive as it sounds. Except maybe the Leper King, which I had hoped was a fast food restaurant.

But the gem of Angkor is Angkor Wat.

It is so wonderfully, mind-blowingly cool, and stuffed with things to see, I visited three times.

My first visit was the most memorable. A storm approached as Katrina and I crossed the massive moat surrounding the temple, turning the sky a strange, trippy purple. Horses dressed up in chain mail for photographs with tourists started fidgeting, urging their owners to get them somewhere covered. By the time I got inside the world's largest Vishnu temple, it was pouring. Rain whipped in through the windows. Kids played in the temporary waterfalls that formed under drainage grooves. Adults slipped and fell. I sat next to a bas relief carving depicting a team of devils, including the twenty-one-headed demon king Ravana, working with a team of gods to churn an ocean of milk using a long serpent wrapped around a mountain propped up by a giant tortoise—an incarnation of Vishnu.

The culture of Cambodia has been torn to shreds by imperialism, American anticommunism, the Khmer Rouge, and the post–Khmer Rouge struggle for power. But the cultural forces that led to the temples of Angkor are still around somewhere. Cambodia is wounded, but not dead. So Cambodia will go on. After all, the rain has to stop sometime, right?

VALI: This Is Embarrassing to Admit

Cambodia: Capable of Turning a Couple of Sarcastic Jerks into Doe-Eyed Teenagers. That should be the slogan used by the Cambodian Tourism Board.

After several days of spending twenty-four hours within arm's reach of each other, watching each other's backs in

Phnom Penh, exploring Angkor Wat in the rain, trying to buy alligators, and drinking beer in a terrace hot tub in Siem Reap, Katrina and I had almost fused together.

Objectively speaking, it was pretty gross. At one point, after agreeing to run separate personal errands in Siem Reap, we reconnected on the street, each having decided to join the other and run our own errand later.

Katrina and I also started referring to each other as husband and wife. I know this has happened twice during my half of the Ridiculous Race, but you must trust that I never initiated the practice. With Katrina and I, it began when she insisted that we go to a photo studio, dress up in traditional Khmer costumes, and have our picture taken. After about a day of badgering, I agreed.

When we got to the studio, "traditional costumes" suddenly became "wedding costumes." Why did I agree? Who knows. Why did *she* even want to do it? Cambodia does crazy things to your brain.

At some point during our travels together Katrina mentioned that she was a descendant of Napoleon Bonaparte. (It came up during a discussion about how Napoleon's embalmed penis was going up for auction.)

I told Katrina the story about the Chandrasekaran men and Russia and how I narrowly missed being Vali Napoleon. I followed this up with a thought about how insane it would be if (1) I actually had gotten named Vali Napoleon and (2) Katrina and I had children—I know this is weird but please bear with me—because then Napoleon's bloodline would have, strangely, returned to its name.

On our final day in Cambodia, Katrina became ill. I told the five One Hotel staff members waiting outside our room door, "We're going to need to check out a little bit later today because my friend is sick." When I walked back into the room, Katrina, still in bed, burned holes into my head with her eyes.

"What's the matter?" I asked.

"We've been telling everyone that we're husband and wife. Why did you just tell them I'm your 'friend'?"

At five a.m. the following morning, I went to the airport. Katrina stayed behind to continue traveling through Cambodia, southern China, and Uzbekistan for several more months.

I was tremendously bummed. The sadness caused me to find the polite questions of my moto driver particularly annoying. After a few minutes I just pretended I couldn't hear him over the roar of the engine.

At the airport, the immigration official checking my passport sensed something was wrong.

"Is everything all right, sir?" he asked.

"I don't know when I'm going to see my wife again," I responded.

VALI: The Nicest Hotel Room Ceiling in Shanghai

I checked into my hotel and collapsed onto the bed. According to everything I had read in the past two years, the future of the world was in China. But I had no desire to see any of it. Instead, I stared at the ceiling and wondered why I hadn't just stayed in Cambodia longer. I wanted to go back, but decided that was stupid. Then I just wanted to go home.

It had been almost three weeks since Steve and I had met in Moscow. It takes about three days to get from Moscow to London, a week to cross the Atlantic by boat, and three days to cross the United States by train or car. So even if Steve had taken an extra week to enjoy himself a little bit, an absurd amount of time for anyone racing around the world, he should have been back in Los Angeles by now. I thought about how happy he must have felt to return home victorious, thrilled that his plans had succeeded. Surely he was celebrating his victory by now. I imagined him sitting in a hot tub with all of my ex-girlfriends.

I wondered what the scotch tasted like.

After a couple minutes of this, I decided the self-pitying had to end. I needed to do something. Anything.

But I couldn't.

So I turned on the TV and was delighted to discover that the hotel carried HBO. I watched *The Making of Rumor Has It,* a behind-the-scenes look at the creation of the Rob Reiner romantic comedy starring Jennifer Aniston, Shirley MacLaine, Kevin Costner, and Mark Ruffalo. Afterward I watched *Rumor Has It.* I think watching the *Making of . . .* actually enhanced my appreciation of the film. I noticed nuances that would have flown over my head before. Yes, Rob Reiner, it did subvert the standard romantic comedy form! A later, second watching of *Rumor Has It* really made me reconsider some recent life decisions.

VALI: Is That a Wood Carving of a Three-Foot Boner?

I can't say I felt totally fine by the next morning, but I did finally realize being in Shanghai was too wonderful of an opportunity to waste. Also, crazily, HBO was not scheduled to play *Rumor Has It* at any point that day. So I used a little of my trademark Vali Get Up and Go and hit the streets.

I walked down to the Bund, the river that scythes Shanghai into two halves, and made my way to the subway station. There I was delighted to discover that, for only a few extra yuan, I could visit two museums located *within* the station. It seemed like an odd location for museums, but I chalked it up to a Chinese zest for education.

The first was an aquatic museum housing a decent number of fish and a lot of written information. There the Chinese really overestimated how much I care about sturgeon.

The second was a museum of ancient Chinese sexual art. Keep in mind this is located in a subway station. The first item I saw was a several-hundred-year-old stone dildo next to a card, explaining, "An artificial penis that was used to expand the anus of gays." Also on display were stone carvings of apes having sex, a penis carved into a piece of polished driftwood, and a three-foot-tall shiny wooden statue of a chain-bound man with a four-foot erection accompanied by the piece's title, *This Part of the Body Could Not Be Locked.* I suspected, but was never able to confirm, that the museum was curated by a group of sixth-grade boys.

One ticket granted admission to a sex museum and an aquarium. Who, except me, wants to see both of those things in one outing? Based on the number of people entering the museum from the busy subway station, I would guess zero.

VALI: Hello, Class

Not long after leaving the sex museum, I walked up to the blackboard and wrote out my name, Mr. Chandrasekaran, then turned to face the eighth-grade English class at the American School in Shanghai.

Just before leaving Russia, Steve challenged me to teach a comedy-writing class before getting back to Los Angeles. Arranging this was much easier than expected, especially once I stopped demanding a twenty-thousand-dollar speaking fee.

The Shanghai American School is brand-new, one of several schools catering exclusively to the Shanghai expat community. Most of the kids were born in America, though a few hailed from Asia and Europe. All of them watched the latest American TV shows on pirated DVDs they bought on the street.

If these kids harbored both a Chinese work ethic and a knowledge of American culture, they represented a real threat to my livelihood. My life as a TV writer was pretty excellent. I didn't want a bunch of hardworking punks coming in and ruining that. *Best to fill my talk with misinformation,* I thought.

"Try and make your television scripts as abstract as possible," I told the class. "Audiences love stories that involve only a funeral urn and a spotlight. And don't forget to give the main character, in this case the funeral urn, a strong emotional arc."

By the end of the hour I was certain nobody in the class

would ever compete with me for a television-writing job. My only regret was not being able to reach more kids.

Just before ending my lesson, I couldn't help giving the students one piece of real comedy advice.

"Swears are always funny."

VALI: Time Is a Very Strange Illusion

A curious fact about flying to the United States from the Far East is that, thanks to the International Date Line, you land before you take off. A flight leaving China at 8:30 p.m. on Saturday will arrive in Los Angeles at 5:45 p.m. the same day. On my way home, somewhere over the Pacific Ocean, the jet engines bent time's arrow back on itself until it broke, instantly giving me back the twenty-four hours that had been slowly stolen from me, in one-hour increments, over the past seven weeks.

I spent most of my newfound time memorizing facts about Air China's fleet.

STEVE: The Home Stretch

At 4:15 in the morning on June 4, 2007, the *Queen Mary 2* missed nicking the bottom of the Verrazano-Narrows Bridge by about three feet as she sailed into New York harbor. Most of my fellow passengers were out on the deck as the Manhattan skyline came into view in the predawn light. I myself was inside, hunched over a plate of hash browns because I didn't want to miss my last free breakfast.

We docked in Brooklyn. The trip from LA to New York—the long way—had taken fifty days.

I was back in the United States. Hopefully Vali wasn't.

Already in this book I've tried to describe the Pacific, summarize China, figure out Mongolia, explain Russia, condense Europe, and contemplate the Atlantic.

But with New York City I give up. Maybe if this was my

first visit, I could try it. But I lived there for two years, and every single day it seemed crazier.

New Yorkers love trying to describe the place. By my count, roughly half the inhabitants of New York have tried to write novels about their city.

They should all give up and go play Capture the Flag in Central Park together, because describing New York City is futile, like trying to describe what chocolate tastes like, or what it feels like to sneeze. I'm giving myself two sentences, and then I'm moving on.

STEVE: New York City in Two Sentences

The average apartment in Manhattan costs one point two million dollars, the net worth of the current mayor is close to four times the GDP of Mongolia, yet once when I lived there I saw a man on the subway defecate into a piece of tinfoil. Like everybody else in New York City, he carried himself as though he were the troubled but heroic main character in an off-Broadway play.

I stayed in New York City just long enough to visit Coney Island, where an elephant named Topsy was once publicly electrocuted and where a midget used to shock ridegoers with a cattle prod.

In one afternoon I defied death three times.

1. I rode the wooden Cyclone, a roller coaster that since 1927 has convinced thrill seekers they're about to get decapitated.
2. I ate a hot dog from Nathan's.
3. I told a cabdriver at rush hour that I needed to get to Penn Station in a hurry.

STEVE: The Lakeshore Limited

Amtrak isn't great at making trains run fast. Our trains are slower than those in, say, France or Japan. This is a national disgrace—we're the United States, and we should have huge trains with flames and lightning bolts painted on the sides that speed along at five hundred miles an hour while blasting the power rock hits of Warrant.

But Amtrak *is* good at naming trains—there's the *Empire Builder*, the *Southwest Chief*, the *California Zephyr*, and the one I was on, the *Lakeshore Limited*, which runs along Lake Erie to Chicago.

I was sitting next to an elderly woman with a voice like a hurt parrot who took my exhausted, dead-ahead stare as an invitation to bring me up to speed on recent developments in her feet, and the swelling thereof. I tried to be polite, and periodically jumped in with an "Oh man" or "That sounds terrible." Every time I did this, she'd stop and look at me as if to say, "Hey—I'm telling a story here, buddy. Quit interrupting." So I stared out the window, and she kept chattering on my right as the Hudson River rolled by on my left.

It was disorienting to be back in the United States and see Cozy Coupes and kiddie pools in backyards. It's easy to forget about how bizarre our own country is. Seeing the stone blocks of West Point across the river were a helpful reminder. Our nation's military academy was attended by Edgar Allan Poe, George Armstrong Custer, Buzz Aldrin, James McNeill Whistler (the guy who painted his mother), Timothy Leary (the guy who invented LSD), and Abner Doubleday (the guy who didn't invent baseball). That's a roster of eclectic achievement no other country can match.

This was all a bit much to think about. So I dozed off. When I woke up in Indiana, my seatmate was telling me about some real bone-headed stuff her son did. This tirade—honest—concluded with the following sentence: "Young people today don't know nothing!"

From New York I could've driven to Los Angeles. It might've been faster. Recently a pair of outlaw racers in a BMW M5 pulled off the 2,794-mile drive in thirty-one hours with the aid of laser jammers, night-vision cameras, and a spotter airplane.

But I was very tired. Doubtless I would've crashed into a schoolbus somewhere in New Jersey. It would've been a tragic and disappointing end to the trip of my life if I'd ended up in shackles on the local news as the anchor said, "They're calling him 'The New Jersey Schoolbus Killer' " and then cut to Vali telling an interviewer, "It's just so sad that Steve chose to be so reckless."

I wouldn't let that happen.

In Chicago I got off the train and was picked up by Sam, my college roommate and a high-intensity road-trip hobbyist. He offered to start driving to Los Angeles immediately. It was noon; he believed we could make it in twenty-four hours and arrive by noon the next day. His plan involved lots of peeing in bottles and tightly orchestrated gas station choreography. Sam is like the Twyla Tharp of getting gas.

I had what I thought was an even better plan. This race for me had turned into a survey of transportation, of how stuff moves around the world by land and sea. I wanted to finish off with one last adventure on the most American ride of all.

VALI: The Moment of Confession, or, Will Steve Stab Me When He Finds Out I Cheated?

In the cab on the way back to my apartment, after fifty-two days on the road and in the air, I wondered how Steve would take the news of my cheating. I imagined he would want to spend the first few minutes of our meeting gloating about his victory. Maybe he would gloat so much and I could act so bummed about losing that I wouldn't have to tell him for a couple of days. On the other hand, we would probably want to start trading stories immediately and I wouldn't be able to tell him much about my trip without raising some serious suspicions. (For example: "Wait. How did you get from Moscow to Egypt to Dubai overland?")

There was no way around it. I needed to tell Steve right away. My only hope was that his trip wasn't miserable enough to make him hate me for having a truly great time.

But Steve was not there when I got home.

I was shocked. How could he have not gotten back from Moscow in three and a half weeks?

In true Steve form, he had pulled a "prank" that fooled exactly zero people for zero seconds. His glass of scotch was empty and in it was a note claiming he had already returned to Los Angeles, having circumnavigated the globe in forty-eight days. We had agreed before the start of the race that the winner would meet the loser in person, so I'm not sure what Steve thought the note would accomplish.

He is an idiot.

But at least he was a gentleman idiot. He had refused to drink the Victory Scotch himself, instead gifting it to my roommate.

I lifted up my own tumbler of scotch, swirled it around, and savored the spicy aroma.

But I couldn't drink it.

Since Steve was actually racing around the world without taking airplanes, I decided to pretend I hadn't gotten home yet. I wanted him to feel the moment of victory, even if the moment would be quickly followed by seething anger.

STEVE: Truckin'

"Hello, I'm a truck."

So goes the opening lyric from my favorite country song, entitled, "Hello, I'm a Truck," written by Mr. Bob Stanton and performed by Red Simpson during the Golden Age of American Trucking Songs, the 1970s. Back then there were so many songs about truck drivers that these gentlemen responded with a song from the truck's point of view, complete with a request to park next to pink trucks with pretty mudflaps and double-chrome stacks.

Smokey and the Bandit sealed the deal on truckers being America's last true independent working-man heroes, modern-day cowboys of the open road. I wanted to finish the race by rolling across America hauling freight in an eighteen-wheeler.

What I was picturing was a slop-gutted fella named Bower or Kennesaw whose T-shirt was spotted with year-old chili stains, who dodged smokeys, chewed tobacco, and popped handfuls of pills from a bottle labeled Energ-X or Awake-o-tol as we pulled eighty thousand tons of turpentine and Schlitz from Bangor to Bakersfield, blasting Buck Owens. We'd arrive on Sixth Street and see Vali pulling around the corner in a Rolls-Royce, knock him off the road, and watch him shake his fist at us as we blew both stacks and won the race by seconds.

I did not know how to make this happen.

I figured hitchhiking would be too risky—timewise, I mean, not dangerwise. I was perfectly happy to get murdered, provided my corpse made it to LA ahead of Vali, and that someone buried me with the Victory Scotch.

But instead what I decided to do was write a letter to the American Trucking Association.

> Dear Sir or Madam [it said],
>
> I'm competing in a race around the world without the use of airplanes [etc.] adventure [whatnot].
>
> I'd love to tell the story of the challenges facing America's truckers, [blahblah], skills and methods the trucking industry employs in its crucial mission to keep America moving [etc. etc.], can I please have a ride, and can he be named Kennesaw?
>
> Sincerely,
> Steve Hely

The American Trucking Association is not stupid. They

probably knew exactly what I wanted—stories about crystal meth and ninety-hour hauls. They wrote back and said, sure, but the driver they gave me was not named Kennesaw, nor was his shirt stained.

Bill Burton is a senior driving instructor for Jevic Transportation. He was selected as one of America's Road Team Captains, which is the highest honor you can get in trucking, at least until the Pulitzer folks revise their archaic prizes. Bill is also, I realized soon after I climbed into his cab, some sort of folksy Zen monk of the American road.

With his bushy rancher mustache, he looked like the actor Sam Elliott. In fact, I hereby declare that casting Sam Elliott is a must for *The Ridiculous Race Movie*. He wasn't slop-gutted; he was in great shape for sixty-something. His shirt was spotless. He ate salads. "There are no guarantees in trucking" was his mantra.

To Bill, trucking wasn't just a sacred

profession—although it was also that. It was an entire philosophy, and from Chicago to Davenport he laid it out for me.

1. "My job isn't to move things. My job is to protect life and property."
2. "A schedule is something two people agreed on without talking to me."
3. "I solve problems with planning that other truckers solve with speeding."
4. "You never miss a chance to eat, shower, or go to the bathroom."

I bided my time, patiently waiting until I could ask about amphetamines and prostitutes. There was plenty of road ahead of us.

Of all the odd and wonderful traveling companions I'd had on this trip, Bill might've been the best storyteller. Our drive was peppered not just with trucker tales, but with stories from the whole thick narrative of his life. From his days as a Baltimore city cop, Bill taught me how to hostage negotiate (establish a bond, play for time), how to talk down a potential suicide (start by asking "what are you doing?"), and how to respond to a bank robbery (try not to wet yourself).

All that was just the preview to his stories about the road: wild, American stories, like the time he passed through two miles of locusts. He had quiet stories of misfortune and courage and redemption. He told me a story about a hitchhiker he'd once picked up, befriended, and later visited in Georgia's state prison. "I promised him I'd pray for him." He waited a minute before telling me the end: "I found out later he was executed."

Bill was a lot sunnier on his favorite subject, trucking. Behind us was something like 79,000 pounds of resin, rubber sheeting, and "inedible fatty acid." I don't want to know what that is. It comes in huge cans.

He told me how snow on an eighteen-wheeler can add six hundred pounds to a load, and showed me spots on the highway where truckers pull off to wait for weigh stations to close. He told me how truckers generally have lots of home time, but it's unpredictable—you can't promise to be at your son's Little League game or your daughter's graduation. He pointed out how the driving is the easy part, but a lot of a trucker's time is eaten up loading and unloading—for which they don't get paid. He said it's impossible to completely avoid accidents while doing all this loading, and by way of example he showed me where a pallet had chopped off a chunk of his finger.

Bill explained the complex federal rules that regulate how much driving you can do, rules that can leave drivers stranded, forced to "reset their clocks," and take a thirty-four-hour break, often states away from home. He told me how the first question any trucker asks before taking a job is whether he's going to have to deal with the nightmare of driving into New York City or Boston.

He also talked a lot about his favorite singer, Sarah Brightman. I mean, a lot. Kind of a creepy amount. He would put on her CD of "Time to Say Good-bye" and scream encouragement at her through the dashboard.

Most importantly Bill taught me trucker lingo:

Evel Knievels—motorcycle cops
City kitties—local cops
Full-grown bears—state troopers
Wigglewagons—double and triple trailers
Stagecoaches—cars with trailers
Nice set of seat covers—a pretty lady in a car
Watering your wheels—peeing
Chicken coops—scale houses
Bedbuggers—household movers
Georgia overdrive—throwing your gear into neutral for a fast cruise downhill
Nebraska earthquake—the feeling you get in your stomach after eating too much Subway. (This one I made up.)

As for the amphetamines and prostitutes—*lot lizards*—Bill claimed those days are mostly over. He credited the rise of female drivers with driving hookers out of truck stops, and pointed out that many trucks these days are operated by husband-and-wife teams.

One thing I was disappointed by is the quality of CB radio chatter. Bill doesn't bother with it, mostly, but I kept asking him, so he gave me the handle "U-Turn" and let me give it a try. When there was chatter, it tended to sound like really bad amateur talk radio. There were lots of attempts at funny accents. Truck drivers are into funny accents. Even Bill himself wasn't immune to this. During a tricky maneuver outside a Denver loading dock, it was necessary for him to assume the persona of "Guillermo," *zee greatest driver in zee world.*

Because we had to make a stop in Denver and dodge some thunderstorms in Kansas, our route took us along I-80 through Nebraska and Iowa. I can't say this was the most exciting scenery I'd passed through on my trip. Compared to the Aleutians, say, there were way fewer whales and volcanoes. But it's not a bad slice of America. We passed by the former headquarters of the Strategic Air Command, and within a few miles of the birthplaces of Ronald Reagan, Herbert Hoover, John Wayne, and Bob Feller, and near Riverside, Iowa, which claims to be the "future birthplace" of Captain James T. Kirk. The landscape out there on the plains may be boring. But it's pleasant boring. Silos and ball fields boring. I think most people in Siberia would get down on their knees and thank God above for land that boring.

After making our Denver drop-off—citizens of Denver, you can thank me anytime for helping to deliver your much-needed rubber sheeting—we climbed through the Rockies, along highways cut by riverbanks, before swooping down into the striped red deserts of Utah.

Drive I-80 and I-76 after seeing the rest of the world and it's easy enough to understand why this country inspires such deep, religious devotion. It *looks* like a promised land.

Bill was a born-again Christian, and up in the mountains we got to talking about religion. This "talking" was mostly me making rewarmed smartass college kid arguments, and Bill responding in a thoughtful and considered tone that showed he knew more than me about both science and religion. To prove a point that the Bible doesn't actually contradict the big bang theory, he put on his CD of the Book of Genesis. The mighty language of God forming the Earth, heard as you pass through canyons and rivers, doesn't prove anything. It did, however, shut me up.

I've told this story—about riding in a truck as Bill put on his Bible CD and warned, "I'm going to pause this frequently"—at meetings and parties in Hollywood. I always get the same knowing "Aren't the country rubes ridiculous?" eye roll.

But I rode next to Bill for three days. I slept in the bunk above him in the back of the cab for two nights, once in Aurora, Nebraska, and once by the banks of the Colorado River. You learn a lot about a guy doing that. Bill drives a truck and lives in Indiana, but he was wiser, healthier, and—this is the most important—happier than anybody I ever met in Manhattan or Hollywood. He slept easy.

Except when my snoring woke him up. He claimed that happened several times a night.

I don't think America is the only place where you can find guys like this—honest, upbeat folks who take their work seriously and believe 100 percent earnestly in one-word values. I do think, though, that we have more of them than any other country in the world. And I think that's a big part of why our last hundred years wasn't nearly as miserable and cruelly ironic as everybody else's.

Bill was also super into Broadway musicals. I'm not ashamed to admit that somewhere in Nevada the two of us had an enthusiastic *Les Miserables* singalong.

STEVE: One Thought on America

All along the way from New York, I'd been trying to come up with some kind of insight about America versus the rest of the world. After all this traveling, I should have some deep perspective, right?

Well, the best I could do came to me after a series of truck stops, where I was constantly reminded of how amazing this country is. It's not even the variety of stuff for sale, although that's certainly amazing versus the rest of the world. It's the size of the bags. I mean, your average, ninety-nine-cent bag of Fritos in America, after seeing food in China and Russia, is just *stupid* huge.

I got to thinking that America isn't like a bully, or a jock, or a cool kid. In the high school of the world, America is like one of those girls that's just effortlessly beautiful. So beautiful you can't even have a crush on her. A girl like that isn't deliberately mean, it's just that she can't possibly understand how lucky she is. And people always do what she wants, without her even realizing it, so she never bothers becoming smart, or savvy about the other kids in school. Just with her airhead remarks, she's always accidentally screwing up the whole order of things. She doesn't even realize it.

Now, when you have a girl like that, the other kinda-pretty girls sort of like her but sort of hate her. That's maybe Germany, or France. And the ugly girls talk about her in the locker room, but are still totally afraid of her. That's Venezuela and Iran. The regular-looking dudes can't help but be awed by her. Maybe they try to woo her with poems. That's Great Britain. And the real twisted kids develop unhealthy obsessions about destroying her, just because they're so infuriated at how unfair things are.

Anyway, that's the brilliant geopolitical metaphor I came up with after two months of world traveling.

It seems to work. Then again I have no idea because there weren't any girls at my high school.

VALI: You Have Got to Be Kidding Me

A few days went by with no sign of Steve. Through some friends I learned he hadn't left London until after I arrived back in Los Angeles. He had taken about twenty-five days to make a trip, traveling from Moscow to London, that could have been easily accomplished in three. He wasn't racing at all.

At least I decided at the beginning that I was not going to race seriously. I wanted to see the world. Steve, on the other hand, continuously made a big show about how dedicated he was and how seriously he was taking the race. One of us failed at what he set out to do and it wasn't me.

Then I learned Steve had spent his extra three weeks gallivanting around western Europe. I lost my mind.

Really, Steve? Mr. gentleman adventurer? In 2007, you picked one section of the globe to explore in more detail and you chose the wilds of western Europe? How were you able to find your way around these uncharted territories? What sort of crazy things did people eat in Italy?

Steve's actions were the adventurous equivalent of Sir Francis Drake taking a nap in his apartment.

It was clear Steve had taken the race aspect of the Ridiculous Race no more seriously than I had. Additionally, I felt Steve took the adventurous spirit of the race far less seriously than I did. Freed of my guilt, I headed back to my apartment for a drink.

VALI: The Kinclaith

Normally one can guess what a better version of an experience will feel like. A person who has pretty good pizza can imagine how great pizza might be different. In our heads we have a list of pizza characteristics—greasiness, cheese flavor, crust quality, et cetera—that we could assign numbers to. Decent pizza might score a five or six across all these criteria, and we can imagine what a slice of pizza that scored all tens might taste like.

The scotch was different.

I lifted the glass up to my mouth and took a careful first sip. It was like a completely different beverage than any other scotch I had tasted. No, a completely different liquid. There was something more to it than taste. It was an experience.

Many days later, I would pour Steve his first glass of the

scotch. He insisted on drinking it with ice, like some sort of savage. Not me. I took the scotch like it was meant to be experienced: neat. Drinking something this delicious with ice was like eating caviar with your feet.

The scotch was spicy upon first hitting the tongue, then mellowed out into a rich taste that lasted forty seconds after swallowing. I timed it. During this period a warm sensation started in my mouth, radiated out all the way to my feet, then just held. It felt like the sun had moved a few thousand miles closer to Earth.

It was incredible, a fitting prize for the winner of the Ridiculous Race.

STEVE: The Last Leg

Driving with Bill had been great, but because of the federal restrictions on how long a trucker can stay on the road, it had taken a lot longer than I'd expected.

On June 12 we reached Ontario, California. We were forty-four miles away from my finish line when Bill hit his daily fourteen-hour driving limit. Federal law required him to stop. It didn't say anything about me.

I called my buddy Doogs, who'd driven me to Long Beach 21,400 miles ago. He picked me up for the last leg of the race.

I was nervous, so I asked Doogs what he'd been up to since I'd seen him last.

"Oh, not too much. I'm thinking about breaking up with this girl I'm seeing."

My brain tracked back, across America, over the Atlantic, through Europe and Asia, back across the Pacific, to the Bake 'n' Broil in Long Beach, fifty-seven days earlier.

"Wait a second," I said. "That's what you said to me the last time I saw you."

"Yeah," said Doogs. "Not a lot's happened."

Finally I couldn't take it anymore. I asked Doogs if Vali was back.

"Yup."

"Dammit." I wasn't crushed exactly. I knew my various exploratory excursions might cost me.

"Yeah," said Doogs, "he's been back for weeks."

Wait a second. Weeks? I did the math in my head.

I'm really bad at math, so I had to do it several times. Finally an equals sign appeared in front of this sentence:

That bastard took an airplane.

STEVE: The End

The end of the Ridiculous Race was impossibly anticlimactic. But maybe if we describe it honestly it'll prove that we've been telling the truth about all the crazy stuff in the last few hundred pages that really did happen.

I went to a bar while Doogs called Vali. While I waited I ate some Pizza Hut. Vali would want me to play some prank on him. Screw that guy. I wanted some pizza.

Vali came in. We yelled at each other and had an awkward hug/handshake. I demanded to know how he'd crossed the Pacific. He refused to tell me, until we got back to his apartment.

"Okay," he said. "I cheated."

Fine. I'd figured he'd might puss out on the Pacific.

"So I win! You took an airplane!"

Then Vali laughed like a corrupt mayor in an old movie and leaned back against the wall. "Oh, I took, like, ten airplanes. I cheated the whole way."

STEVE: Why Didn't I Punch Vali in the Face?

It's a question worth asking. Certainly his face deserved a punching right then and there. It would've been a really satisfying end to this story if I just leaped across the table and popped him and he slumped to the ground cold. Or—better yet—if I shoved his face through the window. That would've been great.

I didn't. It might've been satisfying for you, Reader, but at the moment it seemed like ungracious behavior for the winner. I'd won. Despite my easily distracted style of racing, I'd won fair and square in a race around the world.

And despite sticking to the rules, it sounded like I'd won the Awesomeness Contest as well. From the stories he babbled, it sounded like Vali had mostly hired women to protect him as he checked his Blackberry in between jetting to various hotels in popular tourist destinations. The guy didn't even ride a jetpack. No self-respecting man should go visit a jetpack dealer and come back with a lot of excuses about why he *didn't* ride a jetpack.

This will disappoint Vali, because I'm sure he spent most of his trip giggling as he pictured seeing steam come out of my ears when he revealed his treachery. But Vali's cheating had worked out perfectly—he'd serve as the buffoonish comic relief to my actual tale of adventure. After all, every Matthew McConaughey needs his Steve Zahn.

More than anything, after the places I'd seen, the only emotion I could have was gratitude for the lucky accident of my circumstances.

So I wasn't mad at Vali.

But then I saw that he'd drank about half of the Kinclaith 1969. *My* Victory Scotch. That I'd won. By doing it the hard way.

"Oh my God, you gotta try this, it's *so* good!"

VALI: Why I Didn't Punch Steve in the Face?

True, the end of the Ridiculous Race was impossibly stupid and anticlimactic. Steve arrived about three weeks later than anyone with a serious intention of racing around the world should arrive. He also orchestrated the incredibly lame "prank" of having me arrive at a bar expecting to see my friend Doogs, only to find *him* there playing video poker.

I was livid. This was how Steve wanted to end the most exciting experience of our life to date?!

We walked to my apartment, where I set aside my annoyance for a moment and came clean about the ten airplanes I took. Steve's reaction was to start babbling about his grandchildren and how he wanted to tell them about the race and how I ruined that story.

My face broke into a grin, my chest started trembling, and then my body exploded with laughter.

What was he going to tell his grandchildren? Was he going to tell them that at the end of the race he was too embarrassed to show up at my apartment and face me so instead he went by himself to drink Miller Lite and eat Pizza Hut?

No, but I would.

I sat across from Steve at the very table we met at to start the race, unable to stop laughing as he grew more and more irate.

"What is so funny?" he kept demanding.

I looked forward to sitting in a rocking chair at Steve's house in my sixties with little Vali Hely (I assume all his grandkids will be named after me) sitting on my lap.

"You know how your grandfather talks about going to the Aleutians all the time?" I'd ask. "That's just Alaska. He's trying to make it sound more impressive than it was."

Of course, then Steve would snatch up my grandson, Kan-Yan Napoleon, and whisper into his ear, "Your grandfather is a cheat, a scoundrel, and once accidentally set my second wife on fire."

The fun we would have.

STEVE: Alone, with a Bottle Fairly Won

I withdrew with half a bottle of the Victory Scotch. To my surprise, within a few minutes my anger at Vali was gone.

The accomplishment of winning a race around the world—that might've been what gave my Kinclaith an extra, ephemeral, indescribable, luscious richness that Vali seems not to have tasted.

We'd had a gentleman's wager, and one of us had proved to be a cheat, a man who couldn't understand honor. There's no explaining anything to a man like that.

As I had some more Kinclaith—it was like a pair of soft, warm hands massaging the inside of my mouth, but in a good way; I couldn't stop drinking the stuff—my mind turned, as one's mind so often does, to the *Guardian*'s obituary of the late British explorer Sir Wilfred Thesiger.

"Thesiger recognized," I quoted from memory, "that satisfaction in attaining a goal was directly in proportion to the hardship and challenge involved in getting there."

It's possible that one of my grandchildren—the stupidest one, the one who's always implanting nanobotic stimulant chips into his rectum (or whatever else replaces TV by the year 2067)—won't understand this idea. He'll foolishly follow Vali's style, shirking from difficulties, taking the easy way.

But I hope my other, smart grandchildren (all medical students at SuperOxford–Beijing Campus) will understand why moving around the world the slow way, the hard way, might have a value all its own.

I hope I have a chance to explain all that to them before I'm murdered at age ninety-six by a scorned lover.

Acknowledgments

The authors would like to thank the following people for their advice, guidance, and positive attitudes: The Dalai Lama, Amgalan, Captain Auerbach, Alex, Oliver and the crew of *Hanjin Athens*, Amy B., Shawn Badlani, the Boyle family, Jennie Carlzon, Suma Chandrasekaran, Danny Chun, Wendy Crumrine, Ben Dougan, Durbs, Maria Guarin, Ken Gulko, Filip Hammar, Carolyn Hely, Sam Johnson, Andy Jones, Richard Jones, Julia Kingsford, Min Lieskovsky, Laura McCreary, Chris McKenna, Aisha Muharrar, Liz Phang, Nithya Raman, Leila Strachan, Matt Warburton, Fredrik Wikingsson, the Yanks, our superiors at *American Dad!* and *My Name Is Earl*, Little Bar, Jay Mandel, Sarah Knight, U.S. Smokeless Tobacco (specifically the people who work in the Skoal division), and everyone we spent time with and who came before us at the *Lampoon*.

At one point or another, each of these people saved the authors from certain death.

About the Authors

Vali Chandrasekaran writes for television's *My Name Is Earl*. In 2006, his script "Jump for Joy" was nominated for a Writer's Guild Award. He was an editor of *The Harvard Lampoon* and his comic prose has appeared in *McSweeney's* and *The New Republic*. He currently lives in Los Angeles.

Steve Hely is an Emmy Award–nominated television writer who has written for *American Dad!*, *Last Call with Carson Daly*, and *Late Show with David Letterman*. He was twice president of *The Harvard Lampoon*.